BARE

An Unveiling of My Naked Truth

RAINA O'DELL

LANDON
HAIL
PRESS

*This book is dedicated to my daughters,
Mckenzie & Ella.
You were an unwavering light that illuminated
my path, no matter how dark it felt.
With every page turned, know that you are the
inspiration behind every sentence,
every chapter, and every life.*

CONTENTS

Tell your story.
Shout it. Write it.
Whisper it if you have to.
But tell it.
Some won't understand it.
Some will outright reject it.
But many will thank you for it.
And then the most magical thing will happen.
One by one, voices will start whispering, "Me, too."
And your tribe will gather.
And you will never feel alone again.

—L.R. Knost

Introduction: ME

I Am My Inspiration

Journal Entry: Thursday, April 28, 2022

I've got several things to get out. I'm starting to think this may count as my workout. Haha. Maybe I will just have the house-cleaners start upstairs so I have more time to write.

I had therapy yesterday and she challenged me to start this new journal with an intentional question, an uncovering of: Who is Raina?

My last journal ended with me writing out who I need as a partner and the question of - who is "she" though? - popped in.

She loves deeply. Feels deeply. And loves smiling.

Go deeper.

She craves adventure, new sights and sounds.

She is affectionate and loves to go into deep thinking and conversation with those who flow with her.

She is scared of letting people in, creating a wall. Which is funny because she's in desperate need of someone to break down that wall.

She's nervous and constantly in her head, craving a disconnect to pull her out.

Go deeper.

She craves the feeling of being carefree, a wanderlust, a woman who wants to sit on the edge of a cliff simply to breathe.

She's nurturing, craving the little things like cleaning up after dinner and straightening the pillows every morning.

She loves deeply and deeply wants to be loved.

She finds deep release when surrounded by animals and nature.

She recharges there.

Feet barefoot on the ground.

She wants to plug in her phone and leave it for the day, following the urge of complete disconnect.

She wants to be held. Embraced.

She values adventure and joy, laughter and humor and balance.

She's creative, always in an entrepreneurial headspace and growth mindset.

She's curious.

She's authentic, craving a space to be vulnerable, authentic and peaceful.

She thrives on the feeling of security and safety, realizing she'd have a lifetime of providing that for herself.

She's driven and highly motivated to succeed and prove her negative spiraling thoughts wrong.

She's open, willing, and moldable.

She loves people, the energy and the community yet she recharges solo.

She's a dreamer, craving the things people label unattainable.

She has a strong intuition and internal sense of knowing that she often fights.

She has hardened - and tears well in her eyes at the thought of releasing and breaking those walls.

She wants passion and has spent a lifetime creating an environment to support that, even if it hasn't come yet.

I now feel like I'm rambling and reaching.

And now question, did I even do that right? Yesterday felt like an absolute whirlwind of emotions from anger to sadness - fear to worry to curiosity to an inner realization of where I'm not being true to myself.

Who is Raina?"

Exhale.

When I think about my life, it feels as if I've lived twenty of them in the thirty-seven years I've been on this planet. It's like my soul made a bet with another soul before coming into my human body, with a mission to test how much an Earthling can actually handle. At the same time, it knew we could handle it all.

When I tell my story, it often starts in 2005, after I graduated high school, even though my *many* lives started well before that. Graduating was a pivotal time for me, as it is for many people. We leave the safety net of home, spread our wings, enroll in college and begin the future we have had carefully planned out with our parents and school guidance counselor over the last couple of years.

Let's call this Life #4. If I'd had anything to do with it, *that* was exactly how it was going to play out for me. I knew I wanted more in my life, so I moved out of my mom's house just a couple of weeks after graduating high school, with a couple hundred dollars I'd saved. I enrolled in a technical college, got a job at Applebee's, and rented a cute little house with three other girls I had known throughout high school. Eighteen-year-old Raina was living her best life.

Little did she know it was simply a season. She had no idea that, over the next couple of months, she would meet a boy. The boy would have a drug problem that would turn into a quite serious drug problem, but that was nothing to worry about in Life #4. She didn't know that only six weeks after meeting this boy, they'd find out they were pregnant and, nine months later, would welcome a baby girl into the world. Another baby just a year after that.

She had no idea she would spend a decade fighting for *his* life and their marriage, all while raising two daughters, working multiple jobs, living paycheck to paycheck, and trying to keep her head above water.

In Life #6, eating disorders and depression consumed me.

In Life #13, I took a stab at entrepreneurship and rocked it.

Life #21 became the season of divorce.

Each year that passed seemed to bring with it another season, as I dealt with a nearly life-ending battle with ulcerative colitis, single parenting, and bankruptcy.

I've lived a lot of lives in my thirty-seven years, and I know there is so much more to go. The only difference between where I'm going and where I've been is the life lessons I've collected and the experiences that have caused me to fall more and more in love with myself. I have always been *my* steady, *my* constant. It just took me a long time to realize that.

I knew I had a story to tell. I was aware that, over the course of my thirty-seven seasons, I have gone through some crazy things, navigated some hard shit, and maneuvered through many obstacles that most people won't encounter in their entire lives.

Those things, the hard shit and the obstacles, didn't leave a bad taste in my mouth; in fact, they grew me. They warped themselves into lessons and tools I have carried with me ever since, inside an invisible toolbelt I wear on my waist every day. I believe I'm here to be a teacher of sorts, sharing the tools and lessons I've collected along the way for other women, for other souls who feel like they're stuck or craving more in life.

When I began biweekly meetings with my publisher, it felt like therapy session after therapy session, doing a deep dive into my life, so we could uncover the direction I wanted to take and the key points for the book I'd be writing. I'd meet with my actual therapist a few days later and share all of the *new* things that came up in our book meetings. She'd take notes, jotting it all down, since it all felt important.

It felt important to notice all of these things, not just for the book I'd be writing, but for my journey going forward. I am in a constant state of healing and growing.

"Who was your biggest inspiration growing up?" my publishing team asked me over Zoom, as I sat in my fluffy office chair, palms sweating. I really had to take a minute to think about this.

How embarrassing, I thought, *not having an immediate answer to this question.* Most people would respond with something caring and thoughtful, like, *my mom* or *my dad.* Maybe it was a teacher who really made an impact or a mentor who shifted the trajectory of their life. I filtered through it all, trying to come up with the name of someone who made that kind of impact on me and kept drawing a blank.

"I don't know… Honestly, I guess it's me. *I* am my biggest inspiration," I said, and continued before she asked me to explain. "I feel like I've spent a lot of time in my life *waiting* for someone to come and save me, to rescue me, to take some of the burden away or some of the weight off my shoulders and that person has never come. I've navigated some crazy things in my life, and looking back, through all of them, *I* made my way out. *I* changed the trajectory. *I* learned the lessons. *I* held my own hand and lifted my own chin when things got hard."

"I'm my biggest inspiration because not only did I make it out of some really hard situations, I took those experiences and changed my own life. I created forward motion, a positive trajectory, and not just for myself but for my two kids, as well."

One of the exercises we did together was to identify the highest version of myself. I have talked a lot about this with my clients but never really done that deep work on myself before this.

"When you think of that highest version of yourself," she said, "the most confident, knowing, passionate version of yourself… name her. What's her name?"

"*Jane*," I said, trusting my intuition and replying with whatever came to me first.

"And when you think of the other version of you, maybe she's the quieter, timider, more people-pleasing version…?" she asked.

"*Sara*," I said with confidence. "No *h*."

We smiled at each other before she asked me important questions about Sara and Jane, and then I followed her journaling prompts in order to discover more about the women who were *me*. Here is how that experience went and what was revealed to me:

Who is Jane? *How does she talk, walk, see the world, embrace adversity, and interact with others?*

Jane embodies *knowing*. She knows she is held and safe. She speaks with confidence and peace, knowing that her words are true, real, and genuinely her. She walks tall, full of belief in herself and her vision. She holds her head high. She smiles, makes eye contact, and doesn't question or worry about how she's being perceived.

To Jane, the world is full of potential and abundance. She sees herself as a magnet for that abundance and feels held by the universe. She's not naive enough to think that everyone likes her or agrees with her outlook, yet she has the self-possession to release what doesn't serve her or align with her vision. She appreciates her past and her journey and the lessons they have brought to her. She trusts that she's right where she needs to be.

Who is/was "Shadow Jane"? *Is she really Shadow Jane or angry little Sara?*

Shadow Jane holds a little anger and bitterness toward those who play the victim and aren't stepping into their power. She looks at life as a board game she's winning at; she looks behind her at those others who make excuses or are trapped in *"woe is me"* beliefs as weak players. She says she doesn't *give a fuck* about what people think of her.

Meanwhile, her actions are cold and hard, causing others to think of her as standoffish and unapproachable. Also, she cannot stand to watch people get away with wrong-doing; this makes her blood boil and her face red. If you don't agree with what Shadow Jane is doing, saying, or believes, she will block, delete, and cut you out, so your words don't slow her down or affect her energy. She lives in "fight" mode, not in "freeze" or "flight" response.

Who is Sara? What are her fears, wounds, doubts? Attempt to tie these back to memories from your past.

Sara lives in fear, worry, doubt, and freeze mode. She has some people-pleasing tendencies, but it feels more like, "If I don't go there, I'm safe." Pure avoidance of anything that can go wrong.

Sara craves validation and confirmation. She doesn't believe she can do life, business, parenting, etc. on her own, and she is fearful of making the wrong choices. She tends to think in worst-case scenarios as a protection mechanism, believing if she considers all the ways life can fall apart, when it actually does, it won't throw her off too much.

"See, I knew that [bad thing] would happen…"

Sara has a deep-seated fear of losing everything, because, in previous seasons of her life, it felt like she did. She's white knuckling everything: old ways of living that *worked*, old businesses or ways to earn money that *worked*, and she has a fear of letting go of those.

Doubt creeps in whenever she starts to act on her vision. She's fearful of the unknown and nervous about navigating the *how*, because her belief in herself has been crushed. Sara is tearing up as she writes this, because she knows it's holding her back from living in the now and enjoying the journey she's on.

Who is Raina without Sara in charge?

This is what I've spent the last thirty-seven years trying to figure out.

Every season of my life feels like a lifetime lived; each has left me with ideas, beliefs, and knowledge to fuel the next season. I've developed habits, rituals, and practices that have allowed me to keep my chin up during seasons when I should have crumbled.

I've released myriad old ways of thinking and created new traditions that have aided in healing myself and my two kids. I've kept two children alive, while most days it feels like it's they who have helped to keep *me* alive. I have been aided by some of the places I've traveled to, some of the people I've met, and my animals, each having contributed to the little fire I've always had inside of me.

I've lived hard, loved hard, fell hard, cried hard, grown hard, and become hard.

I've also learned how to soften, to slow down, and to establish boundaries that allowed me to show up for myself and my family gently, yet with intention.

My story isn't like anyone else's; it's mine and only mine to tell.

In the same manner, I don't have a family who looks like everyone else's. My childhood, my marriage, and my businesses are all unique.

In 2018, while I was navigating divorce and questioning how much of my story, our life, I should share on social media, I read to my mother-in-law at the time a quote that said:

"You own everything that happened to you. Tell your stories. If people wanted you to write warmly about them, they should have behaved better."

— Anne Lamott

She giggled, responding, "Yep!" And so, I went on to share my life online, being vulnerable and open. I believe that having done so allowed me to connect with so many of you on a deeper level.

With that, the following pages are *my* story.

They're my memories, my experiences, and my points of view. I'm not here to tell my parents' story or that of the men I've loved or even my children's story. They have got their own stories to tell on their own timeline.

Yet, I believe that each individual who picks up my book will be able to resonate with my story in some way. You may see yourself in some aspects on the pages. Maybe you relate to pieces of my parenting style or the relationships and people who have crossed my path. Maybe you will see yourself in my energy or my mission, the values I developed, or the sense of humor I have.

Maybe you're Jane.

Perhaps you are Sara.

I hope, by reading my story, you'll identify with some of my tools and thought processes, so you'll be eager to make shifts in your own life that create forward motion.

I hope you realize, deeply and to your core, that where you are now in this moment isn't where you always have to be. There's so much more.

Life #1

Glue

I don't believe this is a conscious memory of my own, but I'm going to share it anyway. It's probably one of those unconscious ones that I've stuffed down *below,* along with the recollection of my birthdays and holidays, all of which I feel have been wiped from my memory like my to-do list from last week.

In 2022, my dad came to visit me in Colorado, like he had almost every year since we've lived there. While we were sitting and catching up, something made him share a memory he had.

I was about five years old, sitting on top of our kitchen table in the single-wide trailer I grew up in with my little brother, Mark, who had to have been only a year or so old at that time. Surrounding us, as we sat cross-legged on top of the table, were cereal bowls, a box of Fruit Loops we'd spilled both inside and outside of the bowls, and milk. Some of that had made it into the bowl, but most of it was just pooled on the table, as we ate and giggled.

When my dad brought up that memory, the visual popped into my mind, clear as day. I could see my straight, blonde hair, tossed from my solid night's sleep, my bangs cut straight across my forehead. I could see the mismatched pajamas I was still rocking, while I laughed at my little brother's reaction to the entire situation. I could even picture the dried milk in the corner of both of our mouths as we ate breakfast, carefree.

I could even feel how I felt: in charge. I was his caregiver. Mom wasn't home, and Dad was still sleeping. If we were awake,

I'd decided I might as well take care of Mark and get our day started. Step one, cereal.

As the unconscious memories flooded my thoughts, my dad, with a note of laughter in his voice, went on to say, "Yeah, you may not even remember it. Your mom and I had split up, and I was hungover after a night out of drinking. I heard you and Mark laughing in the kitchen and will never get that sight out of my head—you two on the kitchen table, surrounded by cereal and milk. It was pretty cute...," he finished.

When my dad tells stories nowadays, they start out with a little laughter in his voice and end with a look of sadness. When I turn to look at him, I can sense the emotions he's carrying and the situations he's been unable to forgive himself for. I can see the glimmer in his eyes that tells me he's holding back tears. But most of all, it's the tightness of his lips as his cheeks quiver, like he's holding on so tightly to keep the emotions inside.

Sometimes, I just wish he'd let it all out.

I believe, like most of us, that my parents did the best they absolutely could. I am, however, one of those woo-woo women, even though I was raised Missionary Baptist, who believes that my soul, before coming into this body in this lifetime, handpicked them as my parents. Growing up, I didn't always see *why*, but there is a lot of clarity in hindsight, and looking back, they were exactly who I needed them to be.

I'm not here to tell their story. I'm reminding you of this—and mostly myself—because theirs are not my stories to tell. I do, however, want to give context, which I believe is relevant as I share my childhood and life growing up. These details are all from my memory; they are things mentioned when I was younger, and I'm sure pieces of the larger puzzle are missing. I can only share what I recall.

My mom, Mary, grew up in Sacramento, California. Her parents split up when she was young, so I have no memory of them being together. I know my mom didn't have a great childhood; in fact, it was pretty fucking horrible. Her mom, my grandma, was a stripper, and her dad was an alcoholic. My step-grandpa was a rough man, and the physical and sexual abuse my mom and her siblings had to live through feels just... unimaginable. I've tried many times to put myself in her shoes, and each time, it just feels like too much to handle. The woman was hardened at a very young age and forced to live and grow through so much.

I had a reading with a psychic not long ago who looked at me and told me that my kids I had *lifetimes* of generational trauma to heal from my mother's side, and we would for generations to come. I believed her. I don't think this is something I realized until I had kids of my own.

When she was fifteen, she left northern California and headed to Missouri. I assume she left to live with or find her dad, my alcoholic grandfather, but I'm honestly not sure. I do know she enrolled in high school in a tiny town in southwestern Missouri, the same high school I attended, and fell in love with a boy named Tony.

Tony was seventeen, also a child of divorced parents. His mom, my Grandma Sharon, is to this day one of the sweetest women I've ever known. I have so many beautiful memories with her as a grandma; it's hard to imagine she was any different as a mother to my dad. His dad, my grandpa, is someone I have few memories of, but the ones I do carry feel beautiful. He was a bodybuilder, I remember, and had a battle of his own with alcohol.

When Mary and Tony met, it was apparently love at first sight. Like magnets, they fell in love. And also, like most high school relationships, I'm sure it felt like it was going to last forever. As I know the story, they were very much in love and wanted to get married. Being that they were only fifteen and seventeen, my grandma said no, encouraging them to live their teenage lives, understandably. When they didn't get the answer that they were looking for, they decided, if they got pregnant, they'd *have* to get married.

So, the scheme commenced. It happened on one summer night in 1986. They found themselves on a dock at a local lake, consummating their relationship without care, as my little soul, on a mission, was planted in the womb.

Glue. Even in the womb, I realized the role I'd play in my parents' life: I'd be the glue that allowed them to stick together. What pressure to put on a little ball of life that hadn't even developed fingernails.

I was born on February 10, 1987 at around 9 a.m., weighing nearly ten pounds. I'm an Aquarius sun, Cancer Moon, and Aries Rising, in case this gives you a deeper understanding of who I am. It's also okay if you have no idea what any of that means; again, I'm a little woo-woo.

Like most sixteen- and eighteen-year-olds, my parents were poor. Neither came from families with much money. I'm not sure what my parents really did for work at that point in my life or where our money came from, but I do remember the theme of it never being enough. My mom had dropped out of high school when she got pregnant with me, and my dad graduated with a goal of going to college to be a math teacher. He later gave up that dream in exchange for being able to pay the bills.

Barely scraping by, we lived in a little single-wide trailer at the bottom of a long hill, surrounded by trees. I felt so safe there, so comfortable. I remember feeling like nature was hugging me from every direction. It was like the forest had swallowed us whole, and I was only reminded that other humans existed when we got to the top of our driveway and saw the town.

I remember walking through the woods behind our house with my dad, exploring the property we had. There was a creek in the back of the property, and I helped (at least a little) my dad to build a bridge out of logs, so we could cross the little stream during our explorations. I felt so proud of us, when it was done. He went back years later and told me that only a log or two remained.

I have random, vivid memories of this season of my life, before I was five years old. I can close my eyes and see myself lying in my little bed inside my bedroom, behind the first door on the left as you headed down the hallway. As my dad put me to bed, I would flip onto my stomach and beg him to tickle my back. He'd float his arm in the air and glide his fingertips up and down my back gently, sending shivers all over my body as he sang "Sweet Child o' Mine" by Guns N' Roses. My eyes would fall shut, and my mind would drift off to sleep. This was one of my favorite things in the entire world.

I remember watching *Bozo the Clown* on TV, if my parents weren't watching MTV (back when they actually played music videos). Also, go Google *Bozo the Clown!* How fucking terrifying. I can't believe I wasn't scared to death of that clown.

Our neighbor, Mr. Haney, had horses. I don't remember what he looked like, but I do remember his energy and how I felt, as he led me on his horse around the pasture. I would melt into the horse's back, fearless. Something in me even then knew I had some kind of connection to these magical creatures. During my teenage years, my dad told me our neighbor had actually shot himself in the head at his home. I remember wondering how anyone with horses could be sad enough to kill themselves. I just couldn't imagine.

I remember one VHS family video made by my mom and her camcorder. She followed me and Mark around the house, MTV blasting in the background, until she panned over to my dad, who was sitting on the couch in our living room, watching us with a sad, disconnected look on his face.

"What's wrong, Tony?" my mom asked, the camera zooming into his face, uncomfortably close.

He responded, "Nothing..." in a tone I now recognize as unhappy, unsatisfied, and numb.

I also recall a memory of my little brother and me, sitting on our green couch, as my parents tried to explain what divorce was and how our life was going to look, going forward. Even as a five-year-old, I felt disappointed by how easily my parents had given up on each other.

The safe spaces I'd fallen in love with began to dissolve after that conversation, and along with that, my trust in people.

Life #2

Eruption

I got a glimpse of the safety and security I craved, but it never lasted long. I knew I'd needed to create that safe space within myself. Looking back, it's probably why I developed such a fear of "losing everything" that I carried into adulthood. Nothing I cherished ever seemed to stick around. My parents went on to date and marry other people, which, I believe added to any instability I felt.

I was six years old when my dad met Laurie. She was the cashier at our local grocery store, and I fell in love with her angelic personality. She felt like a unicorn, with such magnetic energy. They had not dated long before I knew my dad was just as in love with her as I was, probably more. That's why it hurt so much when he sat me down to share that she had died suddenly in a car accident and wouldn't be around anymore. To this day, I tear up thinking about her and the life she didn't get to live with us.

My mom met John and moved in with him pretty quickly. I don't have a lot of memories of John and don't remember him being around much. He had a Rottweiler named Bear, who looked *just* like a bear. He lived in a home with a big chunk of land; if my little brother and I weren't playing in the mud pits where his front yard should have been, we were climbing on stacks of hay bales or creating imaginary forts and homes in the woods behind his house. We were always outside, walking to the river or playing with Bear, exploring the land.

My mom and John got married, but their relationship lasted only a few years before they filed for divorce. Again, what had felt comfortable and safe was suddenly stripped away. I learned as an adult that this was an abusive relationship; my mom told me he had actually been running a meth lab on the property.

I lived with my dad the majority of the time and visited my mom on weekends. My dad worked full-time for his stepfather, so I spent most days with my babysitter, Christy. I loved being at her house. She had the longest hair, which she let me brush and style for fun. She'd also rub lotion on my back and write words, having me guess what she was spelling.

Christy's daughter, Crystal, was seventeen, and even though my dad was almost a decade older than her, twenty-six, she was whom my dad was interested in. He attended her high school prom, which had to of been a bit awkward. Not long after she graduated high school, they got married. Even though I was only nine years old at the time, I knew something about it felt *off*. This girl, who was just ten years older than me, was now my parental figure, and she took it way too seriously, which annoyed me. I had trouble trusting the idea that anything I fell in love with would stick around, so I subconsciously blocked her out of my heart from the beginning.

Crystal's family was very religious. They were Missionary Baptists, and my dad started attending church with them regularly. Within a couple of years, he was preaching sermons and baptizing people in the river down the road. He almost became unrecognizable.

My mom remarried not long afterward to a man named Tim, whom she had met at work. Tim had two kids himself, a son a year younger than me and a daughter half my age who used to call me Araina (uh-Raina), which I thought was the cutest thing. Tim was perfect, in my eyes: a good-looking man with a solid job and supportive family. We spent a couple nights a week at his parents' home for catfish fry's and then headed out on their four-wheeler, tearing up the fields. On Sundays, after they went to church, we'd have a family lunch at his grandparents' home, where I tried to learn to play Pitch, a card game the adults played.

Tim and my mom lived in a double-wide right behind a dirt race track, a couple of towns away from where my dad lived. Every Friday night, we'd hear the rumble of cars making their way around the track. It vibrated the house, and I fell asleep to the rumble.

I loved Tim. He treated me with respect, care, and love, as if I were a daughter of his own, even though my brother didn't get the same treatment. I remember Tim busting into my brother's bedroom a few times and spanking him with the belt, though I don't know why. My brother was always getting into trouble.

My dad's sister, Aunt Megan, and I were best friends, too. She was only a year older than me, and we went to the same school, where we were always together. Once, she came over to help me paint one of the sheds outside of our house, and on a break from painting, my mom called me inside and seemed upset. She shared that she and Tim were getting a divorce.

I remember not being okay with this, deep down. *She's taken it too far, running away from people and situations,* I thought. I was tired of moving, and *Tim was perfect.* I felt so frustrated at this turn of events, unsure where to place the blame I held. Later, I heard that Tim had had an affair, and then my mom did, too, to get back at him. Of course, trust had crumbled between them, and I had to mourn the loss of not only a stepdad, but also a brother and sister, his kids.

Meanwhile, at my dad's house, he and my stepmom seemed to be thriving. They'd moved to a new home he had remodeled, and it felt like a mansion compared to the trailer we'd been living in. It was two stories, with a master bedroom upstairs and a loft that overlooked the rest of the house.

The only holiday I remember as a child was in this house, my ninth Christmas. We had a giant tree in the corner of the living room, with lots of presents underneath. I woke up that Christmas morning and saw a Barbie House as tall as I was, which Santa had apparently delivered in the middle of the night. It was heavenly:

pink, a few stories tall, and came with an awesome convertible for Barbie, parked right in front.

It could have been labeled the best Christmas ever with just that, until I saw the saddle sitting on a stand in front of the TV. I had been wanting a horse of my own, like every little girl, planting seeds for my dad every chance I got. My dad turned on a VHS tape that showed a white Shetland Pony that was now *mine*! I couldn't contain the joy I felt. I sat on the saddle, watching Buddy, my new pony, run around on my TV.

I felt as if I had two different lives: one with my dad, and one with my mom. Each was dramatically different yet exactly what I needed. But this could have been when Sara and Jane were born: I had to be Sara with my dad and Jane with mom.

After my mom and Tim divorced, I lived full-time with my dad, Crystal, and their growing family. They soon welcomed a baby boy, my brother Ivan, and a girl, Bobbi, a couple of years later. We lived in that house until they quickly outgrew it and sold it, buying an old farmhouse in the next town over. My pony Buddy didn't come with us. In fact, my dad sold him not long after I got him, because he was mean, biting and misbehaving to the point where I couldn't ride him. Another loss.

The farmhouse we moved into needed a lot of work, but my dad and Crystal had a vision. Room by room, they gutted and remodeled the house, turning it into a quite adorable home. The attic was transformed into two bedrooms and a large closet for me and Mark to share. Those walls were left unfinished, unpainted, and raw, making it feel like the stepchildren's quarters.

I tried to replicate the feeling of my bedroom back at Tim's house, so I cut out photos from magazines and books and covered my walls with a collage that made me happy. I'd sneak my new Eminem CD upstairs and listen to "The Real Slim Shady" as low as my player would go so my dad wouldn't hear, lip-syncing every word while I taped pictures to my wooden wall. One time, I brought home a Red Hot Chili Peppers CD, and my dad broke it in half, so angry that I would listen to such music.

This felt like a weird transition period for me, and it didn't help that I felt like an outsider in my dad's family. Who my dad became and who I knew him to be were different people, with one being a stranger to me. Even now, calling it "my dad's family" makes me feel like *I* was the stepchild. It felt like his world was growing, and I was simply strung along because my mom's house wasn't the best place for me to be.

I found safety in my solitude and with my Grandma Sharon. She was soft-spoken and gentle, with a smile on her face every time I saw her. She worked for the health department in our town and always had healthy food in her house, apart from the pitcher of sweet tea in the fridge. I frequently rode the bus to her house after school, then busted in to make a big bowl of Grape Nuts or a bagel with melted cheese on it. I'd sit in front of the TV or talk to strangers in chat rooms with my Aunt Megan, until Grandma got home or my dad picked me up.

My mom moved from house to house, not staying in one place too long. At one point, she moved into a big yellow house right on the edge of town. She let me paint my bedroom walls whatever color I pleased, so I picked blue and yellow, a disaster that I loved. She even had a capuchin monkey that lived with her in a tall cage she had built in the living room. That monkey hated me. It would squeal and try to bite; so cute but so mean. My mom's house felt like a field trip. I never quite knew what to expect when I spent my weekend with her.

As much as I felt like an outsider living with my dad, it felt constant. I had a sense of safety and security there; I knew what to expect and what I was getting, even if it felt painful. We had farm animals and land, so I felt grounded, even in the midst of chaos and loneliness.

I was in middle school when I started to participate in band, picking up the saxophone and taking it quite seriously. After school, my stepmom made me practice my sax, but because she hated the noise, I'd have to go out into the barn to play, regardless of the temperature. If I complained or talked back, she'd threaten, "Oh, you just wait till your dad gets home..." And, true to her word, I paid for it. My dad would come home from work and I'd have to meet him outside, picking the switch from the tree to spank me with for talking back or lying. I can still see the look on my dad's face as he made his way over to me. It was similar to his face in that home video I'd seen from years before. Sadness.

Over the next few years, it felt as if my relationship with my stepmom got worse and worse. I grew resentful and nervous around her, feeling like I never knew what version of her I was going to get: the nice woman with the fake voice? Or the person she was when the doors closed?

It was always something. Once, I came home from school and realized that clothes were missing from my closet. When I snuck down to her closet while she was in the kitchen, I discovered she'd taken them and hung them up in her closet. I grabbed them and returned them to my own closet and when she caught me *disrespecting her space* or *stealing,* as she sometimes claimed, I was sure to be punished. One time, she took all of the clothes out of my closet and made me wear the same thing to school for a week. As a middle schooler, this was humiliating.

Every week, I was forced to attend church with my dad, while my stepmom stayed home. I always resented her for that, too, feeling like, if any of us needed Jesus, it was her. I spent Sunday mornings, Sunday evenings, and Wednesday nights at church with my dad. As much as I resisted it, I enjoyed being away from home and loved the attention I got from my grandparents and all the old people attending service.

As much as it weirded me out and felt borderline cultish, I liked being around those people, who never had a bad thing to say to me. Once I got used to the old women who threw themselves down on the floor and flopped around, crying and howling as loud as they could, because *the spirit* had consumed them, it felt like a fun place to be. I'd tune out the preaching with daydreams and then snap back into the moment when we started singing hymns. My aunt or my grandma would go up and play the piano, while my dad or the primary preacher played the guitar. I loved singing. I stood right next to my step-grandparents as we all sang, in and out of tune. My grandma always told us what great singers we were.

By the time I started high school, I felt numb to the fact that my stepmom had become my *step monster*, and I was convinced my dad had been brainwashed. My mom took me and my Aunt Megan shopping one afternoon and allowed us to get our belly buttons pierced, even though I had been asking my dad for weeks and he'd always said no. Looking back on it, I can see where that could have created some tension, but as my daughter now says, "I'm just a teenage girl."

Megan got her belly button pierced, and because I was fifteen years old, I could only do it with my mom's consent—so I did. Nervous, I went back to my dad's house with a new hole in my body.

I will never forget that day; it was an experience that changed my life's trajectory. I knew in my gut that what I'd done was probably going to make someone unhappy, but I didn't have any regrets. I think of this as a life pivot my soul knew would happen and it created a lot of *issues* for me, even still, far into my adult life.

As I walked through the front door, with Megan and my mom behind me like my bodyguards, I noticed Crystal and my dad sitting on the couch. My face must have told the story before my voice did.

"Lift up your shirt," Crystal said, staring at me blankly.

I looked at my mom and Megan and then, hesitantly, pulled up my shirt just above my belly button before quickly covering my shiny new stomach accessory. Tears started to sting my eyes. Then, my attention snapped back to the couch.

With her cold eyes on my mom, Crystal shouted, "You manipulative bitch!"

I didn't know what the word "manipulative" meant, but I was definitely familiar with the word "bitch." I looked at my mom as the shouting started and then at my dad, who was sitting next to Crystal on the couch with his head down, not saying a word. I remember feeling very confused. There was so much anger being spat at a woman he'd once loved and the mother of his children. *How could he just sit there?*

In the commotion, my mind and body just shut down. This trauma response caused me to sort of black out, I can't recall a lot of what happened next. Other than shouting—so much shouting and name-calling.

I was flooded with fear and worry, along with disappointment, once I realized my dad wasn't going to stand up for me or my mom. This reinforced my feeling that I was on my own. No one would be saving me. I knew I shouldn't have pierced my belly button, but the chaos that erupted felt over the top, like there were words at the tip of both women's tongues, waiting to be unleashed, once this opportunity presented itself. I was no longer the glue, I realized. There was nothing I could do to keep this situation from erupting.

Next thing I knew, my stepmom was yelling at us from the porch, as we were pushed out of the house. My dad stood behind her, asking everyone to calm down. And my little brother and I cried, as everyone continued to scream at one another. Then, my mom kissed me, got in her car with Megan, and left to go home.

Once my mom was gone, I was afraid for what would happen next, so I stayed outside with my brother, while my dad and Crystal went back inside. I hid in the ditch of the gravel road we lived on, crying and paralyzed.

I didn't have a cell phone back then, so I don't even remember how we contacted her, but the next thing I knew, my mom came back to pick up me and Mark. That was the last time my stepmom and I lived together.

Life #3

Independence

I moved into my mom's house after that. At the time, my mother lived a block away from my high school, in a two-bedroom house she'd rented. It was a small, white house, but we didn't need a lot of room, so we made it work. I did what I could with my tiny budget to make my room comfortable, cozy, and welcoming, which I strongly felt I needed in this time when everything around me was shifting. I always had a desire to make my space *mine*.

I didn't see my dad for several months after that. I've never asked for clarity on this, but at the time I heard this was because my step-mom didn't want me over there. It was rocky with my mom, so he had no choice but to stay away from me and my brother.

What a coward, I remember thinking. Later on, in EMDR work with my therapist around this situation, feelings of abandonment came up. It felt as if he'd chosen someone else over me. I still feel the pain and realization of that in some present moments.

"Crystal was always upset, saying I needed to *make* you and your brother respect her," my dad said during his trip to Colorado in 2022. "I always told her, respect has to be earned…"

That was the most I'd ever heard from him, when he talked about our relationship, or lack thereof, with Crystal.

When we lived in the white house, my mom introduced my brother and me to her next boyfriend. And while he was an okay guy, my inner voice and knowing told me not to let him in because nothing lasts.

Darrell was nice, but he was also very weird. I feel like I have been pretty good at reading people for most of my life. Something about him felt off, so I just kept my distance. *It is best for all of us*, I thought.

Living with my mom felt night-and-day different than living with my dad. My dad had rules, religion, and structure that felt like quite a tight ship most days.

I always saw my mom as a free spirit and a little witchy. She'd always have tarot cards, a bookshelf full of Stephen King books, and a "fuck it" attitude that I loved. I felt free with her. Because she was such a young parent, I don't really think she knew how to lead us, which I didn't hold against her at all, because it felt like a mutual trust, a friendship.

I think I grew up to be a combination of both of them.

A couple of years into their relationship, my mom and Darrell decided to open a pet store in our hometown. I don't know if this was my mom's dream or his, but together they opened Pet Stop right on the square in my hometown. My grandparents had lived in a house on the square, and we moved in right as they moved out. Mom and Darrell converted the front of the house into the pet store, separating me from the mice, snakes, fish, and rodents with a single door labeled *PRIVATE*.

At first, it felt like a cool idea, living in the back of a pet store. My mom started working on growing the business and developing the pet grooming side of things, and the line between home and work started to fade. Before long, the entire house smelled like a pet store, and I began to resent it, feeling embarrassed to have friends over. A few times, I came home from school with a couple of friends, and they thought the shop was the coolest thing ever. Then, Darrell showed them our parrot and fed it straight from his mouth, while everyone laughed. I resisted, horrified, and started inviting friends over less and less, insisting we hang out anywhere else but my home.

I didn't *really* have a curfew or structure. We didn't eat family dinners or connect at the end of the night. So, I felt independent, craving adventure and escape from what "normal" life looked like.

Around this time, my curiosity about the opposite sex started to bloom. I was a freshman in a high school with an average class size of fifteen to twenty, so it felt like, if any boy looked my way, I should probably consider him as a mate, given my limited options. I had innocent crushes on a few boys who were a year or two ahead of me, and when one of the seniors at school split up with his longtime girlfriend, I didn't hide my interest.

Dustin was *the* main attraction at school. He played all the sports and excelled at each of them. He was tall, dark, and handsome with the best smile.

I'm sure if he was interviewed now, he'd admit that dating me was some sort of bet with the guys, but at the time, it felt like we were meant to be. I was addicted to the feeling of being wanted, sought out, and taken care of. In hindsight, daddy issues, I'm sure.

He would drive me to his home after school each day, to a small, white house that was just as messy as mine. We'd head to the couch to make out, unless his dad was home, which caused us to move it to the bedroom. His dad was scary, not someone I'd want to be alone with. Just weeks into our relationship, while we were making out in his room, he asked me if I wanted to have sex.

"Sure." I shrugged, like he had just offered me a sandwich. I lost my virginity that afternoon. I was fifteen, and it was nothing like I thought it would be. He went slow and was careful and considerate, continually asking me if I was okay.

"Yep," I responded as I just laid there, looking up at the stains on his ceiling. I remember going to the bathroom right after to pee and seeing a little blood as I wiped, thinking, *Hmmm, I guess I did it.*

Of course, I told some of my girlfriends, who told some other friends who told some people, and when I got home from school a few days later, my mom asked me to talk.

"Sure…," I said hesitantly, sitting down at the kitchen table as I wondered if this was another "divorce" talk.

"I got a call from one of your teachers today…" she started.

Not where I thought the conversation was going.

"From who? And what about?"

She told me that one of my teachers had heard some students at school talking about me and Dustin and the loss of my virginity. She'd wanted to make sure my mom knew. *Kinda fucked up.*

Mortified, I palmed my red face as my mom giggled and asked, "Well, how was it?" I looked up, shocked and also not surprised at her reaction.

Tentatively, I answered, "Oh my God. It was fine!"

She laughed some more, trying to comfort my awkwardness before heading back into the store for work.

"Just be safe," she added as she resumed grooming a dog.

That was it. Was *that* the "sex talk"? I'd imagined it going very differently but felt relieved she hadn't made it a big deal, like I was sure my dad would have done. My dad would have gone into the other room to grab his gun and held it in his lap while he talked, as I absorbed the terror and fear of him possibly shooting my boyfriend in the face.

I felt like more of an independent woman from then on. Sex became yet another piece of my life that I'd just have to figure it out on my own, and I accepted there'd be no one to guide me. I could have sex with my boyfriend whenever I wanted and had the freedom to be out with friends when I wanted. I even got a part-time job.

Darrell bought an old race car and participated in the races on Friday nights at the local dirt track. My mom had friends working the concession stands who got us a job there on the weekends, which was truly so much fun. We'd get there early to prepare the space and food, opening and heating the cans of chili for the chili dogs, getting the pretzels and canned nacho cheese heated, and organizing the candy and soda. When the rumble of the cars started, we opened the window, and it was race time. It was always busy, always consuming, and really fun to meet all kinds of new people. Even on the nights when my mom couldn't work, I still did, loving how I got to leave with cash each night, after being paid under the table.

During the summer, I worked at a little bait-and-tackle store near the lake one town over. My role was to stock shelves, clean up, and eventually work the cash register. I was paid under the table there also, at an hourly wage that was definitely less than minimum wage, but I didn't care. I felt independent, responsible, and kind of a badass, learning how to count change back to a customer without a calculator.

As a teenage girl with hormones raging, I also loved the fact that, all summer long, tourists were in and out of my shop with their own kids and teenagers. I was convinced that some teenage heartthrob was going to walk through the door and sweep me off my feet. He'd surely save me from the situation I called life. But I waited all summer, and he never came.

The love affair with Dustin ended within months. Afterward, I spent the next year or so searching for the same *love* and connection I'd had with Dustin, plus the attention I didn't get from my father. My freshman and sophomore years were consumed with boys and "giving up the goods" quickly, assuming it would lead to a deep love connection. It never really did.

My friends and I went to parties on the weekends, and since I didn't really have a curfew, we'd take our time driving down the gravel roads, drinking cheap beer and smoking cheap weed. I'd spend the night with friends, and we'd sneak boys through the window, spending the night with some random guy I'd thought might be my next love story. They weren't.

I don't know why we moved out of the house behind the pet store, but we did. We moved into a two-story white house down the road that someone in the family had owned before us. It was a pretty cool house, way bigger than the prior one, and I got my own room, instead of sharing a space with my brother, our rooms separated by a bedsheet hung from the ceiling. It felt luxurious.

As we moved in, my mom again gave me permission to paint my room by myself. I picked a hot-pink color and spent the following few days putting up primer and splattering pink from floor to ceiling, claiming it as my own.

Again, my bedroom became my safe place. It still felt weird, sharing a space with Darrell, while my mom was rarely home, since she spent most of her time at the pet store. My brother was at an age where he was more annoying than anything else. I felt so turned off by Darrell and my brother's presence that I declared the rule that no one could enter my room without permission. The door was always closed, whether I was there or not.

Quickly, the luxurious feeling I'd had about the home we lived in faded. We got a couple of dogs, a Yorkie who yapped a lot and a Mastiff named Kato, who had strings of slobber hanging from his mouth at all times. I have so many memories with Kato, though I acted really grossed out by him, which I regret.

We also had a few cats. One was named Kitty, who was always a bitch, swatting at anyone who tried to pet her; she mostly hid under my mom's bed. We also had a couple of other kittens who were Munchkin cats, with the body of a regular cat and legs one-third the size. They were so funny to watch, even though I never quite fell in love with them. I'm still not a *cat person*.

Because of the animal takeover and the fact that my mom was never home, the house got dirty and stayed dirty for the majority of the time. I don't remember ever seeing Darrell clean, or doing anything, really. Every once in a while, I'd catch a glimpse of him sneaking in or out of his bedroom in his tighty-whities, which made me cringe in disgust. I think he felt weird getting caught, too, because he scurried when he caught a glimpse of me, which also made me wince.

For all of those reasons, I always made a beeline from the front door to my bedroom upstairs, never really looking around much. If I needed to use the bathroom or shower, I put my metaphorical blinders on and quickly navigated my way downstairs to the bathroom, where I shut the door. It never failed, when I had to shower, I'd pull back the curtain and spend a minute or two cleaning the cat shit out of the tub before showering.

Because my mom wasn't really home, we were on our own for most meals. My go-to meals at the time were a bowl of cereal or slices of cinnamon-sugar toast. I'd take it straight up to my room to eat, so I could be in a clean space, with my music on in the background, and without animals.

Anytime I had friends or boyfriends over, which was rare, I'd warn them, before we walked into the front door, to put blinders on and not look around as I led them up to my bedroom. I was always embarrassed by the piles of clothes, dirty or clean, the stained carpets, dirty floors, messy kitchen, and the dog hair covering the couch.

I know most of them looked around, curious to see what my home looked like. Even if they followed my instructions, I'm sure the smell of cat urine, dirty dogs, and cigarette smoke gave them an idea what I was living in. I would never have admitted that to my mom, though, as it would have hurt her feelings. Even at that age, I knew she was doing the best she could. I could acknowledge she was a young mom, working with what she knew. I mean, shit, when I was fifteen, she was only thirty-one. She was navigating her own life issues.

When I got my driver's license, I got a job waiting tables at a restaurant fifteen to twenty minutes from my house. It was a little ma-and-pop business that specialized in homemade pies. I have vivid memories of picking the hard little bits of meringue off the lemon meringue pie every time I was back in the kitchen. I ate most of my meals there after work, taking advantage of the discounted food.

I worked there until I graduated high school, and I loved it. I also loved not being home. I worked most of my shifts after school until the restaurant closed on weekdays and during evenings on the weekends, until I became skilled enough to take the open shift. The morning shifts were my favorite. Most of the time, I was the only server on the floor. The cook was a tall, lanky woman who looked like a skinny Mrs. Trunchbull. Had I ever seen her outside of work, I would have thought she looked terrifying.

When we opened together, she'd invite me back into the kitchen and teach me to cook. She taught me how to crack an egg and open it with one hand, a skill I still use. My focus was to work and save as much money as I could. If I wanted gas money or food to eat, it was going to have to come from what I made working.

I still didn't see my dad a lot during this time in my life. He would show up randomly during my waitressing shifts and order food. It made my day to see him. I think he probably held back tears, like I am now, writing about this. This was one of his only opportunities to see me without my stepmom knowing. He'd pay his bill, hug me, kiss me on the forehead, and say, "I'm always praying for you," as he teared up and walked out. Every single time, when I cleaned off his table, I'd find a $100 bill under his plate that he'd left me as a tip.

I'm sure it was his way of supporting me at the time, and I don't think I'll ever forget it. In those moments, I could see the older version of my father, the one I loved and missed deeply.

I loved my job. I made incredible friends from all over the area. I learned people skills and leadership abilities that propelled me during this season of life. I could pay for my gas, put money in savings, buy my cap and gown to graduate high school, and even swing for a class ring. A couple of days each week, after work, I stopped at the grocery store and bought a couple of boxes of cereal, so my brother and I had food to eat for a few days. It felt like adulting.

After I bought our food, I always kept it up in my room in a plastic container, to keep it fresh and out of sight. When my brother came up and knocked on the door, asking for some cereal, I couldn't say no. It just became the norm, just like it was when we were little, sitting on the kitchen table, while my dad slept.

My days were spent at school, my afternoons at work, and my evenings were spent with my friend group. I was never a girl's girl, as I hear so many women say now, as an adult; my group of friends consisted of four boys, and I didn't want it any other way.

I had known each of them since kindergarten, and we'd developed really good friendships over the years.

Preston had hair as red as fire and a beard that fell to his chest. He was the only sixteen-year-old I knew who had a beard that made even my dad jealous. Preston always made me laugh. I remember that well. If he wasn't working on cars, riding his motorcycle, or listening to old rock music, he was roaming around town with us, shotgunning beers.

Buddha was a short kid with gentle energy and a beer belly, hence his nickname. Hell, I don't even remember what his real name was; we all just called him Buddha. He was always super-quiet and chill, until he wasn't. He'd randomly say something hilarious or out of character, making us all laugh. I was then reminded that he was just a teenage boy.

Andrew was a hottie in high school and always had a girlfriend. He was a cute, stereotypical kid who was good at all sports. I had a crush on him for a few years, but it faded as we became closer as friends. He had some health issues that he didn't talk about often, but he never let it get in the way of having a good time.

Then there was Nick. Nick reminded me of Dustin: he was popular and a starter in every sport he played. He had dated many girls throughout high school, and during our junior year, we grew closer and closer, blurring the line between friends and lovers. His mom had been born and raised in Thailand, and his dad was American, so Nick had dark hair and caramel skin, with a smile that stole my heart every time.

There were a couple of other boys and a few girls who made their way into our small, safe circle, but our core group stayed solid as people came and went.

Nick and I grew closer and closer, and like a lot of relationships in high school, it became very sexual. I felt like we were magnets, consumed by each other. I'd urge him through the door at my house and up to my room, where we'd spend the afternoon in bed, if neither of us had to work. If we weren't at my house, we were at his, pretending to study, but usually making out or having sex instead. And when we needed to come up for some air, we'd meet up with the other guys and spend the night laughing, smoking, and enjoying our youth. It felt like we were invincible, and with the freedom and independence we all had, I felt ready to fly the coop as soon as I graduated.

I had been working to save money for things that most kids have their senior year, like my class ring and cap and gown. A growing panic at not having the things I needed to help me blend in, forced me to save and budget more than a normal teenager, but I am thankful for that lesson.

Graduation day came and went, and all I could think about was leaving. I was ready to leave my little brother, my mom, Darrell, and the home where we lived. I wasn't as close to my dad as I had been at earlier points in my life, but he poked his head back in enough that it annoyed me, and I felt ready to leave that, too. I couldn't see my dad without his asking me to come back to church, which I resisted. It felt like a cult (still kind of does to this day), and it was the last place I wanted to be in my free time.

Life #4

Freedom

Two weeks after graduating, I moved out of my mom's house and decided I was never going to look back. While I loved that I got to leave my family behind, I realized, years later, when I left, my little brother's decline began. He became the annoying little brother who sold photos of me to his friends, when I moved out.

He spent the next two decades in and out of prison for theft, drugs, and a list of other things. I didn't realize my self-blame around my brother's decline, which I had stuffed down until recently, until I was able to talk to him about his journey and what had happened.

I signed a lease with one of my early childhood friends, Ashley, and two of her friends, who all went to a different school than I had. We got a little house in Springfield, Missouri, a college town with a population of about 150,000. It felt massive compared to the 497 people who lived in my hometown. Nick and I decided to keep our relationship going, since he was planning to move to Springfield later that summer for college.

We moved into the house, which felt so fun to organize and settle into. I had my own room, which I also organized and decorated with excitement. I had gotten a little money from graduation, and along with some I'd saved from working, I had a little cushion to play with, as I started to settle into my new city. I enrolled in community college, and even though I hated school, I was excited to start in the fall, knowing it would increase my ability to make more money.

I felt so sad to leave my waitressing job. I sobbed all the way home, after giving my notice. However, I now had a skill and two years of work experience as a waitress, so I started applying around, and I landed a position at Applebee's. I thought I had really made it big, getting a job at a chain restaurant.

It's funny, reflecting back on how big this job felt to me, at my age. I worked with men and women in their late twenties and thirties, bartenders and cooks who seemed to have it all together and were making the *big* bucks. I knew I'd made it to the big leagues, to the top, and I took it very seriously.

I loved my job. It was everything I'd enjoyed at my little ma-and-pop restaurant, but amplified and with more people, conversations, fun, and excitement than I ever realized I could have in a job. Plus, it came with a pay increase. Back then, as a waitress I made $2.13 an hour plus tips. It felt like robbery for the work I put in, but the tips at Applebee's, after the $1 and $3 tips at the old restaurant, created a huge pay increase for me. My new life was an hour away from everything I used to call home and my independence turned into full-blown adult responsibilities.

While the changes felt very big, I had an innate belief that I could change everything about my life and be okay. Not just okay! I could thrive, creating stability for myself.

If I wasn't working, I was at home, settling into my new space, filling my gas tank, or preparing to make the hour drive down to see Nick. I missed him, and it was a hard adjustment to go from seeing him every single day to once or twice a week. I felt secure in our relationship, because we'd had so many conversations about our future. I hadn't had any real experience with cheating or someone being unfaithful, either, so my naive view of life blinded me to the reality of what was really going on back home, while I was a world away.

I pulled into Nick's house one night after spending the hour-long drive listening to Ja Rule and thinking of what I would say when I surprised him with my visit. I thought about the fact that his dad probably wasn't home, which would give us free rein to play house. This usually meant we'd turn on "Slow Motion," a song by Juvenile, on repeat, while devouring each other.

I didn't anticipate seeing a driveway full of cars or hearing other music coming from the house. I hadn't imagined he'd be having people over and not invite me. I didn't envision a world where he'd be making out with other girls as I walked in, or my being asked to leave, when I showed up.

I sobbed for sixty minutes as I drove back to the city, alone, heartbroken, and angry, while blaming myself for what transpired.

I shouldn't have left...

I should have waited and moved when Nick moved.

What did I do wrong?

I wonder what I could have done differently...?

I beat myself up for days, mourning the loss of a relationship I didn't see coming to an end. I understand now how this event robbed me of my sense of self, some of the vision I had, and the values I carried. I'd never wanted kids but with him, we'd had those conversations. Looking back, they were simply connections and dreams we were sharing, make-believe ideas of what life might look like beyond high school.

I smothered my sadness with work, and I stayed late after we closed to sneak drinks with coworkers. Slowly, distractions were successful, and my mind settled a little bit, allowing me to move forward at a snail's pace.

If I go slow, I'm safe.

If I go slow, I'll see the next bad thing coming, before it can surprise me.

When my dad found out what had happened, he swore he'd find him and give him an ass whoopin', but we all eventually moved on. I'd laugh when he said that, with part of me wanting to give him Nick's address and the other part wishing it would just all go away.

In August that year, I got a text from an on-and-off friend I'd had in high school, whom I'll call Carol. We didn't go to the same school, but we did attend the same vo-tech program specializing in graphic design. She and I were like magnets during my sophomore year, and I would drive twenty-five to thirty minutes on the weekends to hang out with her, smoke weed, and attend whatever parties were going on in the area. She became one of my best friends, standing up for me when the bullies at vo-tech threatened to kick my ass on the bus. (I'd had sex with one of their best friend's ex-boyfriends, which automatically put me on their shit list.)

Vo-tech was a wild time for me. I dated another boy there who, after we broke up, made 8x12 fliers on white printer paper that said, *"Raina is a slut."* He put them into the hands of every student, and even taped them to the school bus windows, which I saw as I left school one day. I was humiliated, angry, and so ashamed, regretting I'd let him get that close to me. My tracker was off, my judgment, which caused self-doubt, and I had a hard time rebuilding it. I didn't realize till recently that this was a common theme: of someone else telling my story and telling other people who I was through their lens.

I was surprised by how close she and I got as friends. It had been hard to let women get close to me, to open up and be vulnerable about life. Carol and I kept in touch, but because Nick consumed me the rest of high school, our friendship faded.

When she sent me a text message that it was her birthday weekend and she wanted to hang out, I bit at the opportunity to reconnect with her. When we saw each other, it was like there was no time lost. It stayed that way into our adulthood. We were immediately gossiping, laughing, and singing—I had missed her so much.

On her eighteenth birthday, we met up to get tattoos. It would be my first of many, a Chinese symbol meaning *strength*, and took me three minutes to pick out. As we sat there, getting tattooed, she told me about what we would be doing that night: meeting at her boyfriend's friend's home for some pre-drinking, and then we'd head to the club around midnight. I yawned, and then rallied, excited to get out of my house and go along for the ride.

She had just started dating a boy named Ty. Ty's best friend, Bret, had just had his twenty-first birthday the week before, so they were having a bunch of people over to celebrate. We pulled into a small, worn-out apartment complex in the middle of the city and climbed three floors to knock on the door. We didn't wait for anyone to answer, because the music we could hear from out in the hallway was too loud for a knock to be heard inside.

When we walked in, several people were standing around in the kitchen, with others splayed out on the couch, and some on barstools, doing lines of cocaine. They looked up as we entered, and then a couple of girls ran over to greet Carol, excited for our arrival.

She hugged her friends and introduced me as we made our way over to Ty for an introduction. He was as tall as Carol, which made her insecure about the relationship. He had blond hair and muscles upon muscles that showed through his jeans and T-shirt. When we hugged, I caught a glance of the boy who had to be Bret right behind him. Carol had warned me about how *hot* Bret was, but also, she'd told me, he was *no good,* He smiled, I smiled, and we were introduced by Ty as we nodded awkwardly at each other.

Holy hotness, I thought. *Nick who?*

Bret was taller than Ty, with honey-brown eyes and a head of the thickest dark hair I'd ever seen. He styled it messy, like a lot of the boys in 2005, and it fit his outgoing, confident personality. *Damn, he even smelled good.*

Bret kept my attention, and I kept his. Every time I glanced his way, he was already looking my way. More drinks were poured, and everyone settled around the kitchen, talking about everything and nothing. Carol introduced me to Bret's girlfriend, Kapri, and I felt my face flush.

Damn, he's off limits—I don't wanna be that girl right now, I thought, still pissed about the girl Nick had been making out with. As I shoved the thoughts of Nick out of my mind, Bret claimed the empty barstool next to me and made himself comfortable. I could feel the heat run through my body from my face down to the throbbing between my legs.

The heat never left my face, and it felt as if I was sucked into a vortex as I noticed Bret's hand on my leg. *What in the fuck?* I didn't push him away, though. My body froze while my mind was going 100 miles a minute.

He has a girlfriend.

Oh Raina, don't be that girl.

Oh fuck, though, he's so hot.

He has a girlfriend.

Raina.

Raina…

I tried to hush the thoughts with another drink and conversation with Carol, who was on the other side of me, while Bret's fingers traced outlines of imaginary pictures on my leg. Then, it stopped. I looked behind me and saw him walking down the hallway, where I assumed his bedroom was. With a deep breath, I reset.

A few minutes later, Ty came up the hallway toward us and bent down to whisper in my ear, "Bret wants to talk to you."

I looked into Ty's eyes, confused and flush, then I slowly stood up. He nodded for me to follow him. If this were a movie, I'd be yelling at the screen, "Don't goooo!"

I turned the corner and walked into the room where Bret was standing. We froze in eye contact, and I heard the door gently shut behind me. In the next moment, Bret was in front of me, palms planted on each side of my face, as he kissed me. Not just a kiss… An all-consuming exchange of saliva, breath, and urgency.

I melted into it, feeling hypnotized and out of control. It felt like thirty minutes, but most likely it was just thirty seconds before we were separated.

He pulled back, and I smiled, letting out a little huff of breath, insinuating *What in the fuck was that?* And also, *Wow…*, as he put his hand on my arm, moved behind me, and led us out the door with a smile pasted on his own face. *Oh, he is trouble…* I thought.

But the good kind of trouble. The kind that will convince you to break all of the rules in the name of love.

I took a couple of minutes to get my shit together and catch my breath before heading back out to the kitchen. I saw Carol and smiled with my eyes wide. She was smiling, too. Caught. I just shook my head at her with an exciting confusion.

We all left the apartment after another hour or two and piled into a few cars to make our way to the club. When I walked in, I could feel the beats vibrate through my whole body. I was definitely drunk. Aware, but drunk. Carol and I made our way around the club with big, black X-marks on our hands, indicating we were underage, and I told her about what had happened with Bret. She didn't disapprove but also quickly reminded me that he had a girlfriend and a potentially concerning drug habit.

I didn't have any experience with drugs. In fact, I'd only ever smoked weed. I had been with a couple of short-term boyfriends in high school who'd had drug problems but had managed to have decent relationships with them. They were mostly meth users and dealers who'd eventually made me feel dirty.

Bret didn't feel like that. Carol told me he owned his own business and was a functioning drug user, which felt like a definite step up. Drugs weren't really my concern; it was more that we had just made out under the same roof as his girlfriend.

It wasn't lost on me, how I had just begun to heal from the trauma of a boyfriend cheating on me and there I was, being the *other girl*. I continued to zone out, letting my body move to the beat of the music, when I felt a warm body come up behind me. I wasn't a dancer. I hate dancing, actually—still to this day.

If you see me dancing, it's because I'm pretty fucked up, which I definitely was that night. As I quickly turned around to see who was touching me, Bret grabbed my hand and pulled me off the dance floor. I followed him through the crowd, apologizing to everybody I ran into and laughing just as often.

We made it to the back of the bar, where he palmed my face and kissed me with everything he had. I kissed back. We stumbled all over the club, catching glimpses of Kapri here and there, then raced away to stay hidden from her, like it was a game and we were the only players. Every forty-five seconds, our mouths would meet, and we'd melt into one another until reality brought us back. We continued this until Carol and Ty found us, snapping us out of the trance, saying we were all heading back to the apartment.

Feeling like a sloppy mess, I joined Carol in the back seat of a car, unable to wipe the stupid smile from my face. When we made it back to the apartment, she and Ty claimed a bedroom, while Bret and Kapri went off into another, and a group of us piled onto the couch and living room floor, before drifting off to sleep. *Weird. What a weird - and exciting - night.*

I peeled my eyes open the next morning when I heard rustling in the kitchen. From my couch, I could see Bret in his FedEx uniform, grabbing his belongings off the counter and shoving keys into his pocket. We made eye contact. He walked over to the couch and leaned down to kiss me on the cheek, whispering, "Call me," before he walked out the front door.

No, really. What in the fuck happened?

I waited a solid twenty-four hours to reach out to him, because I didn't wanna come off as clingy or desperate. I knew my roommates wouldn't approve of Bret's and my *happening,* so I spent the next day connecting with Carol and Ty as they told me about Bret's plans to break up with Kapri.

When I dialed the number and heard, "This is Bret…," on the other end, I instantly wanted to hang up and act like nothing had happened. Instead, I said, "Hey, it's Raina…"

"Who?" he said.

Fuck. I thought. "Raina… From the other night?"

"I'm just kidding, I know who you are. I've been waiting for you to call," he replied.

An obnoxious smile spread across my face.

He was driving his FedEx truck with headphones in, so we spent the next hour or so talking as he delivered packages. He had purchased a FedEx route with his dad; drivers make money based on the number of stops and other things. He was operating an insanely successful business, which was really attractive to me, as an eighteen-year-old from a not-so-successful family.

From that moment forward, we didn't spend a day apart. Part of me thought this type of love wasn't possible, after the heartbreak I'd gone through with Nick, but Bret sparked me back to life.

We truly felt like magnets, attached at the hip. We took pride in the fact that we waited to have sex. Although I say "waited" — it was only for three weeks, but it felt like months. During that time, we focused on our connection and getting to know each other. For an eighteen- and twenty-one-year-old, it felt like a mature decision and a daily struggle to resist.

I'd never really done drugs outside of smoking some ditch weed in high school, so when Bret, Carol, and Ty asked if I wanted to do Ecstasy with them, I was intrigued. I didn't want to take something that would cause me to walk around like some psycho, trying to catch fireflies that weren't there, like I always envisioned, when I passed homeless people in the street. They assured me we would all stay in the apartment living room together, and that wouldn't happen.

The four of us did Ecstasy together nearly every night. Some nights, we'd stay home; on others, we'd migrate out to friends' places, enjoying the trip with other people. I met some interesting and amazing people, but slowly lost touch with my three roommates, since I was never home. Either I spent the night with Bret or the two of us stayed over at a friend's home.

Within a month, Bret and Ty had signed a lease at a new apartment called The Greens, located on a golf course in our city. Once we had sex for the first time, our relationship snowballed. After that first time, Bret and I laid in bed, looking at each other for a long time.

"Say it," he said, nudging me.

I smiled. "You say it first."

We went back and forth until Bret said the first, "I love you." We yelled for Carol and Ty, who opened the door.

"We love each other!" we said simultaneously from under the covers, and we all laughed so hard.

While I was at Bret's new apartment one afternoon, my three roommates showed up. It felt like an intervention. As Bret stood behind me, they expressed their concern about the relationship I was voluntarily drowning in.

"Guys, I'm good," I said confidently, as Bret put his arm around my waist.

My old roommate looked at me like I was making the worst decision of my life. But as I shut the door on the girls I'd lived with, I truly felt nothing. They didn't see my vision, they didn't believe in us, and I didn't want that energy in my life.

I packed up my things that week and moved in with Bret. Ty had also asked Carol to move in, so the four of us settled into a two-bedroom, third-floor apartment that felt like an insane upgrade compared to the homes I'd lived in prior.

We were young and dumb and having fun, doing Ecstasy every night. Carol and I would clear off the coffee table and sit on it, facing each other while we tripped. We held and rubbed each other's hands, talking for hours, with Garth Brooks playing in the background, while the guys sat on the couch behind us, laughing.

One night, when Bret came home from work, he dropped a little baggie on the kitchen counter. It didn't look like Ecstasy, and he told the three of us it was called "ice." My gut turned. *Crystal Meth?* I loved Ecstasy, but everything in me resisted the idea of snorting something up my nose, so I didn't partake. My gut turned as I watched my friends participate, though, and I fought the feeling that I was being left behind as they experimented.

I stuck with weed and Ecstasy while my small group started to experiment with other drugs. Acid, meth—nothing was really off limits.

The following night, when we all went to a friend's house, my gut was still turning. I pulled Carol aside and told her I wasn't going to do anything that night. I just felt off. A couple of other people joined us outside and jumped into the conversation about how I felt.

Someone asked, "What if you're pregnant?"

Ha! Yeah, right. I took birth control—inconsistently, but I took it. It was still in my system, right? I couldn't be pregnant. I wasn't done being young and dumb.

Two days later, Carol and I were staring at a positive pregnancy test while Bret sat in the shower, crying, the water bouncing off of his skin. She hugged me as the nausea became overwhelming. Bret stayed balled up like a little boy in the corner.

"I can't talk about it right now," he said, and let the shower run for an hour. We didn't talk about it for a day or two, and I could see the fear of what was to come hit him hard. I knew he was scared, but I knew I could do this.

We lay in bed each night, staring at the ceiling, nervous about the future. Night after night, he begged me to have an abortion, offering me money (which he'd get from his parents) and begging me to make this *go away.*

There it was again: the loneliness, the feeling of not being wanted. The same feelings I'd felt when I moved in with my mom. The same feelings after each boy I'd loved decided the feeling wasn't reciprocated. It all came flooding back, as I angrily declined his requests each night, cradling my still-flat stomach and offering a silent apology to the little planted seed.

I had grown up in a home and a city where having an abortion was not an option, so I felt offended he would suggest such an idea. As much as I resisted my family and the environment I was raised in, the beliefs were deep-seated and engrained. It was a no. The pregnancy was something *we* had done, and *we* would deal with the outcome.

We had been together for six weeks at that point, and now we were expecting a child.

My drug use stopped that day. Bret's only increased.

Life #5

Girls

All through high school, I believed I didn't want any kids. They seemed like a burden, little annoying creatures who would consume all of your time, energy, and money with their little sticky fingers.

My mom had always seemed inconvenienced by me and my brother. And I often felt how stressed my stepmom and dad seemed to be, because of us and the amount of friction we caused. There wasn't a part of me who thought that would be a fun life experience.

At the same time, I didn't ever have "the talk" with anyone about how to prevent pregnancy. Of course, I knew how babies were made. I just didn't realize how easily it could happen. In my small town, young women just appeared pregnant and made it work, so I knew I would, too.

After realizing I was pregnant, I spent the next several months fighting for a new vision in my head. One where we maybe got married, maybe had a beautiful child; where maybe we could be happy and healthy together.

Instead, reality continued to cripple me. I'd tag along with Bret to his drug binges, not wanting to be left out of his life. I was constantly surrounded by people who were high and fucked-up; being the only sober person in a room was a living hell. The first time Bret dropped acid, I sat on the couch and watched with disgust through the strobe lights in the single-wide trailer. I stayed with him all night, fighting my urge to sleep, so I could keep an eye on him. When he sat outside in a lawn chair, watching the sun come up, he said the clouds were talking to him. I pulled over a chair beside him, noticing the flies that were crawling on his face, his eyes wide open in conversation with the clouds. I sat quietly and started to cry, again feeling like the glue keeping my life together.

Reality was setting in hard. It shifted the vision I'd had for our cute little future family.

Is this always going to be a fight?

Will drugs always win?

What more do I need to do to help him wake up and realize what he's got in front of him?

I sat there in silence, watching the flies cover Bret's face, feeling in my "Sara" identity: the quieter, timider, more people-pleasing version of me. But what I really wanted to do was be Jane: to jump up and scream loudly, yelling at Bret to wake the fuck up. But I couldn't. I just sat there, paralyzed by fears and what-ifs.

With this new pressure ahead, I realized I needed a steadier, more "serious" source of income. Ty worked for an Alltel call center at the time and put in a good word for me. I went through the interview process when I was just *weeks* pregnant; fearful they wouldn't hire me, I didn't tell them I was expecting. I got the job.

I hated that job. I can be a little dramatic sometimes, but really, I hated the job. I was the person people called when they either wanted to pay a bill or had an issue. Ninety percent of the time, it was an issue, and we all know how customer service reps are treated on these calls. I don't know how many people I just hung up on, because I was tired of getting yelled at.

We also worked on commission, so I was expected to attempt to sell a car charger to any person who called in to cancel their account. I just kept working, accepting the reality I'd created.

Every single week, I begged Bret to stop the drug use. It quickly became something he started to hide, along with the affairs he began to have. Carol and I would chill at home while he and Ty went out, not coming home until 3:00 or 4:00 a.m. the next morning.

Week after week, my heart broke a little more. Inconsistently, Bret attended some meetings for addiction that a couple of his friends had invited him to. I tagged along one night. After the meeting, Bret went back out to party, unaffected and unbothered by having just been in a sobriety meeting. It was like he had checked a required box but then went right back to numbing out.

I started to cry, begging him to stay, but he peeled out of the parking lot. I started to head home, but as I exited the highway, I had to pull over to the shoulder, unable to control my sobs or keep my eyes open. I held my belly, my big, hard, round belly, and just kept saying, "I'm sorry! I'm sorry."

I felt so guilty that I was going to bring my baby into this world and into such a fucked-up situation. "I'm so sorry," I repeated as I wept. I wish I'd known then about the realities and depths of generational trauma, because, in that moment, I decided to break the cycles without even knowing it.

The next few months were filled with more inconsistency. There were nights when Bret would "run to the store" and not come home until 11 a.m. the next day. I started to accept that, in this life, I'd just be a statistic.

My mom had me at a young age, so I guess that was what I'd do, too. My parents didn't have a great marriage, so maybe I wouldn't, either.

I barely had the capacity for school plus work a full-time job, let alone do it with a newborn baby, so I dropped out of college just weeks after I started.

Life is hard. It's all I've ever seen, all I've ever known. I don't know why I thought this would be easy.

Mckenzie Layne was born on May 12, 2006 with a full head of dark hair, just like her dad, that fell automatically into a mohawk on top of her head.

For Bret and me, *this* was love at first sight. I'd never seen him so consumed by anything other than drugs, so to see him hold our daughter and stare into her eyes just melted every bit of the resentment and walls I had built up.

I thought I knew what love was, but I really had no idea until I held our daughter for the first time. It was the deepest, most pure love. In an instant, I knew I'd do and survive anything to make her world a good one.

I took the six weeks of paid maternity leave, soaking up the reality of becoming a mom. Bret's mom came down from Kansas City and stayed with us for an entire month after Kenzie was born. It was the biggest help, and I appreciated every second of it. I could have stayed in that space forever, being home with Kenzie, just watching her sleep and playing with her all day, but the reality was we needed money, especially now.

I stayed in my call-center job for a while. While Mckenzie was in daycare and Bret was at work, I was working away, too; pushing for sales quotas, trying to convince pissed-off people that they needed a new phone case for their phone, and playing dumb while angry customers vented. When I look back now, I can see the pain I was in, not only in a job I hated, but as a brand-new mom in a relationship that was just as painful. Bret's drug use was through the roof during this season, and when it felt like my life was out of control, all I could do was hold on.

As a new mom, I felt like an alien in my body, and *skinny* became my goal and with depression on my side, I developed eating disorders. I kept a box of Cheerios in my desk drawer at work, so when I felt hunger pains, I grabbed a handful and ate them one at a time, as slowly as possible, in between calls. I would go home and make dinner, usually Hamburger Helper, and before bed, I would purge it. I stepped on the scale every evening before my shower, and as it read just over 110 pounds, at 5'6", I felt like a disgusting slob.

I spent the next six months completely sleepless and unhappy, yet obsessed with the little creature we'd created. I was in full-on survival mode to keep us both alive, while also being in total awe of my daughter. Her birth didn't stop the drug use like I had hoped it would, but it did make Bret's time at home a little more special. I fell deeper in love with him and his love for Mckenzie.

My days were spent at work and with Kenzie. I'd lie on the floor and videotape her as she started to crawl around. I'd follow on my hands and knees, just obsessed with the tiny human we'd created.

Once, after I put her to bed, I hopped into the shower as Bret told me he would go pick up some diapers at Walmart. History had me convinced I would not see him again until the next morning, so when I heard the front door open and shut, I was surprised he had come back so early.

Then, Bret walked into the bathroom and immediately stepped into the shower with me, fully clothed. I was so taken aback; I had no idea what in the fuck was happening! He pulled out a little, plastic Pretty Princess ring from his pocket, kneeling on one knee as water soaked his clothes, and asked me to marry him.

The shower water dripped into my tears and bounced down my body. I said yes. Mostly because it was a part of my vision: I wanted my daughter to have a married mom and dad. I also knew my dad would be happy to know that we were married. It just felt like the next needed step.

We ended up getting married a few months later in Kansas City, when Mckenzie was nine months old. It was a small ceremony with just immediate family and a reception for extended family and friends. My stomach was in knots on my way to the church. Bret had done drugs the night before, he admitted to me. I wouldn't have put it past him to show up high to our wedding. But I walked down the aisle over many red flags, right to the altar.

Just three months later, on Kenzie's first birthday, I peed on another pregnancy stick, which was a positive, and we celebrated the fact that we were going to have another baby. *At least this time we're married*, I thought, battling the ingrained beliefs from my childhood and family.

The second pregnancy didn't change much in our relationship, though. I was a single parent most of the time, between Bret's being at work or out with friends. Kenzie became my best friend immediately, whether she wanted to play that role or not. With another baby on the way, I began to savor these moments I had with her, just the two of us. I knew life would be shifting even quicker than I had expected. As my belly grew, I knew life would pivot yet again.

With another baby on the way, I reintroduced food back into my diet. It was easy to pause my disordered eating, knowing I had a human growing inside me. Without food to control, though, I felt like things spiraled more. I walked into work one day when I was six months pregnant (and carrying the insurance for my family), and I quit my job. Something in me had snapped. I gave my notice and never went back. It felt, if I stayed, I'd quite literally break.

Bret wasn't happy about my choice, but we made it work. He had always made decent money for his age. Even with his outlandish drug use, he made more money than I'd ever imagined making, so we let that carry us for a month or two. I think he was most unhappy because it cut into his drug budget quite a bit.

I applied for Medicaid because of having no income and got approved. It felt like I could exhale for the first time in a long time, but I always felt so embarrassed, walking up to the checkout lane at the grocery store with my Medicaid food coupons, knowing this wasn't what I wanted life to look like.

Things were changing so fast that any vision I had for my life started to fade. I felt like I had surrendered to a big wave, allowing it to carry me wherever it may. After spending the last year trying to control everything, it felt like God was just laughing in my face. This was one of the first seasons of my life when I allowed myself to be fully present and in the moment every day, mostly because a vision for the future felt impossible.

Those nine months were up and down with emotions. One day, Bret seemed like a dream partner and ideal spouse, catering to my every need. The next moment, I'd be sitting in a ball in my closet while Kenzie napped, holding my belly and screaming into a pillow, because he hadn't come home for two days.

I'd spend those evenings on the phone with Bret's mom, crying, venting, and problem-solving with no real goal in mind. It felt like, once a month, I'd leave my house with Kenzie in tow and make the three-hour trek up to Kansas City from Springfield, Missouri, so I wouldn't be alone. I'd stay the night with his parents, and when he got home and realized I wasn't there, he'd call me, sobbing and apologizing, promising me how much he'd change. This cycle never truly ended.

With a one-year-old and being pregnant with another, I decided to figure out what I could do for income that would allow me to keep them home with me. So, I put up neighborhood signs promoting myself for in-home daycare. This from the girl who didn't want her own kids and would have liked not to be invited to any parties with anyone else's children. However, I knew it would be a way to make money and pay my bills while staying home with my kids.

I consistently had two to three kids in my daycare business. It felt good to contribute to my family's finances again. However, I didn't enjoy the work. I'd be up earlier than I preferred and then be counting down the hours until the parents returned to pick up their little ones. A couple of months into my new business, with my exploding pregnant belly, I was talking to one of the parents about my vulnerable situation. I told her about my work history, current situation, and the lack of vision I had for what I'd like to do with my life.

If you would have asked me, after graduating high school, I would have said I was going to move to New York City and be a fashion designer. Bret's parents laughed at me when I shared that out loud one time, which changed my mind pretty quickly.

This parent explained to me that she was a phlebotomist, working for an insurance-exam company locally. She drew people's blood, collected their urine, got paid per visit, and had a super-flexible schedule. I didn't know how to draw blood and handling people's liquids sounded a little less than pleasant, but I wanted something different that also had flexibility.

When she offered to show me how to draw blood, I looked at her like she was crazy.

"No, really!" she said. "It's not as hard as it looks."

We sat out in her truck, with our kids in the back seat, and she pulled out her work bag. On the middle console, she lay out a needle, a vile, an alcohol pad, a tourniquet, gloves, a cotton ball and a Band-Aid. She asked if I was afraid of needles, which I wasn't, then she started the process of drawing my blood. I watched every detail like my life depended on it.

She put on her gloves then put the tourniquet on my arm. She pressed gently inside my elbow, feeling for my vein, then wiped the spot with an alcohol pad. I watched her put the vial into the shoot of the needle and poke without hesitation. She set the cotton ball on the needle where it'd entered my skin and removed it in a flash, applying pressure to my new puncture with the cotton ball.

After she applied my Band-Aid, she softly brushed my arm off the middle console and plopped hers there in its place.

"Now do me," she said.

I looked at her like she was out of her mind. But then, I smiled and said, "Okay."

She spent some time helping me feel for her veins and taught me what to feel for. She didn't want me dependent on the *look* of the vein, since that wasn't always reliable, she explained.

I put on my gloves, applied the tourniquet, and wiped with the alcohol pad. Then, I grabbed my needle and vial and poked. A flash of red streamed into the vile, and I gasped, mostly in awe that I had done it, though another part of me was grossed out.

As the blood filled the tube, I held as still as I could, thinking about my mom the first time I filled up her gas tank. I'd had the gas nozzle in the tank when a boy walked by, and she'd watched as my eyes followed him into the gas station and my hand pulled away from the tank, spraying gas everywhere, including all over me.

I snapped back into the moment. Gently, I pulled out the needle out and covered it with my cotton pad.

We practiced every day for a week before she got me an interview at the office where she worked, after convincing the lady who ran the company that I did, in fact, know how to draw blood. I was hired and planned to work up until I had the baby.

I loved the job, and I loved being able to interact with adults again. We found inexpensive yet dependable childcare for Kenzie, a woman in the same neighborhood who watched a few other little girls Kenzie's age.

Right before the holidays, Bret's family drove down from Kansas City to spend the week with us. His mom, Danelle, talked about the fact that Jerry, his dad, would be going out of town for a couple of weeks after the holiday.

"I wish you could have the baby before he leaves!" she kept saying. I was due on January 6, so it would be close, if I made it to forty weeks.

Feeling the pressure to perform, we looked up ways to induce labor early. I knew thirty-eight weeks wouldn't be *too* early, so, when I found articles about a castor-oil cocktail inducing labor, we went to Walgreens to buy some. We stopped at Sonic for a Dr. Pepper to mix it with.

We sat in the parking lot at Sonic, and I poured some castor oil into my soda, which bubbled up at the top, unable to mix properly. *Gag*. Ty, Bret's brother, made throw-up noises in the front seat, but I downed the entire drink, pausing only to catch my breath. It smelled like cheap lipstick and sweet caramel and didn't taste pleasant, but I downed the concoction anyway.

We drove home and went about the evening with no big changes. I was lying in bed, about to fall asleep, when the gurgling started in my stomach. *Oh God.* I ran into the bathroom, making it to the toilet just in time to have diarrhea, with my stomach cramping like crazy. When the diarrhea stopped, the cramping continued and turned into contractions.

"It worked!" Bret yelled down the hallway as we woke the rest of the family, grabbed bags, and headed to the hospital.

I had a quick birthing experience with Ella Grace. Now, I joke about it, saying I grunted twice and she popped right out, compared to Mckenzie, who I was sure would *never* come out!

Kenzie loved being a big sister to our little blonde baby. She always needed to be involved, whether we asked her to or not. Ella felt like a different child than Kenzie was. She struggled with colic for a month or two as a newborn and had a hard time sleeping in the evenings. Very different from my first baby.

Without taking a full six weeks at home, I dove back into my phlebotomy, eager to return to work. I asked for a full-time position and for the first time in a long time, I felt real joy around the work I did. I connected with men and women who were applying for life insurance, and I got to hear their stories, meet their families, and share in their sorrow or joy, depending on their season of life.

Life #6

Restart

Acouple of months after Ella was born, Bret and I decided that the city where we lived no longer aligned with the direction our family needed to go.

We were in a college town, where Bret and I had met and where we'd fallen apart. The connections and friendships he had there weren't serving him anymore. I couldn't leave the house without being triggered, reminded of his drug binges and my lonely nights since we'd met. I would feel nauseated at my memories on every street, whether they were of his drug use or affairs. I couldn't get rid of the thoughts, and Bret seemed to agree that we needed to start over somewhere new.

As I gave my notice, I asked my boss if she'd be able to send me a referral to a sister office in Kansas City, so I could keep doing what I was doing when we moved. We packed up our things, sold all of our furniture, and moved to Kansas City. Bret's family lived in the area, and I had found true comfort and love, being a part of his family. I didn't have the best relationship with my own, after moving away, but his parents quickly welcomed me as a daughter. They soon felt more like my family than his.

We moved into the basement of their home while we searched for our own house to rent in the area. I got the job as a phlebotomist for the lab there, which really excited me. It was a commute of about thirty minutes each way, so I'd wake up early, leaving the kids with their grandma. They loved this time just as much as she did. A house hunt and a daycare hunt were our two focuses, as we settled into our new city.

We did find a home, but we had less luck with childcare. We found places that worked temporarily but quickly discovered things we didn't like. Our daughters would come home smelling disgusting, with dried snot and slobber all over their faces, or we'd realize the home or facility wasn't as put together as we liked. Eventually, we found a daycare facility run out of a nearby church, and the kids settled in nicely.

I felt like a single mom during this season of my life, even though I was married. And I still identified as Sara, in my personality and relationship to life. Bret felt more and more distant, focused on his work while settling into his new friendships.

I went to work, picked up the kids, and spent most evenings at home, trying to decide what flavor of Hamburger Helper I was going to make for dinner. This was about the only thing I knew how to make. After the kids went to bed, craving the escape, I'd watch an episode or two of *True Blood*, falling into a fantasy land.

I loved my job, too, so it was something to look forward to each day. Instead of driving around to people's homes, I was hired to stay in the office for appointments and/or walk-ins who showed up. I loved having a desk, being in charge of a filing system, and sharing space older women in the office, with whom I could eat lunch, laugh, and grow. Some of those women really shaped who I became, teaching me their techniques and lessons after having worked in the field for so long.

After a while, though, I began to feel bored, realizing I was kind of hemmed in at my position. I spent my lunch breaks searching for different phlebotomy positions in the area and stumbled upon a children's hospital that was hiring in their lab. It felt like a long shot, applying for a position in an actual hospital, with people who had actual degrees, certifications, and schooling, but even as imposter syndrome flooded in, I went with my gut and submitted my application.

I was called in for an interview not long after, given a tour of the in-patient and out-patient labs, and loved the busy energy of both. Boredom wouldn't be an issue, if I got this job, so I gave it my all: I connected with everyone I was introduced to and used my smile to seal the deal. I was hired based on my work experience and spent the first week or so shadowing one of the OGs of the lab.

She was a slow-walking, fast-talking, African American woman who used a needle the way an old cowboy draws his pistol. I had never seen anything like it. She was so smooth in her technique, confident in her skills, and friendly with every single patient who sat in her big, blue chair. I watched in awe, just like I had with my friend in the front seat of her truck, that first time I learned to draw blood.

I liked to think of myself as her protégé. As the months went on, my skills improved and improved. I was even requested, on occasion, for the *hard draws*, patients whom others were having trouble with, and I had some regular patients who only trusted me to draw their labs. Then, the old lady retired, and I felt like the reins were handed over to me. I became the employee who was shadowed in order to train new people coming in. Eventually, I even hosted some trainings in the hospital for nurses who were learning how to do phlebotomy.

A year or so in, I was asked to move up to the endocrine clinic of the hospital, as their clinic phlebotomist. I had my own little office and would sometimes see patients in there; other times, I went to their room for a change of scenery. Being in the clinic setting felt like a cool club, and I developed close relationships with the nurses and doctors. We'd eat lunch together and spend happy hour together; those friendships eventually evolved into pub crawls and date nights. I'd sit in my office, waiting for patients' lab orders, while reading my *Twilight* book or paying bills between visits.

I look back and feel honored, lucky, and blessed to have fallen so seamlessly into that role at the hospital and to have made those amazing connections. I felt so inspired by the women in my clinic that I enrolled in college again, with a goal of getting my nursing degree. I worked at the hospital all day and then drove to school a few nights a week, while the babysitter watched the girls for me.

I hated school, even high school, and I felt the same when I went back to college for a second round. I didn't belong in the classroom, but I pushed through it anyway, knowing that getting my degree would open more financial doors for me.

Life #7

Disruption

For the first time in a long time, I felt like I was right where I needed to be, work-wise. At home, though, things felt like they were falling apart. On the outside, it looked like our cute, little family really had it together, but behind closed doors—we were a mess.

Bret's new friend group from work became his new drug group. I always felt so naive when he defended his friends, trying to justify the extra-curricular activities they shared.

"Raina, it's not like I'm snorting coke in a back room with meth-heads. I am hanging out at the houses of doctors, lawyers, and people who make a lot of money," he'd say when he felt I was judging his decisions.

Disgusting, and so disappointing, I thought. As he became more and more inconsistent, I felt the need to pick up the slack. I got a part-time job at Applebee's in our new city, so I could work there after my shifts at the hospital, between school, and on weekends.

Nostalgia hit. I loved waiting tables again. I loved the energy, I loved the people, and I slowly started to develop my own friend group at both jobs. Most of us only shared the common thread of working at the same place, though. I had pretty steady babysitters for the kids and help around the house when I worked, and I spent every moment with the girls when I wasn't working. I remember thinking how wild it was that my husband made six-figures while I worked two jobs, yet we were still living paycheck to paycheck. Drugs were expensive and prioritized under our roof; it didn't matter if I disagreed.

This disagreement caused a lot of friction between us. To cope, I found myself on anti-depressants just to survive each day. It was the first time I'd taken anything other than ibuprofen since I was pregnant and they made me feel so numb. Even if the house was on fire, I would have slowly made my way to the front door, unbothered.

One weekend, I had a rare day off and was home with both girls. We made cupcakes and I took pictures of them with pink frosting all over their faces, sitting naked with just their aprons on. The three of us were having so much fun, when I got a call from an unknown number. It was Justin, one of Bret's friends and coworkers.

"Bret's here and needs to be picked up," he said. "He's been up all night and isn't listening to us. He's just been fucked up for hours and can't drive, but he needs to go home..."

I felt nothing, as I loaded the kids in the car, thinking, *Why don't I feel anything?* I had a voice in my head saying, *You should be freaking out right now,* but my body and emotions were just numb.

While we drove home, Bret was annoying and out of control, but I kept calm, while engraining this memory without any reaction in the present moment. Raina normally would be flipping her shit, but she couldn't. My Jane part, who was confident and knowing, seemed trapped inside, unable to speak, while Sara had taken over through the anti-depressants.

Bret and I were always unpredictable. I think that's just how life is with an addict. One week, he seemed like super-dad, and I'd feel more in love than ever. Then, the next week, I'd be packing my girls up and sleeping at my in-laws' home for a couple of nights, because I couldn't be around him.

Those instances happened more than I wanted them to. In the car ride to their grandparents' house, I'd frame the spontaneous trip as a fun little getaway for just us girls. Inside, I couldn't stand the fact that Bret was choosing drugs and other women over the little family he'd co-created.

In the morning after one of our *sleepovers* at grandma's, I'd packed the kids up and dropped them off at preschool with a lingering heaviness in my chest that trickled down into nausea in my gut. Those were always my signals that something was off. I always listened to them. Still to this day, I recognize the same warning signs. They're never wrong.

I kissed the girls goodbye and told them I'd see them right after I got off work. They were running off before I had a chance to say another word, excited to spend the day with their friends.

Some instinct inside of me told me to swing by the house to check on Bret. He'd been out for a few days, drinking and doing drugs, but before I went to work, and I just wanted to make sure he was okay.

I flashed back to the moment when I'd surprised Nick after graduation. My stomach was in knots with nerves.

I pulled into our driveway and made my way up the stairs to the front door, walking in without hesitation. We had a split-level home at the time, so I slowly walked up the stairs toward our kitchen, calling "Bret...? Are you home?"

On my kitchen table, I saw a purse. *Not my purse,* I noted. *Whose fucking purse is that?* I made my way down the hallway, past the girls' room on the right, half-smiling because I already missed them. When I opened my door, the heaviness on my chest fell out of my ass and right onto the floor. I found the owner of the purse.

She was standing on my side of the bed with her pants halfway up to her knees, struggling to pull them up, but not fast enough. I saw Bret doing the same on his side of the bed.

Can I be honest? From here, my memories of what happened next are spotty. But by the time this woman made her way to the doorway, where I stood in, hoping to exit quickly, I'd grabbed her by the hair at the crown of her head.

"Get the fuck out of my house!" I chanted. "*Get the fuck out. Of. My. House!*"

It wasn't acting. I was deeply hurt and broken, when I opened the front door and pushed her out of it by the hair, as hard as I could. I slammed the door behind me and turned back toward the kitchen. There was Bret, standing at the top of the stairs, apologizing like his life depended on it.

I was late for work that day. My eyes puffy from crying and my heart ached. I wish I could say this was the one-and-only instance, but it wasn't. The truth is, I had a husband who was addicted to anything you can be addicted to: attention, drugs, alcohol, women, sex. For years, I thought I could be the one to help heal him, or maybe his two daughters would be the ones to help him wake up. It wasn't until years later that I realized it wasn't our role.

I didn't leave Bret. Not that time or any of the multiple times from that point on. There was a voice in me saying I *couldn't* leave.

It was the voice of my dad and those at my church growing up, who said that divorce wasn't an option and that God most definitely frowned upon it.

It was the voice of my mom and the experiences I'd had with her, as she made her way through multiple marriages.

I didn't want to break up my family. *I was the glue.* I wanted my two daughters to have both parents in the picture, loving and respecting each other, to show them what love looks like. I stayed, I forgave, I never forgot, and I carried on. I did, however, fall out of love that day.

Life #8

Numb

It felt like my life was spinning out of control, and yet, again, I was the glue, clinging to each piece of my life, forcing it to stay together with everything I had. When the stress heightened, I found myself falling back onto old, toxic habits.

Food was something I'd always felt I could control, in one way or another. I grew up in southwest Missouri, and my mom, to this day, still cooks with sticks of butter. Meat and potatoes were a staple, and at my dad's house, I would get punished for not finishing my plate. After I had my kids, I explored the world of eating disorders, mostly dabbling in anorexia, because I hated to throw up.

I'd go in and out of seasons of experimenting with how much I could restrict my food or how little I could eat, while still checking boxes as a parent and employee. Not eating became a struggle while I worked at the hospital; I was on my feet too much and would get lightheaded and nauseated easily.

I turned to binge eating at that point. After the kids went to bed each night, I'd make myself a bowl of Fruit Loops, filling the bowl to the rim before adding milk. As the Fruit Loops spilled over, I'd rush them into my mouth and start eating while I stood at the window, watching for Bret's car to pull up. I knew, if I saw him pulling into the parking lot, I'd have enough time to rinse my bowl, removing any evidence of me eating that late at night. I'd sometimes be able to eat three or four heaping bowls before he got home, and I'd greet him as he walked in the door as if nothing had happened.

I don't know why I felt the need to hide. Probably because of the amount I needed to consume to feel better. I decided to try laxatives. Every morning before work, I'd swallow a few laxatives and head out the door to the hospital. I got really good at timing it all, having just enough time to park my car, ride the shuttle bus to the main building, unlock the doors to the lab, and run back to the bathroom, before letting patients inside. I started to use them more and more as time went on, happy that I could eat plus addicted to the satisfied feeling after it was all cleared out.

Oh man, I wish I could go back and give her a hug.

I was simply over everything. I was over my marriage, my body, and my emotions. I loved my job and my kids, though. That's the only reason I opened my eyes each morning.

While in my office at work one day, I got a call from the information desk downstairs saying I had a visitor. Expecting no one, I hesitantly made my way down the halls and elevators to meet whomever had come to see me. A cute brunette stood by the information desk with a half-smile, looking at me as I walked up to her.

"I'm sleeping with your husband," she whispered, matter of factly.

There it was again, my chest falling out my ass.

We sat together on the main floor of the hospital as I cried. She told me the origin story of her relationship with my husband.

"I didn't know he was married, and I just found out," she said as I wiped away tears, not angry at her but disgusted with him. There was a piece of me that admired her for being the woman who'd come tell me this.

Being the overwhelmed twenty-two-year-old that I was, I agreed to go with her to confront him. I walked into my manager's office with tear-stained cheeks and explained to her that I needed to take the afternoon off due to a family emergency.

We got into her car and drove the twenty-five minutes to his work, brainstorming and strategizing the entire drive about what we would say when we walked in. We agreed that we didn't have to say a thing.

At the time, he worked in sales for a big phone company. As expected, there were employees and customers all over the floor that day, complaining about their bills and shopping for new phones. As we walked in, naturally, our eyes locked on Bret.

His eyes went so wide, I thought they might bulge out of his head. I kind of hoped they would, leaving them just dangling outside of their sockets from shock. She and I just stood there, side by side, saying nothing. He lowered his head and pointed outside. "I'll be out in a minute…"

I spent the next hour listening to his bullshit, which my numb Jane soul filtered, realizing I cared less and less about him and his actions. I couldn't even cry anymore. Deep in my subconscious, Jane closed my eyes and ears, so I wouldn't remember the interaction. I don't recall what was said. I just know that, even after that, I didn't leave him.

I felt myself slipping away after that. I'd go out with friends from Applebee's a couple of nights a week for drinks, always to bars with either live music or karaoke. We would all laugh and talk, doing our own numbing out.

At a bar one night, I made eye contact with the guitarist in the live band and held it for the entire night. He was adorable, giving off a Chris Daughtry vibe. When the band took a break, he got off stage and motioned for me to come over. I sat in a booth with him, talking and sharing a little about our lives, while the world carried on around us.

His name was Jeremy. He was dad to a little boy and had recently divorced. I closed down the bar with him, and we spent thirty minutes making out outside, after all of my friends had left. I just wanted to feel something again.

I arrived home around 3 a.m. and was met outside by Bret, who was screaming at me, "You're such a whore! *Where have you been?* I knew it. I fucking knew it!"

Numb and feeling disgusted by him, all I could do is laugh, "You're such a fucking hypocrite!" Toxic. Oh, it became so toxic.

Within a few weeks, I couldn't fight the urge to give up on what Bret and I had together. It felt impossible to continue with him, cleaning up his messes, hearing his lies, and putting on a smile in front of our kids and to the outside world, while I felt like life was falling apart.

Life #9

Bottom

For over five years, I had hidden everything from my family. Bret's parents knew the majority of what had gone on—the drugs, the infidelity. Even his cousin and aunt knew, having confronted me with my mother-in-law one evening about the fact that they thought Bret was having an affair with one of his cousin's friends. Overwhelmed, it all just felt like a disaster that I no longer wanted to be a part of.

While Bret was out one night, I called my dad and told him everything. After the initial, "I've got a gun, I'm on my way...," from my dad, he settled down, so I could share, vulnerably, what life had looked like over the past several years. I cried, and he cried. I got mad, and he got mad. And before we got off the phone, he agreed to help me put down a retainer so I could file for divorce.

It was the first and only time I had asked my family for financial help. Bret was spending every paycheck we had on his habits. Every week, I'd sit down in my office at the hospital, in front of my computer with my little five-inch notebook, where I tracked all of our bills and budget. I'd scratch off bills paid and make phone calls to request extensions for those we couldn't pay. Every single week flowed the same way.

When I filed for divorce, my fifteen-dollar-an-hour income from the hospital and a couple of hundred dollars each week from waiting tables was my only source of income. I could afford daycare, my car payment, and had a little extra here and there for groceries and random bills. But nothing left for a place of my own.

I hated him. I hated what he had done to our family.

One of my best friends from work, Trisha, knew about my situation and had been telling me for months that I needed to leave Bret. She'd offered an empty room in her home to me, where the girls and I could stay, if I ever made the decision to leave him. I took her up on that offer immediately after filing, and we moved in with her, her husband, and their two kids.

The girls and I shared a queen bed in a tiny room with a tiny closet, but I felt free. I felt like a weight was off of my shoulders, even though some pain still remained. My friends tried to set me up with other people, but *mom* was the only role I wanted to play for a while. I'd take the kids to preschool, spend my days at work, and then pick up the girls, drive home, spending the night with a glass of wine glued to my hand.

I had heard that Bret was staying with his family. They'd let him come back to their house temporarily, while we "worked things out." I felt so betrayed, getting messages from his mom that talked about how he'd *changed*. Days... weeks... He hadn't changed. He would never change.

I had been staying with my friend for about four months when Bret asked me out to lunch with the girls. The four of us sat at a small restaurant, eating, and I could feel the hardened expression on my face. Numb and mindless, I sat there, letting his words flow in one ear and out the other.

"I got saved," he said to me.

"Ha!" I laughed. "You don't even know what that means."

I felt the nausea come back as I flashed on those evenings at church with my dad. My dad truly believed, if you weren't "saved" by God and forgiven of all of your sins, you'd be on the 5 o'clock train straight to hell. Listen, I'm not here to mock religion or make you question your beliefs. I just feel that back then, I was part of a small-town, culty church group and that has affected how I show up and think about religion daily.

It's taken a lot of exploration, unlearning, and rewiring since then, but at that point in 2010, it was still very fresh. The cuts and fear ran so deep, it was hard for me to listen to him, let alone believe him.

"I'm serious," he said. "And I'm getting baptized in a couple of weeks. I'd really like you and the girls to be there."

I had watched my dad baptize many, many people in a river that ran down the road from our church growing up. He had baptized me in that same river, after I spent hours kneeling down on the altar in front of him while he preached, crying because everyone else was crying. That water was so fucking cold.

"No. I'm not going to watch that bullshit." I start to cry, which pissed me off even more. "Why now? Why *now* are you going to become this godly, healed man? Why now, after everything you've put me through? It's not fair."

I cried. He cried. And by the end of our lunch, I agreed that I'd bring the kids to see it. "I'm going to sit in the car, though. I'm not going inside to watch it." He accepted my terms.

The following week, I was scheduled to have a tonsillectomy. I had spent months over the last year with strep throat, so frequently it was really putting a damper on life. Weeks out of each month of the year, I'd be in so much pain, I'd call into work, be glued to bed, and was unable to talk. When Bret found out about my surgery, he begged me to stay with him in the apartment he'd just signed for, to heal.

"You're not going to be able to heal, to take care of yourself and the girls... Let me help you," he pleaded.

Looking back, I was still desperate for that healed family. I had so much anger toward him, but it wasn't as strong as the desire I had for my girls to have their family together. I said yes. After my surgery, I was lying on the couch in his apartment, healing, while my kids laughed and played with their dad.

What if he has changed?

What if, this time, me leaving, filing for divorce, moving out — what if this time it was enough to wake him up?

My mind raced, the internal dialogue a war between the devil and the angel sitting on my shoulder.

I spent a few days healing on the couch, watching my family be back together. Bret was getting baptized in a week, and I didn't know what to believe. I couldn't believe the voices in my head, and I couldn't trust him. There were too many stories in my mind; it felt as if there was no room left for my own.

I doubted his family and the friends in my life, who were yelling, "Run the other way!" when I told them I was going on a three-day trip with Bret after his baptism. He had rented a little cabin a few hours away for the four of us. We were going to check in after church and return midweek, after reconnecting with each other, lakeside. I was moving into a new season, but I did not know what it would hold. Just that I couldn't be who I'd been anymore.

Life #10

Recommitted

Nervous, I walked into the church, signed my babies into the kids' area, and sat down on a pew toward the back, hoping none of the hypocrites who filled the seats would speak to me or make eye contact.

There was preaching, there was clapping, there was woohooing. When the singing started and everyone was asked to stand, my stomach dropped. This was about the time at my dad's church when I would sneak out to the bathroom—an outhouse—and chill for a while, until I heard the singing stop, which meant church was dismissed. Hanging outside in an actual outhouse that smelled exactly as you can imagine was preferable to sitting inside, listening to my grandparents, aunts, and their friends sing off-key, as they took turns coming up to me to ask if I was ready to find Jesus.

Bret sang alone, swaying from side to side, lifting one hand in the air as he closed his eyes. Inside, I was curled up in a little ball, wishing time would speed up, so I could get the fuck out of there.

As I people watched, I made eye contact with a man who was walking toward us with a woman close behind him. *Husband and wife, maybe?* I thought. *Maybe they're just leaving? Maybe they're off to the restroom? Together? No.*

They made their way over to Bret and me, excusing themselves as they shimmied past people in the pew. When they stood in front of me, shaking Bret's hand, I crumbled and immediately started to cry. It wasn't *God* bringing me to tears; it wasn't the *Holy Spirit* taking over. It was fear and trauma.

They introduced themselves as the associate pastor and his wife, leaders of the Young Marrieds group at the church. They told me that God had put it in their heart to walk back to me and Bret and to see if we wanted them to pray for us.

He held his hands in front of him like he was under arrest, saying, "I don't know anything, but I think God wants me to pray for you guys. Is there something I can pray for you for?"

Bret looked at me and said, "Our marriage. She filed for divorce, but it's not yet final, and I want to stay married. Can you pray for our marriage to heal?"

Part of me felt like he was throwing me under the bus, blaming the idea of divorce on me, and the other part of me just accepted that.

And so, they prayed. Placing one hand on my shoulder and another on Bret's, they formed a little circle, and I cried as the pastor prayed for our marriage to be healed.

Fuck was all I thought, wishing my brain would stop running a hundred miles a minute. After the singing ended, they transitioned into baptisms, asking those who were going to be baptized to come up to the front. Bret kissed me on the cheek before making his way up to the front of the church, where he stood in line patiently, awaiting his chance to be dipped into the pool.

I stood there by myself, watching it all play out.

Bret approached the above-ground pool, stepped up the ladder, and then lowered himself into the water, joking about how cold it was. The crowd laughed. That was Bret, the people person, the jokester, the guy everyone liked, always prepared with a witty one-liner.

The preacher asked Bret if he wanted to share anything. Bret took the mic and jumped into sharing a piece of his story, his journey, including his regrets and his hopes, and then thanked God for all of it. I winced.

The pastor put one hand over Bret's face and the other on his back, then lowered him into the water. As he was submerged, I blinked, feeling the impact of the water through my body as if it were washing away pieces of me. *What the fuck was that?*

When Bret resurfaced, the crowd cheered, applauded, and cried. He stood up, smiling from ear to ear. I took a deep breath and exhaled whatever felt stuck deep inside of me.

Later, he and I did a little video interview for the church, where I shared, "As soon as he hit the water, it was like everything washed away in me, too. Every memory, every doubt, every fear—gone, in an instant."

And I meant it. He got out of that water, and I felt like I was the one washed clean.

Then, it felt like Jane and Sara were at it again. Jane felt a sense of frustration: *Oh, we just get to be wiped clean now? Just like that, all the shitty things you've done are forgiven?* While Sara sat there in the pew as tears rolled down her face, washing me away into nothingness.

We left church and went on our little family vacation. We had a little two-bedroom cabin to ourselves, where we played games, grilled food, and walked to the lake, where the girls played and splashed in the water in their little toddler bikinis. The photos from that trip are some of my favorites. We made beautiful memories that weekend.

And right there, the next season of our life came into focus. The girls and I moved back in with Bret, into his two-bedroom apartment and out of my friend's house. Unfortunately, that ended our friendship; she explained how she couldn't support us getting back together, not after listening to me cry in frustration for months. I'm pretty sure she thought I was brainwashed, and I couldn't argue that. I felt kind of brainwashed, but I didn't fight it. I surrendered to whatever this next season would bring, going with the flow of the baptismal waters.

We started going to church every Sunday. We grew closer to the associate pastor and his wife and even attended some of their Young Marrieds group meetings out of their home. Within a few months, we'd broken the lease to Bret's apartment and moved about an hour away, to Overland Park, Kansas, much closer to the church and the new friendships we were creating there.

For the first time in a long time, things felt good. Bret swore on everything holy that he was sober and done with the life he'd been living before. Sins were washed away, and I believed him. It felt as if I finally had a happy marriage, along with a good job and great kids. What else was there to search for?

We settled into an apartment complex that we loved, unbothered that our two-bedroom apartment felt small for the four of us. We'd make it work until something bigger was available.

We enrolled the kids in preschool there, and Kenzie prepared for her first year of kindergarten. I couldn't believe how fast they were growing; it was all flying by faster than I was comfortable with.

The area where we lived felt "yuppie," as my mother-in-law would say. The streets were lined with two-story homes and perfectly groomed lawns, filled with husbands who worked full-time and wives who stayed home to do *who knows what* during the day, while their kids were at school. I was still working full-time at the hospital, but all of my new friendships at church were with stay-at-home moms. I envied their lives and the slowed-down, family-focused world they lived in.

One evening, when Bret got home from work, I met him on the couch with a handwritten list of the pros and cons of my becoming a stay-at-home mom versus working a full-time job. Some of the work cons included the fact that I was tired and burnt-out by the schedule, plus, after paying for childcare and gas, I wasn't netting much money. We were already living paycheck to paycheck but this could be an opportunity for us to really shift things, cut back and start saving.

"Imagine having dinner ready when you got home," I argued and went on with more potential benefits for my husband. And, it worked.

I gave my two-week notice at the hospital, though a little reluctantly. Half of me was convinced life would be better with me at home, as just a *wife and mom*, but the other half loved and felt deep purpose for the work I did. I knew I'd miss it.

The women at the hospital threw me a "retirement" party, with cake and décor all over the lab, and I felt my heart break a bit. I had grown beautiful friendships there, and I felt guilty leaving. I did feel like I was leaving behind a piece of me. Yet, I walked out on the last day and didn't look back, fully embracing my new season.

Life #11

Renewed

I lived on cloud nine for the longest time, joining the women for coffee and kid dates, zoo adventures, and all kinds of random activities midweek. It felt awesome to have that freedom, to wave goodbye to my husband knowing I could do anything I wanted while he was gone, so long as I earned my keep by keeping the kids alive and having dinner ready when he got home. Shit, I'd go above and beyond: I would have cobbler or some other dessert ready to dig into, after dinner was done.

After a few months of pool dates and Lunchables, Kenzie started kindergarten. We were within walking distance of the elementary school, so, when the weather was nice, I walked her to school each morning, while both kids scootered their hearts out on the sidewalk in front of me. When Ella and I got home, we'd load up the car, and I'd drop her off at half-day preschool, prepping her for kindergarten the following year.

While the kids were in school, I cleaned, cooked lunches, prepped for dinners, baked, twiddled my thumbs, and watched TV, bored and ready to pick up the girls. I'd snag Ella from preschool and smother her with kisses, after missing her company.

The boredom of being a stay-at-home mom slowly crept in. I could feel it in my body, an uneasiness followed by the urge to prove my worth. I had flashbacks, remembering how much I'd hated running a daycare out of my home, although it wasn't as bad this time, because I had only my own kids. But I noticed the same emotions coming up, day after day: not the need for more money, but the urge to do *anything* besides sit and play with children and clean.

I realize many moms would kill for that opportunity. But still, I was bored, no matter all the great things I got to do with my kids.

Shouldn't I have been grateful? I'd fought hard for this opportunity.

Then, one day, I noticed a tutorial on Facebook about how to make T-shirt scarves. They looked so cool and unique, piquing my curiosity. From Bret's closet, I snagged a T-shirt he didn't wear too often so it wouldn't missed, and I began to follow the tutorial, step by step. Thirty minutes later, I had created a scarf from an old T-shirt. When I slipped it on, I smiled, thinking this was exactly what I needed to do: to *create*.

Life #12

Create

I needed to create for myself first, though. I didn't even think about sharing it with anyone else. It just felt like a beautiful gift to myself. Bret and the kids thought it was the *coolest* idea, which gave me the confidence to make a few more.

I wore one to church that weekend and got compliments left and right. One of the older women there insisted I make one for her, and when she wore it to church the following week, it felt so cool. She told Bret how much she loved her scarf and suggested I think about selling them on Etsy.

I was a little taken aback. First, I didn't know what Etsy was! And second, I thought, *I could sell these?*

The truth was, I was tired of just getting by. My entire life had been a series of years of *just getting by*. I was tired of having to spend a couple of hours clipping coupons before I went to the grocery store. I was frustrated each time I walked in with my Ziplock bag of coupons and a $25 budget for a family of four. I was tired of filling my cart with canned vegetables and trying to get the kids excited about new flavors of Hamburger Helper.

One afternoon, after running errands, I rolled into the gas station with my tank nearly empty and sent a quick text to Bret, *Can I put $5-10 in gas?*

No, he responded. *We don't have it until Friday.*

I felt the heat rush into my cheeks. I was hot with emotions and the embarrassment about the life I was still living. I made it home and parked my car till Friday.

I created an account on Etsy. After I picked the girls up from school, we drove to Goodwill and searched the aisles for cool T-shirts to use for my new hobby. After dinner each evening, while the girls played, I sprawled out on the floor, cutting T-shirts and tying and hot-gluing pieces together to create a really cool accessory. I got creative with styles, ways of tying them, and even figured out a technique to create wavy strands that looked so fun. I could feel my creative juices flowing and the joy that evolved from a place deep inside, something I had never experienced before.

Within a month, I had posted thirty to forty scarves for sale on Etsy and shared them in special albums on Facebook that directed people to shop. I had orders rolling in from other women at church, as well as strangers on the Internet. Each time I heard the little *cha-ching* notification on my phone, signaling a new sale, my stomach fluttered with excitement. My entrepreneurship journey was taking off!

The girls and I became regulars at Goodwill on our hunts for new T-shirts. I spent naptimes and evenings collecting my shirts, fulfilling orders, and packaging them up to be shipped.

That winter, I ran a Black Friday sale that was really successful. I think this sparked my Jane flame!

Smiling, Bret looked at me and asked, "So... How much did you make?"

After checking my phone app, I replied, "Just a little over ten thousand dollars." *Yep, entrepreneurship is my jam,* I thought.

The day before Thanksgiving, we got the greenlight to move into a three-bedroom apartment in our complex, so Black Friday was a shopping marathon for our new space.

Within a few weeks, we were settled in. The girls still wanted to share a bedroom so I converted our spare bedroom into my office. I even had room for a mannequin, which improved the quality of my photos and staging, though the girls insisted on being models, too. That inspired me to make some smaller ones that I sold as "kid's scarves." It became a legit business, which lit me up.

I lived about three hours away from my family, so they didn't make the trip often. Typically, Bret and I loaded the girls in the car and made the drive down there, so they could spend the entire weekend, sharing time between my parents. But on our drives home after picking them up, it never failed: one or the other would throw up, because they'd been eating anything and everything Grandma and Grandpa let them. We quickly learned to stock the car with wipes and towels, in anticipation.

My dad and stepmom made the drive up one weekend after we moved in, to see the new space and, honestly, I think, to check on me. My dad knew everything about our marriage, and I'm sure he needed to be convinced that Bret had *found God*.

During this season of my life, I wasn't close with my family. We spent the majority of our time with Bret's family on weekends and holidays. I hadn't had a relationship with my stepmom since I'd moved out of their house beyond the occasional hello when I dropped my kids off to spend time with them.

When I opened the door to my office during their tour of our apartment, I was so proud of the setup for my small business.

My stepmom looked around with a half-annoyed, half-proud look on her face and said, "I swear to God, Raina. You have always had this ridiculous ability to turn shit into gold."

Was she jealous? Or annoyed at my ability to do that? I've always been good at reading people and absorbing their energy, so a part of me felt offended.

At the time, I didn't really know what she meant, but as life continued, this became something I truly believed about myself. It became a hidden ability that I was deliberately focused on proving. I connected it to my marriage, to my upbringing, and now to my journey in entrepreneurship. My new little *inner entrepreneur* knew how much the money I was making would change our life. It was the first of a lot of *shit into gold* moments.

While the extra income was amazing, somehow it seemed to leave our pocket as soon as it arrived. We'd spent the last several years barely scraping by, and now, I still felt like that, even with all my new income. For years, I'd been paying bills with a little less than enough, so it felt frustrating to still be in this position, even after Bret had *changed.*

Bret had never been someone to follow a budget or really think twice about buying new shoes or a new shirt, if and when he wanted it. While I cut coupons, he lived life. My resentment built up in the background of our lives, but I just continued to work, finding joy in my creative outlet and trusting that my *renewed* husband was doing the right things for our family. There was always a promise of a bonus coming or a light at the end of the tunnel. He said we were saving money, and I held my breath every month, hoping it was true.

While our finances were still a constant worry, I reminded myself of the things I had control over. I could lean into my business, lean into my girls, and appreciate the *healed* marriage I had in front of me. I did feel the love. Our relationship felt like it was right where it needed to be, plus we finally had a community of people our age and all newly married, to lean on, if and when we needed it.

Bret and I prioritized date nights weekly and focused on rebuilding our relationship. One evening, he took me out for crab legs, something I had never had before, at an expensive restaurant in the city. After we finished eating, we walked around the Plaza, holding hands and talking when I felt him tug me to a stop.

He knelt down on one knee and held out a diamond ring. Tears welled up behind my eyes.

"Will you re-marry me?" he asked.

"Yes!" I said through my tears, not even thinking twice.

I heard cheering behind us and turned to see my family there. My dad, my stepmom, my mom, my brothers and sister, aunts, uncles, grandparents, and new close friends had been invited by Bret to witness his re-proposal and, hopefully begin to earn their trust back.

My dad gave me a hug before shaking Bret's hand. My friends asked to see the ring. I thought, *this is what it was supposed to feel like.*

We'd rushed things the first time, when we were young, naïve, and ignorant to what was in front of us. *This time,* I thought, *we'll get to do things the right way.*

A couple of months later, more friends and family gathered with us again in the same spot, by the fountain on the Plaza, and we renewed our vows, led by the associate pastor who'd connected with us at church. As Bret read his vows, my heart expanded and contracted, healing cracks that had once felt so deep.

We all took photos, ate dinner, and celebrated our reconnection and recommitment.

Life #13

Entrepreneurship

For the first time in— well, *ever*, I felt like I was in a good space mentally. However, I didn't feel comfortable in my skin. It felt like my body didn't match my new life or energy. Once I wasn't working at the hospital anymore, I'd slowly stopped my laxative usage and felt like I'd adopted a healthier, more balanced relationship with food. But this came with a bit of weight gain. I was a breakfast, lunch, and dinner kind of girl, now that I was spending more time at home, fueling my babies.

In hopes of riding this confidence train, I decided to check out the gym that had just opened across the street from us. It was a Lifetime Fitness and one of the biggest gyms this small-town girl had ever seen. When I walked in, it felt like fitness heaven. The kids ran into the childcare area without even looking back. I knew this membership would allow me to take my self-love to the next level.

I started going to Pump classes a couple of times a week. I didn't want to stroll on the treadmill or flop around in the free-weight section with others who seemed to know what they were doing. But I felt safe in the back of a class, following along with everyone. Pump is like lifting weights, choreographed. I really enjoyed it and started to feel that little ping of joy on my way to class each week.

Slowly, my body and mind started to change. Both became stronger. When I took the girls on field trips to the library, I also checked out books like, *The Rules of Weightlifting for Women,* and anything else I could get my hands on that could help me gain knowledge about fueling and taking care of my body.

I don't quite know where this motivation came from. But I continued taking little action steps toward wanting something more. It's almost as if, subconsciously, Jane was preparing me, sending me to boot camp to be ready for what was to come.

While we were driving one afternoon, Bret and I started to talk about finances. I had begun to question our money's *disappearing act*, which had always been a sensitive subject between us. After year after year of living paycheck to paycheck because of his drug use, my trust had been broken. But now, I just didn't understand how we were in the same situation, when he was finally sober and both of our incomes had gone up.

He shared how we had been in debt and insanely behind after our spending in previous years. This seemed odd, since he still so freely spent money on himself or went to get drinks with friends so often. It didn't add up, but I knew not to push him, and I was working on trusting him again.

My old beliefs and my Sara self were constantly in the back of my head. *Trust your husband. Wives stay silent. Let him control the finances. He's a godly man. He will do what's best.* I silenced each worry I had or any gut intuition that popped up using these inherited thoughts from both sides of our family.

I wanted a solution. I wanted to be able to save and grow. I wanted someday to be able to buy a house and not have to struggle.

"I'm tired of struggling," I told him.

He shared how, earlier that week, he'd met with a lawyer to get some information about filing for bankruptcy.

Immediately, I said, "No! What? It's not *that* bad. How could we be in a situation bad enough to file for bankruptcy? We just need to get smart about things!" I started to cry.

I could feel it again, in my gut. We had a friend who had filed for bankruptcy, and I'd heard her and her husband share about how hard it was on their family, how they couldn't buy a home for a long time. It took nearly a decade before they felt like they were finally okay.

"It just feels like the last option," I told him.

"It's the only option," he replied.

Devastated and embarrassed, I attended a meeting with a bankruptcy lawyer and my husband, staying silent and signing on the line agreeing to a Chapter 13 bankruptcy.

Trusting my husband and having his voice in the back of my head that *this was a good thing,* I let go of the stress and worry. I surrendered into just trusting that the decision we'd made was for the best. It would take us time to pay off the debt accumulated, but afterward, we'd be free and clear. I clung to what it would feel like to be *free and clear,* focusing on growing my scarf business and raising my daughters.

"She wasn't a person to whom things happen. She did all the happenings."

—Muriel Spark

My weekly Pump classes became my outlet. After dropping off the kids, I'd go and set up for the class, then turn my brain off while I moved. I began to take some photos before or after the class, which I shared randomly on Facebook, my only social media platform at the time. I never had MySpace, so being plugged into Facebook felt like being connected to a bigger world. When I shared my photos, I got a bit of praise from my family and acquaintances, who told me I was an inspiration.

Motivated by this praise, I kept going, fueled to stay consistent on my health journey. I downloaded an app called MyFitnessPal and created an account, making my username: *rainavsfood*. This felt appropriate, given how I'd battled with food for so many years.

Every time I ate something, I immediately logged it. My awareness expanded each time I tracked a meal, and it became a game, hitting my calorie and macro goals each day. Through my food intentionality and consistency at the gym, I fell in love with my body for the first time in my life.

I was twenty-five years old with two kids. I had always put a lot of pressure on myself to not look like I had kids. I wanted to be lean, skinny, and curveless; now, I craved the muscle that told me I was strong.

Always eager to do more and learn more, I spent my spare time scrolling on MFP, which was similar to Facebook, and reading the blogs written by other users, trainers, and nutritionists. I soaked up a wide variety of topics and facts, taking away little things I could try or implement.

One thing I read about was a *superfood shake,* and how it had not only increased the writers' energy but also reduced their cravings for sweets.

On a typical night, Bret and I would stroll through Freddy's Drive-Thru, where I would get me a root beer float and he'd have a Triple Reese's Concrete. Yes—*triple* the Reese's.

I posted to MFP one day, asking if anyone could share details on this *magic* shake. When I learned who sold them, I immediately reached out to her on Facebook.

She had curly red hair, two kids, a husband, and went by the name Leslie. She shared so much of her life on social media, I was sucked in quickly. I sent her a private message, asking if she had any free samples of the shake she could send me. I knew it would cost more than I could afford at the moment.

Within minutes, she responded, "Definitely! I'd love to send you some. Tell me about the health journey you're on!"

We chatted back and forth for about an hour, sharing pieces of our lives and how we'd each gotten started on our paths. I loved Leslie and became so inspired by her story. There she was, a stay-at-home mom who worked with the company whose shakes I was inquiring about. She was earning about $5,000 per week. I was blown away and began daydreaming about the impact that could have on my family.

When she asked about my goals, I shared how, at this point, I was really just craving accountability and community. I felt like it was the missing piece on my journey.

"You should think about the business side of things. It's the best form of accountability I've ever had," she said honestly. I was sold.

Leslie sent me a link to a recording about her full story and that of other regular women, moms and wives who had undertaken this business opportunity after wanting more in their life. They'd found joy in their self-care journey and decided to turn that into a business, which then had transformed their lives.

When Bret got home later that day, I told him about the woman I'd met, the stories I'd heard, and the urge I now had to join them. I explained what was involved and how much it would cost me to start. He was hesitant, because our financial situation wasn't in the best spot.

I continued to describe how much it would mean to me, how much I needed the accountability, and if it worked out as Leslie's had, how much it could financially change things for our family. I contemplated creating a pro-and-con list like before, but I didn't have to.

After about a week of thinking about it, Bret told me, "Okay… Let's do it. We'll put the $205 startup fee on the credit card. But the only thing is, I want you to pay me back."

Sold. It might take me a week or a year, I figured, but I didn't care. I just wanted to start. I sent a message to Leslie and told her I was ready to sign up. She sent me the link, and on April 12, 2013, within minutes, I was signed up as a coach. I had Bret take *before* photos of me, confident that, soon, I could look back at them and compare, as I documented my transformation.

I felt like a sponge, totally unaware of the potential in front of me, while I trusted that I was on the right path. With the title of *coach*, I felt accountability immediately. I thought, *If I'm going to coach people and carry this title, I'd better figure my shit out first.* I downloaded the training materials and plugged into Leslie's team page, while I waited on my workouts and meal plans to arrive in the mail.

As I scrolled through the feed on the team page, I soaked in all of the celebrations, accomplishments, and recognition she had given to people for hitting specific goals. I couldn't remember the last time I'd had acknowledgement like that. I imagined it felt pretty special to the people receiving it. I sent her a message shortly after, explaining how I'd started my deep dive into training and was curious about what my first goals should be, if I were to work on the business side of things.

She called me to explain some of the ranks I could advance to, the income brackets available, and what it all meant. My mind raced and my belly fluttered in amazement: by simply walking the walk, taking control of my health, and sharing it, I could invite people to join me who would then do the same kinds of workouts and plans, and I could make money by doing that. She told me to start posting on my Facebook—nothing crazy, just to share my journey.

"Three to five posts a day," she suggested. So, I did.

Within the first week, before I'd even gotten my workouts in the mail, I had three people join me for support, which advanced me to the first rank above *coach*. Leslie snagged a photo from my page and created a recognition post, praising me on how I'd *hit the ground running*... I couldn't stop smiling.

It felt so amazing to have that praise from her and the team. I paid attention to the page every day after that, noticing the wins, the questions, and the people who were recognized most. At the top of every leaderboard, I'd see the name, *Anita. What is she doing?* I wondered. That was my competition, I decided. Friendly, of course, but I wanted my name at the top, above hers.

Once my package arrived, I dove into my first program, which was called P90X. I read the nutrition plan from cover to cover and then shared about my strategy, workouts, mindset, and food, on my social media, plus some bits about my family. I decided to create a diary of it, to share my process as I went through it, hoping people would watch and be inspired.

When my first paycheck arrived, my jaw dropped: I had earned $243 for one week of effort. I ran into the living room and told Bret he could already have his money back. This was the small win I needed to keep doing what I was doing. Imagine: $243 weekly! That would completely shift my family's situation. That would speed up our debt payoff and help get us out of our hole even quicker.

After thirty days, my body had shifted right along with my energy and motivation. I asked Bret to snap pictures of me in my bathing suit, for a "before and after." I was shocked and so excited to share it. The shifts I'd made in just thirty days, physically, mentally, and financially, were unbelievable. Still, I was a little nervous when I hit *share* on Facebook after organizing those photos.

My notifications dinged with comments and likes immediately. People told me how inspiring it was and how happy they were for me. And there it was again: that shot of serotonin straight to my veins. The Sara in me, that piece of me deep-down that craved external validation and confirmation, was finally getting exactly what she needed.

That Sunday, Bret and I walked through the church doors confidently, with smiles on our faces as we dropped the kids off and made our way into the main room. I felt an energy shift as we said hi to some of our friends, who seemed standoffish in a way.

When the associate pastor made his way over to us, he asked if he could talk to us. Unsure what it was about, we eagerly said yes and followed him off to the side.

He began to explain that some women in the church weren't happy with how I was sharing so publicly on social media. More specifically, they were taken back by the photo I had shared in my bathing suit, vulnerably sharing my body with the world. The women believed that *a woman's body should be for her husband only*... My actions were concerning. I'm not sure what shade of horrified red my face turned, but heat flooded my entire body, a combination of embarrassment and anger.

Bret and I were asked to have a meeting with our pastor and a couple of the women, to talk through the situation. I couldn't find the energy to argue my side. I just sat there, soaking in their judgment, while my thoughts went wild with anger, reminding me of why I'd avoided places like this for so many years. I called my mother-in-law that afternoon, crying and upset about how these women, my new *friends*, felt that way about what I was sharing.

What she said to me stuck with me for decades.

"Raina, if what you're doing and sharing feels good inside your heart of hearts—if it doesn't feel wrong or malicious or for the wrong reasons—then keep doing what you're doing. Allow it to fuel your fire."

And so, I did.

I started to pull away from the church, and by mid-summer, my name had made it to the top of the recognition boards, even surpassing Anita. There was a constant push and pull between us, as we fought for the top spot. I got off on the competition. I had rank-advanced two more times by then, and the couple of hundred dollars I'd been earning each week grew into $400-500. If Bret had needed any convincing, that was it.

I always told my team, "Men speak the language of money. If they're not supportive now, start earning an income, and watch how quickly it changes."

Bret encouraged me to continue and became my biggest fan.

Leslie called me one afternoon to share that she'd been invited to a leadership event in Orange County, California, and she asked if I'd like to be her guest. All expenses would be paid, other than my flight, and if I could make it, I'd just have to meet her in Los Angeles.

This can't be real life, I thought. I'd never been to California; it seemed so exotic, big, and full of possibility. That's where people went to make magical things happen. I said yes to her before Bret had even agreed, and I was on my first-ever solo flight to the West Coast.

I can recall the vision outside of my taxi window as we drove through the hills in California. The houses were stacked on the side of the mountain with such confidence. The warm air, the light breeze, the palm trees. I felt like a different person after being there for just thirty minutes. As I inhaled, I could smell dreams coming true.

I arrived at the resort and met Leslie in person, hugging the woman who'd single-handedly changed the trajectory of my life in ways I couldn't even have imagined. We jumped on the bed like little girls, snapping a photo that we could use on social media to share the story of our connection and how we intended to spend the weekend.

I didn't realize at the time that this event was for the top coaches in the company, with hundreds of people in attendance. I was surrounded by the highest-earning and top-ranked men and women in the company, who'd said yes to the opportunity, just like I had.

Some I recognized from social media, some from training videos I'd seen, and some from the workouts themselves. They were the trainers who led workouts I did from my living room. I was starstruck and inspired.

During the welcome reception that first night, I followed Leslie around as she introduced me to some of her friends and partners in the business. We snapped photos with the CEO himself and some of the fitness trainers, which felt like being surrounded by movie stars, people who had really made it. My small-town inner Sara self, who always felt like she had to play it small and safe, had to remind myself to be cool and not freak out. I felt so lucky to be there.

I was introduced to a group of three or four women by Leslie, who shared with them my accomplishments in the business so far, including my rank-advances and the numbers I was hitting each week. I blushed: I was never great at celebrating myself. Even when I heard it out loud, it didn't feel like she was talking about me.

One of the women sipped her drink and asked, "That's great. How long have you been a coach?"

"Six months!" I said proudly.

"Oh, well, that's why your numbers are so good. You're new. Trust me, that'll go away," she stated, taking another sip from her drink. A couple of the other women giggled.

"Ah, I don't believe that." I responded, expressing my inner Jane. Then, I turned toward Leslie and smiled.

Let it fuel your fire, I reminded myself.

We spent the next few days in training sessions, doing live workouts with the trainers, and sipping cocktails with women whose businesses and lives I envied. I sat there, soaking in every word they said, as if the secrets to the business were kept inside each of them.

On the very last day, before leaving for the airport, Leslie and I took a fifteen-minute walk to the beach. I had never been to the Pacific Ocean before, let alone sunk my toes into the sand or let the waves crash into my body. I peeled off my shoes and stood at the edge of the water, where the sea met the sand in a beautiful rhythm. I closed my eyes, feeling the tears build behind my lids. I had to breathe deep to shoo them away.

This felt like home.

This felt like the life I wanted.

This felt aligned.

And in this moment, it clicked for Jane: all the possibility, a potential way out.

I turned to Leslie and said, "One day, I'm going to move here."

"Hell yes, girl," she replied, smiling. She closed her own eyes as she faced the ocean. Fire fueled.

I arrived back in Kansas City feeling more motivated than ever before. I worked closely with Leslie as I shared my big goals, strategizing my continued growth in the company.

Bret asked me all about the trip, and I shared every detail with excitement and newfound energy. I told him, more serious than nervous, "One day, I'm moving our family to California."

"Okay," he said and laughed.

That was the only word I needed to hear. I didn't care if he believed it or not. I held had fast to that vision that had swooped in on my plane ride home, as I watched the ocean fade into the distance.

By December of that first year, I was making $1,000 a week, and my life never looked the same again.

I decided to close my Etsy shop and retire from making the scarves. It just didn't make sense anymore to spend my spare time working on that business, when my joy was in the other one. I went all-in.

My business began to just flow. After I had completed several of the fitness programs, I felt like I was in the best shape I'd ever been in. I had six-pack abs, and my legs were starting to lean out, something I never thought would be possible for me.

While I was growing up, I'd never felt insecure about my legs. They were *my* legs. When I joined the basketball team my freshman year, we wore our jersey and shorts with long knee-socks circled in purple. During practices after school, though, we ditched the long socks while we worked on drills and ran laps in the gym.

"Oh shit! Raina's got *cankles*!" one boy yelled from the boys' basketball team. Other boys laughed, and that one comment stuck with me into my adulthood.

I had my mom's legs, thick and full, and I knew, by looking at her, I'd have the same legs once I grew up. I was okay with it, until I realized that *boys* found it unattractive.

Bret even said to me once, "You're the only person I've ever seen with cellulite on their calves," and he'd laughed like he'd made the funniest joke in the world. He probably didn't realize it would also stick with me well into my thirties.

With my eating disorders healed and leaner body, it fueled a confidence I'd never had, I was ready for the next level, though I was unsure what that even was. I had watched our old babysitter, Crystal, dive into the world of fitness competitions, and I was very intrigued.

Crystal was our babysitter when Mckenzie was little, and she'd even watched Ella after she was born, until we moved to Kansas City. I loved her as our babysitter and cried when we moved away, because I hated to leave her behind. We stayed in touch via Facebook, though, and I watched her transition into the fitness world. I couldn't get enough of it.

Bret and I drove down to Springfield one weekend to watch her competition. She ended up placing. I became really intrigued by this world, by the discipline each woman had to stand on that stage, and I felt an immediate pull to it.

While we chatted back and forth, she asked if I'd ever thought about competing and offered to help coach me through it.

Me? I thought. *A bikini competition?* I mean, I was already posting before and after photos to my social media. What would be the harm in getting on a stage to do it for a prize and a title? I was in. It felt like the next right step in my fitness journey, and I was excited to begin.

Life #14

Competition

Crystal put me on a handful of supplements, wrote out a meal plan for me, and provided me with a training schedule.

"The only thing is," she said, "I know you're doing this whole coaching business thing, and I love it for you, but you can't drink the shakes. And you need to follow my workout plan. No exceptions, if you really wanna win." After I nodded, she continued, "No more fruit. Fruit is for fat people and runners."

I read over the protein-packed, carb-and-fat-cycling plan she emailed me and thought, *Okay, I can just focus on the business side of things, mentoring other women to work the business, just like Leslie did for me, while I go through the competitions.* I had confidence that I could do both. And not just *do* them, but excel at them.

For the next six months, I dove into competition prep. I spent at least an hour in the gym each day, really falling in love with the energy and the vibe that came with it. It felt like we'd entered into a whole new community when people heard I was training for competition. People became invested in the journey. Bret and I went together every day, cheering each other on.

We took weekend trips down to our hometown area to meet with Crystal and her new boyfriend, who was also in the competition world, after dropping the girls off with my dad. We'd spend a couple of hours in the gym, where she taught me the ins and outs of weightlifting and helped me to increase my body awareness. She sent me to the machine to do rows, pushing her index finger into the back of my shoulder, while pressing firmly into my rear delts, to show me where I should be focusing my energy. I'd think only about where her finger was pressing as I pulled into each rep, flexing that muscle. Learning this body awareness helped me more in the future than I ever imagined.

After the gym, we'd stop by the supplement store to restock our protein powder and pre-workout nutrition, before sitting down for protein-packed meals at their home. We'd talk about the competition world, the science behind the meal plans we were following, and gym life. I loved every second of it. I loved the control it gave me over my body, and in a healthier way than I was used to, on my own.

About half way through my prep, Crystal told me I wasn't burning fat at the rate she wanted, so she suggested I try Anavar. Anavar is an anabolic steroid that I took in the form of an oil, directly under my tongue. For the sake of the sport, I did it, stuffing the feeling that I was a *fraud* as far down as I could. My body quickly shifted from that point forward. My body fat percentage went down, and my muscle definition increased. By the time I stood on stage in my emerald-green sparkly bikini and clear stilettos, I felt like a strong, lean machine.

I did two competitions, one in Las Vegas, where I placed in the top ten out of hundreds. The night before I stepped on stage, I felt like I was having a giant panic attack. Crystal didn't join us in Vegas, so Bret called her to ask what he should do.

"Go get her some Reese's peanut butter cups, now! She needs the sugar!" she urged him. Within ten minutes after eating two cups, I felt better.

The second time was an NPC competition, where I won second place, earning my way into the National Championships in Chicago, early the next year. I was so proud of myself, so grateful for the incredible training that Crystal had provided, and so insanely ready for a cheeseburger on a regular bun with bacon and cheese.

We went out to dinner that night with all of my family and friends who had attended. Even Leslie came to support me, flying in from Michigan and I got my cheeseburger. I had done it, placed in my first bikini competition. Box checked.

Post-competition emotions hit me hard. I felt so good for a week or so after the show. Crystal even met me for a photo shoot, where I felt insanely confident. My issues didn't start until I got home. I didn't want to look at a shake, eat a piece of chicken, or touch a vegetable. Not only that, I felt really burnt out at the gym, so working out didn't excite me anymore.

Looking back, I think it's because the vision was gone. I had *won* already, in my mind. I had no goal of doing this professionally, continuing for years into the future. But it seemed like everyone else around me thought I should.

Bret and I quickly fell back into our Freddy's trips and takeout for dinner, because, well, I just really missed eating food. I'll never forget sitting in my hotel room, pre-competition, eating cold tilapia and broccoli out of a Tupperware dish. I felt numb and just over everything. I still thought about that as I drank my root beer float. I cut Anavar cold turkey and went right back to eating real food, instead of reverse dieting like Crystal had recommended.

Within a couple of months, I'd put on all of my pre-competition weight plus an extra forty pounds. I was heavier than I had ever been, even while pregnant with my daughters. I hid behind cute clothes and my business, thankful that I got to work from social media versus in person. I knew how to pose and what angles to hit to hide the weight gain from a lot of people. Like a storm, all of my insecurities and disordered eating habits rolled back in, and I had a hard time accepting the fact that I'd fallen off.

I told myself and others that I was in the muscle-building phase, continuing the workouts at the gym and focusing on lifting heavy, while I ate higher calories and macros to stack on weight. I lived in this phase for about four months before I had to start cutting again for my next show, the Nationals in Chicago. Around this time, for accountability and the joy of it, Bret decided to compete, also. It felt good, having his support and help at home. I didn't feel like I could do it alone again.

With my next show on the calendar, I restarted a stricter diet and workout routine, trying to fall back into the flow of competition prep. Week after week, I had a hard time noticing my body changing. It felt harder than ever to shed the weight I had gained. I told myself my body was probably *too far gone* and my mindset was struggling.

Despite all the struggles with my body and mindset, my business continued to thrive. It felt like an anchor in my life, while everything else felt like a mess. *I've been here before,* I thought.

I continued to advance, rank after rank, surpassing people who had signed up around the same time I had. Before I knew it, my weekly paychecks were $2-3,000 per week, and I was nearly surpassing Bret's income. We were both floored and impressed at how easily my business was growing.

Bret and I went on a reward trip with the company the following spring. I had so much anxiety around the trip. I felt like I wasn't going to be able to eat or drink or have fun, since I was just a matter of weeks out from my competition. I put on a happy face while we celebrated our accomplishments with the team and sat around poolside. Then, I allowed my smile to fall and the tears to flow when I was back in my room. This wasn't the *restrictive* life I wanted. I knew that to my core.

And then, as if the string to whatever was holding me together just snapped, I ordered a strawberry daiquiri in the pool. Bret looked at me with questioning eyes, like, *Why would you order such a sugary drink?*

"I can't do it... I can't cut, I can't eat like this. I can't mentally do this anymore. I want to give up my spot at Nationals," I blurted out.

Then, I broke. The tears started to run down my face, and I shrugged at him, shaking my head. A couple of my friends waded through the pool to come give me a hug.

"Thank fucking God," they said, as we all laughed.

"*Drinks!*" another yelled.

I needed their humor. I needed their lightness. It felt like such a heavy decision to leave that world behind and disappoint all the people who'd helped me get there. The Sara part of me felt as if I was disappointing a lot of people, but that wasn't really *my* voice saying that.

By blocking that voice out, I spent the rest of our trip enjoying myself, drinking with my friends, and celebrating the decision I had made to come back to myself.

Once we were home, it felt like a weight had fallen off of my shoulders, like I had regained the freedom to eat whatever I wanted, without judgment or punishment, and to move my body in a way that felt good.

Life #15

Vision

I dove back into my home workout programs, excited to be able to work out in my living room again, in all the ways I had fallen in love with.

With this refocus on my fitness came a refocus on my business. I'd felt like a fraud, going to the gym each day, while telling people to drink a shake I wasn't allowed to drink. I felt like this *refocus* would help me in my business, reconnecting me with the people I was helping—and it did.

We picked up the girls from school and sat down on the picnic tables at the park one afternoon, while the kids played on the playground. Bret and I did this a few days a week, letting them run around screaming, "Mom! Dad! Watch this!" over and over again. We'd watch, laugh, and continue our conversation as they lived their best lives.

This time, I'd brought a notebook with me, and I told Bret I was serious about my goal of moving to California. I wanted him to help me make a business plan to get there. We chatted about our goals individually and as a family, and I knew I wanted more for my kids.

I loved the life we had worked so hard to create, but I wanted more. I didn't want my girls growing up in Missouri; I carried a lot of disgust for the place I'd called home my entire life. In my mind, it was a place you either ran from or allowed to suck you in, tie you down, and hold you prisoner. I'd seen what happened to those who stayed. It felt like a guaranteed life of poverty and loneliness.

Years before, I'd thought my future was clear, laid out in front of me. I'd be a mom, most likely divorced, broke, and struggling to pay bills. Everyone I knew around me as I grew up was living that life, so surely, I was bound for it, also.

"Mom! *Watch!*" the girls yelled. I smiled, proud of myself for deciding that their future would look different.

Bret had grown to hate his job—the hours, the money, the environment no longer aligned. He had become such a staple in my business, carrying the vision of being a stay-at-home dad and helping me full-time. He knew a lot about entrepreneurship and running a business, so I felt it was a realistic goal to set: retire him. He was already joining me on team calls and giving pep talks, strategizing business growth, and providing accountability to several of my teammates. They saw him as an extension of me. It just made sense.

We set a goal to replace his income within a year, with a $160,000 goal for me, which I wasn't far from. We felt more comfortable having several months of solid income before he gave his notice.

In just six months, Bret officially became a stay-at-home dad, and our entire flow changed. We spent the day together, dropping kids off at school and then exploring, working out, and collaborating with our team on our business. He'd join me for team calls I hosted and he mentored members of our team in a way I couldn't. He had a magic motivational touch that no one could deny. We were a real power couple.

We were prepping for a road trip to our company's annual event. We planned to leave a couple of days early, so we could take our time, stop in Colorado, and sightsee. In Vegas, we planned to spend each day in training conferences and listening to motivational speakers, and at night, we'd attend parties and dinners with our team and other company coaches.

When I entered a room, Bret held my bags, took any photos people asked for, and smiled the whole time, proud of me and happy to be a part of it all. When I looked at him, I was so proud of the man he'd become. While he may have been on Adderall most days and drank more with the guys than I liked, *it could be worse*, I thought. Things *had* been worse. I had to cling onto gratitude for the progress he'd made.

The girls were spending time with grandparents, so we weren't in a rush to head back home. I talked Bret into extending our four-day trip by a few days, so we could take a drive to California afterward. I wanted to show him why I fell in love. My hope was that, when we left, he'd have the same pit in his stomach, nudging him to the West Coast.

We didn't really know *where* in California we wanted to be, so we just drove west. Before the sun set, we cruised down the main strip of the cutest little town, Encinitas, and parked at a motel, not really caring what the inside looked like. We booked a room and dropped off our bags before heading to walk on the beach and grab dinner.

We held hands as we walked along the beach, the seventy-degree breeze blowing my hair around. *Heaven,* I thought. Bret and I walked, daydreamed, browsed Zillow, and ate at a local restaurant while soaking in the environment.

We spent the following day roaming around other towns along Highway 101, windows down. While Bret blasted his music, I closed my eyes and let the wind blow in my face. I allowed myself to daydream again, and I saw the clear vision of me and my family living there.

I imagined our day, with the girls in their school, palm trees out the window. I imagined our beach-bound weekends and the girls in their little bathing suits, running and laughing as they chased the waves. I imagined walks along the beach like this, happy, with my husband by my side. I opened my eyes and looked over at Bret with a big smile on my face.

He smiled back at me and just said, "Okay... I get it."

When we arrived back home, Bret and I sat down at the park again, to talk about family and life goals. I was earning about $3,500 a week by this point, and my inner Jane had zero self-doubt: I was convinced I could do anything.

He told me, if I was serious about California, *which I was*, I would need to triple my income for us to make the move and live comfortably. I didn't question him. I just soaked in this fact and started to write out a strategy for how to make it a reality. I had retired him with ease, and I was again convinced I could hit my goals.

There was no doubt in my mind. I didn't have negative self-talk or doubt. There was no little voice in the back of my head saying, *Maybe we can't do this.* No, I knew I could.

I felt, if my vision was clear enough, I just needed to put in the action steps to financially make it a reality. Working with my corporate mentors in the business, I created a strategy, went all-in on my social media platforms to help more people, worked overtime mentoring my team to hit their goals, and put blinders on, focusing only on building the business I knew would support the life I wanted to live.

Life #16

Action

With that, my income gradually increased. I worked my business with confidence, reaping the benefits of my intentional work. I'd never seen this kind of money in my life... *ever*. It felt as if I was being rewarded for how poor I had been for all those years, and I celebrated that. For the first time, I could enroll my girls in things like ballet and gymnastics, not questioning if I could afford it. I began to stroll through the grocery store, excited to experiment with other meals that didn't come out of boxes.

That Christmas felt more special than any before it. In previous years, we'd taken out a payday loan in order to pay for the holidays, putting us in a deeper hole come January. This year, we paid cash for Christmas and didn't put a cap on it. I wanted to give my kids a Christmas they wouldn't forget. And as our little family joyfully healed, it only made sense to add a puppy into the mix.

I grew up with all kinds of animals, because my mom owned and ran the pet store when I was growing up. As I think happens to many people, whatever you grow up around, you end up resisting. Same with me.

Initially, I didn't want any animals to take care of. Two kids felt like plenty. But Mckenzie had been begging us for months for a dog. She knew Bret was slightly allergic, and I didn't want a big dog, so she went ahead and did the research for us.

"A maltipoo! That's what I want! It looks like a little teddy bear, and Dad won't be allergic," she told us with her little lisp as she scrolled through photos on Google.

My mom was still in the pet business at that time and referred us to a woman in Missouri who was just about to have a litter of maltipoo puppies. Bret and I made a three-hour drive down to meet the new addition to our family, a month or so before the holidays. We talked about names the entire drive, knowing it would be us who needed to name the puppy or else we'd get stuck with a dog named *Princess Jasmine* or *Barbie Dream Girl.* Bret and I had been binging the TV show, *Dexter.* I was completely obsessed with the character and the storyline, so when I pitched the name, it stuck.

We picked up the little guy a couple of weeks later and planned to surprise the girls with him on Christmas morning. I was trying to give them my own nine-year-old's Christmas, hoping to see that same joy on their face, if even for a single moment. We dropped Dexter off at their great-grandparents' home; they'd offered to watch him until Christmas Eve, so we could preserve the surprise.

Christmas morning felt like a dream. After opening all the presents, Bret said, "Awe, man—we forgot one! I'll be right back..." And he ran out to the garage to make the puppy exchange. He was a terrible actor but good enough to convince two little girls.

They hardly acknowledged him and continued to play, unboxing the presents they'd already received, while he slipped out the door to meet our grandparents and snagged the puppy.

"Here it is... Kenzie, Ella, the last present! You have to close your eyes!"

With the puppy in a little wooden basket with a blanket draped over it, Bret walked into the house with the basket in his arms, while Dexter wobbled around inside.

We made the girls sit on the couch together as they squeezed their eyes shut and bounced up and down in their seats.

"What is it? *What is it?"*

They had the biggest toothless smiles as they squeezed their eyes shut, the crinkles in their face made me giggle.

When they opened the basket and squealed, I thought my heart would explode right then and there. Like when my dad surprised me with a pony.

Dexter became the glue for our little struggling family. I no longer had the burden of feeling like it was only *me* who kept the family together. He played a big role in keeping me together, when I felt like I was about to fall apart. He was always the kids' dog, but I'll remember his connection with me forever.

Once I had made the decision to stop competing, I went into full support-mode for Bret and his goal to compete in a physique competition. We weren't working with Crystal anymore, but Bret found a local trainer whom he knew from his hometown. Grant jumped at the opportunity to help Bret prep for his first show.

Grant was a beast and so knowledgeable in the world Bret was dipping his toe into. I would tag along with Bret to the gym and half-ass my workouts, playing the role of supportive wife, to spot him or encourage him through the workout.

I was even the one who gave him shots in the butt, when he decided he needed to take steroids in order to get to the size he would be comfortable competing at. Feeling like a hypocrite, I hated that he did this, worried about it triggering some old addict instinct in him.

I realized quickly that most people in that world are using some kind of enhancement. There were easy work-arounds when it came to testing, so it wasn't something Bret resisted. Within months, he was so jacked, veins were just spewing from every body part as he lifted more weight than I could ever imagine picking up.

Through this process, he started to deal with some back pain as a result of the heavy weights he was lifting. He got plugged into physical therapy, and after a few doctor visits, he was prescribed some pain medicine for his ongoing issue. I look back on that and wished I'd known that this was the beginning of a long road leading to a dead end.

He needed to slow down, to possibly rethink the goal he had set, yet he kept pushing through, and I didn't blame him. It was the world we lived in.

Nationals rolled around, the same competition I was supposed to be competing in before I withdrew, and Grant thought it would be cool if we all went to Chicago anyway and spent the weekend just relaxing and having fun. I was sold. I had never been to Chicago, and I knew we both needed a vacation. Grant and his wife, Bret and I, and Bret's parents all booked a hotel and flights, meeting in the heart of Chicago for a weekend trip.

I could tell on the flight out that Bret wasn't feeling well. He kept having to stand up to stretch his back, sitting down for longer than he wanted to, and unable to stay in one spot because of the discomfort. I watched him pop a pain medication or two then looked away, knowing he was struggling.

When we landed, we checked into the hotel, and Bret lay down on the bed for a bit, to ease the pain.

How in the hell are we supposed to walk around Chicago all weekend if he's in so much pain? I wondered. I texted Grant, telling him how shitty Bret was feeling, so we all decided to have a relaxing night. We would go out to dinner, have a few drinks, and call it an early first night.

The next day, we had planned a brunch and day of shopping. I was so pumped—my first time in Chicago. Bret's mom, Danelle, had pumped me up about the idea of shopping on the Magnificent Mile, raving about all the high-end brands and stores we'd get to explore. She knew I had another event coming up soon for our company, a couple of weeks after we got home from Chicago.

During brunch, Bret was in so much pain, he couldn't stand. He couldn't sit, either, and walking about killed him. As we sat on a bench near a bus stop, the five of us, watching Bret wince with every movement, his dad insisted Bret go to the ER, to see if something else was wrong.

Reluctantly, Bret allowed his dad and Grant to escort him to the nearest hospital, Northwestern, to get looked at. Truly, I didn't think it would take long. I assumed he'd be pumped with fluids plus more pain meds, and be stabilized temporarily to a point where we could at least finish our vacation, then he could go see his doctor when we got home.

Danelle and I opted for a girls' day of shopping around Chicago, and we had no regrets. We explored every store in that Mile, swiping the card as we pleased. We went to dinner at Giordano's Pizza and had some cocktails while we waited for the boys to give us an update.

When we got the call from Jerry, my stomach dropped.

Bret had been diagnosed with a Pars Defect, a break in his back that was causing a CSF leak, which—we were told—was very serious. He was admitted into the hospital, and we waited for more information after scans and more doctor visits. The cause was unknown, though we all assumed it had been punctured from damage to his spine, due to working out.

He was ordered to lie flat, to minimize the fluid leak going forward. During an MRI, they discovered he had another puncture in his neck. They discussed doing an epidural blood patch on the spaces to seal them and, after several days, decided he'd require surgery to repair the leaks.

Bret lay in his hospital bed for the entire weekend. We ended up extending our stay for a full week. I missed my kids deeply, but I stayed by Bret's bedside until he was safe to go home. It was a whirlwind of a week, full of nerves and fear between bursts of hopefulness and naps. I slept in a chair in his hospital room, only leaving his side when Danelle, Jerry, and I roamed down to the pier, while he had his surgery.

When he was released from the hospital, I was so relieved to be able to roll him out in the wheelchair. I'd battled serious thoughts of *what if I lose my husband?*

Not long after that, Bret was back in the gym, fueled by pain medication and pre-workout supplements. Weeks later, he competed in his first competition, and we were all so proud of him. I also felt relieved it was over. I was ready to leave this world in my rear-view mirror.

Life #17

California

In 2015, life started to feel semi-normal again, and we booked a family vacation: to fly to California with the girls to spend a couple of days at Disneyland, in between house shopping. I took hundreds of photos of them as we walked out of the airport, capturing their first glimpses of palm trees and the smiles on their faces. I couldn't get enough. We found our hotel and wandered to the beach to show them the ocean. I grinned broadly as they all took off toward the water.

Their little screams were so dramatic, as they ran from the waves then chased them back into the ocean. *This.* This was what I wanted every day to feel like. This was a peek into my vision.

When we woke up the next morning, we headed for Universal Studios. I noticed Bret take a couple of his pain meds as we got out of the car, preparing himself for a day of being up and about. I felt a heaviness in my gut, but I ignored it, looking in the other direction and avoiding what needed to be addressed.

If I just avoid it, maybe it'll go away.

Quickly, I pasted the smile back on my face and laughed as Bret went to the line to sign us up for Fast Passes. In true Bret fashion, we were going big or going home: he didn't want to wait in a line.

We zipped through ride after ride, ate all of the churros, and laughed together for hours before the girls were ready to crash. When we left the park, we drove past two or three homes we'd saved on Zillow, while the girls slept in the back seat.

We did this the next day, too, and the next. We reached out for house tours at a few of the homes we loved, but I left each one feeling defeated. None of them aligned with my vision. I wanted to move so badly, so I found myself trying to settle. One home wouldn't work because there weren't enough rooms, but I thought, *maybe we could convert the garage?* The next home only had one bathroom, but *maybe we can make it work with the four of us?*

On the last morning of our trip, we took it slow, waking up at a gentle pace. We didn't have any parks scheduled, just home tours, and they didn't start until after lunch. Bret walked the girls down to the lobby to snag the free breakfast, while I lay in bed with my coffee and grabbed my laptop. I got paid every Thursday, and since it was a Thursday morning, I logged into my online office website to see where I was in my mission to increase my income.

As the girls busted through the door, I looked up at Bret and smiled, crying, "Oh my god!"

$15,000 in one week. I'd fucking done it. I'd done exactly what I said I was going to do.

Bret and I just stared at each other, smiling, while the kids jumped on the bed. I was in California with my family, celebrating the biggest weekly paycheck I'd ever received. *I'd done it!*

This was just fuel on the fire for Jane! I walked a little taller that day, blown away by the powerful feeling of simply making shit happen. I couldn't believe how quickly my life had turned around. It wasn't perfect by any means, but I was holding the reins on the way there.

We spent the afternoon driving along the coast from Los Angeles down to San Diego. We had put pins in different locations, planning and strategizing for times with realtors, trying to fit in as many viewings as we could. By the time we made it down to San Diego, we had looked at five homes and had two more left.

Again, the feeling of defeat had slipped back in. But I stayed positive as we headed toward the last home. When I put the address in the GPS, recognition slammed into me.

Encinitas, California. The house was in the same little town where Bret and I had stayed on our first trip together. These were the first beaches we'd walked and the first restaurants we'd explored. A tingle flooded me.

"In half a mile, turn left," said the GPS.

We made our way to the top of a hill. I was in awe of the palm trees lining each street in the neighborhood. Then, I *gasped* when I saw the Pacific Ocean straight ahead. We followed the coastline down the hill, with the ocean on our right.

This is it, I thought, knowing deep-down this would be the house. I elbowed Bret, and he smiled. He didn't even have to say it: I knew he felt the same way.

When we pulled up the steep driveway to the white house, I got out and looked out to the ocean, pausing for a moment to soak in the idea that this could be home. I told the kids to listen to the crashing waves against the shore. I couldn't wait to wake up to that sound.

The real estate agent pulled in right behind us and unlocked the front door. On the first floor would be Kenzie's room on the left and Ella's on the right. I knew this because they ran into each room, claiming it as their own. There was a perfect bathroom right between them and lots of closet space. As we made our way upstairs to the main floor, again I left out a *gasp.*

Bret gave me a look that said, *What the hell?* He had told me to play it cool. "Don't get overly excited when we see it," he'd say. "We'll lose the ability to negotiate price if you are too giddy about it." I swallowed my gasp.

At the top of the stairs was a big, open living room, dining room, and then kitchen. The balcony was the biggest I'd ever seen, with a 180-degree view overlooking the Pacific Ocean. I felt the sting of tears welling in my wide eyes and made eye contact with Bret, mouthing the word: *YES.*

The girls ran around the balcony in circles as I just stood there, looking out at the expanse. This was it, my vision. I had zero doubts in my mind that this was the house I'd be living in.

We finished the tour, but I could have signed right there.

After a tour of the huge master bedroom, closet, stone-tiled bathroom, and my future office, the realtor asked, "Well, what do you think?"

Bret asked her if we could talk privately for a moment, and she went to chat with the girls.

"This is it," I said. "Don't you think?! This is it. This is the house I want. Holy shit, Bret—the balcony! Please. Do you love it? Please… I want this." I rambled, knowing I wouldn't take no for an answer.

We met the realtor in the kitchen. "We want it." Bret told her.

She pulled the lease out of her bag, and we spent the next thirty minutes talking about logistics, move-in timeline, deposit, and requirements. We signed the lease agreement right then and there, trusting that this place would be ours.

The only hesitation we had was over the move-in day. We'd need to go home, give our notice, start packing, and be back in two weeks to move in. It was a lot to organize and balance, but I didn't care. I was ready.

We got on our flight back to Kansas City, and within a day, the realtor had processed the background checks and records to approve us. We sent the first and last month's rent as deposit. Me, my husband, my two daughters, and our maltipoo puppy, Dexter, were going to relocate to California.

We gave our notice to the apartment complex and shared the news with our family. Bret's family was so excited for us, for the opportunity we had, but sad their granddaughters would be so far away. My dad wasn't excited about the transition. In his eyes, it would pull his daughter and grandkids further away from God. My mom was pretty indifferent.

Whether we had all the support in the world or none at all, I still would have made the choice to move. To this day, it's one of the best decisions I have ever made for myself and my girls.

We spent the next two weeks posting our furniture on Craigslist and packing the things we wanted to take with us. We decided to sell all of the furniture we had, mostly beds and couches, and buy new sets when we got there. We donated a lot of clothes and toys to Goodwill and packed up the rest in boxes for Bret and his dad to drive out to California.

The girls, Danelle, and I all flew out together, landing in California a few days before the boys arrived. We had so much fun exploring Encinitas and shopping around at all of the little boutiques. I walked into one of the stores that had a combination of furniture, crystals, clothing, and knickknacks. There, I fell in love with a beautiful, round, cement-topped table of gray concrete with wooden legs crossed in an X. We bought it, and it became the centerpiece to set the vibe for the whole house.

Something I'd learned about myself, if my space isn't organized, I can't settle. I had been this way growing up and into high school. Between giving birth to Mckenzie and moving to California, we'd lived in ten different homes, and in each space, I had had to settle into it and make it home, whether we were going to live there a short time or forever.

California was the same—but very intensely. This was *it*, my big vision. It was also a clean slate. Everything I used to be, the old versions of myself and her furniture, were gone. I now had the ability to let my girls pick out beds and decor for their rooms, and I let them get whatever they wanted. We picked out a beautiful king-size bed with the best adjustable mattress available, so Bret could find some relief when he slept. We found the perfect chairs to go with my amazing new table, and a comfortable gray couch to complement it. Everywhere, I created a safe space, a cozy nest that was mine.

I woke up each morning and lay there for a few minutes before getting up. I quieted my breath and could hear the soft crashes of the waves along the shore. Then, I'd roll out of bed and take Dexter outside to potty, watching the water until the girls were awake. I opened the sliding doors to the balcony and allowed the breeze to cleanse the house, blowing away whatever energy wasn't welcome.

As I made breakfast, I watched the runners and bikers on the sidewalk that lined the cliffs in front of the beach. I loved the energy of watching people outside moving their bodies. It stirred excitement in me.

After we took the girls to school and waved goodbye, I'd catch a glimpse of Bret grabbing his pain medication from his middle console and swallowing a few. I tried not to make eye contact with him when I saw this. If I did, he'd quickly snap a look back at me saying, "What? I'm taking the amount I'm supposed to," like guilt was already crippling him. He didn't need added pressure from me. I got really good at avoiding this entire situation.

Once we dropped the kids off, Bret and I would head back home to make our pre-workout drink and work out together. He had begun to take it easy, joining me in doing some of the home workouts I promoted, and I loved this time we had together. We'd put on some rap music and lift weights or try to keep up with the cardio moves, laughing and watching the ocean in between sets.

After our post-workout shakes, we'd take Dexter on a walk around the town. Our favorite path was steep and quite the trek for Dexter, so Bret ended up carrying him for half of the walk, but the view at the top of the overlook was breathtaking. We would just stand there, watching the surfers float on their surfboards, patient and in no rush. Once they spotted the perfect wave, they'd ride it into the beach and then fight their way back out to repeat the process.

We had deep conversations there. Conversations about the future, about our past, about the kids and our goals. It became one of my favorite spots in the world.

When we returned home midmorning, and I'd sit down in my office to start my work day. I'd check in with my team, log onto mentorship calls, or create new trainings and/or strategies to continue our team's growth. I loved what I did. This season of my business lit my fire like nothing I'd ever experienced before.

I was good at what I did. Good at mentoring people, good at expressing tough love and connecting with those who wanted to create a business of their own. My inner Jane was in full bloom, and I soon became known for expressing tough love, speaking as a guest on other team's calls, and even participating on company-wide conference calls. I worked every single day and gave it everything I had.

That year, I exploded not only financially, but also in accomplishments and recognition from the company. I locked in the highest rank in the company, creating a team of several other leaders who worked beside me. We earned the title, Millionaire's Club, which meant, in the time we'd been in business, we'd earned a cumulative income of over $1 million. And shortly after, we were recognized for hitting Top 10 in the company, landing a spot at number seven out of nearly 400,000 people.

I was on Cloud Nine. High on life and business, and I felt as if I could truly do and create anything I set my mind to. But my body felt like it was out to get me.

Life #18

Colitis

Since I'd decided to stop competing, my weight gain was consistent. I felt so uncomfortable in my skin, but I hid behind my success in the business.

The weight wasn't coming off as easily as it once had, yet when I reflected, I wasn't taking my wellness journey as seriously as I once had, either. I drank my shakes inconsistently, because I was so burnt out on protein shakes. And other than that, I didn't monitor what food went in. We ate out often, because we could and we were in a new town that we wanted to explore.

I also found myself half-assing my workouts. Bret would do most of it, but I'd piddle around for more time than necessary, propping up my phone to record some of the moves for sharing on my social media platform. I was more focused on selling the workouts than doing them.

In addition to this, I'd found myself using the bathroom frequently. I would tell Bret, "As much as I'm shitting every day, you'd think the weight would just be coming off!"

I was finding myself in the bathroom over twenty times a day with diarrhea. I chalked it up to bad luck or something I was eating. After several months of this, Bret said to me, "I don't think this is normal. You should maybe go to the doctor."

I tossed the idea around and avoided it, but when I started to see blood in my stool, I made a couple of appointments.

I met with doctor after doctor but got nowhere. One doctor told me it was normal, then the next one recommended an antidiarrheal. One doctor put me on HCG, so I could try to lose the extra weight and see if that helped. The next one did an allergy test, which came back with nothing unusual. The next thought it might be food allergies and asked what other symptoms I had. When I thought back to my years of strep throat, hives, and mouth sores, things started to click.

Years before, when I sat by the pool with my family, I had pointed out the hives covering my arms and parts of my stomach, and we'd brainstormed possible causes. We usually ended up blaming it on the sun.

I tried everything I could find at the pharmacy to relieve the pain of the two to five canker sores that were always inside my mouth. I'd curse, if I bit my lip or cheek again in the same spot as a growing sore, the pain vibrating through my body.

After growing frustrated by all the strep throat and missing work because of it, my doctor had suggested we remove my tonsils. They'd promised it would mean I wouldn't have to keep dealing with this.

In California, I eventually met with a doctor who suggested they do a colonoscopy, to rule out some things and just check in on my colon. I went home with the date on the calendar and spent the night before cleaning out with the colonoscopy prep. 0/10 *do not* recommend.

I felt a little loopy after my colonoscopy, so Bret drove us to our favorite breakfast spot to refuel. Within a few days, I got the call with my results.

The doctor diagnosed me with Mild Ulcerative Colitis and emailed me the photos of my colon. "On the left," he said, "that's what a normal colon is supposed to look like. Yours is on the right. Notice how it sort of looks like ground beef?"

Hmmm, I thought.

I had no idea what Ulcerative Colitis was. To me, it just seemed like a label for some random issue where people have to go to the bathroom a lot. I picked up my new medication at the pharmacy and my doctor said it would help control my symptoms, but, I'd "have to take it for the rest of my life, most likely."

Ummm, no, I thought. *I'm a fucking wellness coach. I teach this. I help women get a grip on this, and I can't do it for myself?*

I had known for nearly a year that I was not giving my wellness my all. In fact, I was giving a mere ten percent. I had no idea if committing to my wellness would help my Ulcerative Colitis, but I decided to do my best and see what progress or healing I could do by cleaning up my diet and moving my body more intentionally.

I made an appointment with a naturopath down the street to get some help with the nutrition side of things. I wanted to get some tests done to see what foods would help and which were doing more harm, given this new diagnosis. Together, we created a plan for me to follow. I also signed up for regular IV vitamin infusions; Bret and I did them together weekly. I figured the more nutrients I could get, the better.

My company also had a program called The Ultimate Reset. It was a twenty-one-day vegan program that helped you reset your body and detox your system. The meal plan inside the detox was *very* similar to the program I'd created with the naturopath, so I decided I'd use the twenty-one-day detox as accountability. Twenty-one days at a time. I could do anything for twenty-one days.

I snapped a picture of myself in a sports bra the next morning, declaring that *Day One.* I didn't alter it; I didn't suck in. I didn't throw out a bikini-competition pose that would alter the way my body looked on camera. I just captured my natural body. I decided that, every single day for twenty-one days, I'd take a photo in the same mirror, to track progress for myself.

I told Bret I wanted to take daily walks, because intense exercise wasn't recommended during the detox. But I wanted to get in the habit of moving my body.

By the end of the first twenty-one days, I'd lost seventeen pounds, and my bathroom breaks had been cut in half.

I felt so relieved, looking at my *before* photo next to my twenty-first-day progress picture. I was really proud of myself, and this time it wasn't about my six-pack abs or chiseled legs. It was about health and longevity. I felt like a piece of "old Raina" had returned, and I was excited to regain my health.

I picked another program to dive into, right after my detox ended, and I committed to following it beginning to end. After that, I picked another program and another, continuing this train I found myself on and feeling like I never wanted to get off. I was getting back both my body and my confidence.

When I reflect, I can see clearly how my life has come in waves of good followed by struggle. Hindsight is always 20/20. I wish I could go back to tell that version of myself to pay more attention to the world around her.

I had blinders on. I was focused on my business, my health, my vision, and the paycheck that provided for my family. I did get gut feelings and glimpses of Bret's struggle, but it took a while for me to really wake up to what was happening.

By the time we were settled in California, I'd started to notice Bret's inconspicuous pill popping more times than I thought was normal. We'd be out shopping for the day, and before we'd get out of the car, he'd take his medicine. When we got back to the car, he took more. When we got home, he'd take more. This kept increasing week after week, and when I'd glance his way, giving him a concerned look, he began to get defensive.

"*What?*" he snapped.

"Bret... You just took, like, three pills. You just took some less than an hour ago, when we pulled into the parking lot," I said.

"Raina, it's prescribed by a doctor. My fucking back hurts. What do you want? For me to just be in pain?"

"No. Obviously. I want to make sure you're not taking more than you need," I snapped back. "I see how much you take every day, and it seems like more than a doctor would prescribe, Bret..."

We had back and forth like this often throughout the week. I've always been one to listen to my gut, so, when the nauseated feeling rolled over me, I acted on it. I questioned him to *make sure* my gut was lying, because surely my new and improved husband would be honest with me.

After a few months, this started to create some tension and resentment between us. I'd assume and ignore. He'd notice and continue. When he asked if I wanted to go to the doctor with him, so I could see that he was telling the truth, I said yes. I jumped at the opportunity to see how in the hell a physician could prescribe such a high amount of Oxycontin to someone.

When we walked into the office, I could feel the frustration and anger on my face. *Relax your face, Raina,* I thought to myself. I'd developed a hard exterior over the last several years and was working to release that.

In the exam room, the doctor asked Bret about his pain levels. He explained how he was still in pain and how certain positions and activities helped, while others made it worse. As if putting on an act for me, he added, "But I'd like to start tapering down from the medications I'm on. I'm not sure if they're working, and I feel like I'm having to take more than I'd like."

Internally, I felt like I was being played, and I felt helpless. There was nothing I could do but sit there as the appointment wrapped up.

The doctor looked at his chart and slowly nodded. "Well, you are on one of the highest doses we suggest. I think, instead of tapering down, we could swap you to a different medication that maybe requires you to take a little less."

That's not what he asked, I thought. He doesn't need another medication that's stronger, therefore requiring less. *He just asked to taper down!* My face turned red.

"Great," he said, as if he didn't understand the trade he was saying yes to.

He can't be that dumb, I thought. *He has to understand that this is an even trade, potentially a stronger pain medication he's swapping over to. This isn't an improvement. It's an exchange.*

Bret had been on opioids for *months* at this point. There was a bigger issue underneath all of this, and I felt it in my core.

However, I was really good at avoiding and wishing the problem would just go away.

We walked out with a new prescription in hand. Bret left with a pep in his step, proud of himself that he had had the needed conversation with the doctor. I walked out feeling heavy, flashing back to the evenings I'd spent alone with the girls when they were babies, wondering if my husband was going to come home that night. When he'd roll in at 3 a.m., high out of his mind and telling me how crazy I was for being upset at him. I had this same gut feeling each time he'd tried to gaslight me: nausea with a little bit of weight in my chest. I never knew what word to label it with and still don't to this day. I just know to listen to that feeling.

The subtle grabs for the pill bottle didn't stop or slow down.

Red. Fucking. Flag.

Instead, it felt as if he thought I would care less, since I'd attended the doctor appointment with him. I felt so alone, like there was a battle in front of me I just had to sit and watch. I felt like I was watching the deterioration of the human I'd spent so many years fighting for.

Life #19

Crash

In spring 2016, our entire world changed.

Bret and I got into bed after putting the kids to sleep, like we did every night. I rolled over, putting my back toward him, and tried to quiet my racing thoughts so I could fall asleep.

I was startled awake before the sun came up by Bret's moans. I jumped up, looking over at his sweat-covered body where he groaned and grunted in pain. "What is happening?" I asked.

He curled into a ball under the sheets. "I don't know," he responded. "It all just hurts so bad!"

"What hurts, Bret? What's going on?" I demanded.

"Raina, I don't fucking know. My whole body hurts, and I can't stop shaking." He started to cry.

I stepped back to take him in.

Bret was so pale, his skin almost green. He was covered in sweat, and our sheets were wet underneath him. He was shaking, uncontrollably, like he'd been out in the snow for an hour with no clothes on. The groans and moans started to turn into screams as I told him I was taking him to the emergency room.

I made a quick phone call to my friend, Keisha, who lived just down the street, and asked if she'd come and sit with the girls while I took Bret to the hospital.

"Of course," she said. "What's happening?"

"I think he's withdrawing from his pain medicine," I whispered, as his screams filled the house. *I can't believe this is fucking happening,* I thought.

"I'll be there in five minutes."

I'd opened up to her about my experience with Bret at his doctor and had shared a lot of my story with Bret's drug use in the past, adding how I was worried and fearful we were heading down another dark hill.

When she walked in the door and heard Bret's screams, Keisha's eyes flew wide. I just shook my head, closed my eyes, and mouthed the words: *thank you.* Then, I grabbed Bret by the arm and helped him out of bed. He shook, bent over in pain.

We sped to the hospital, which was only three minutes down the road. There, Bret was admitted and immediately given pain medication and fluids. As the doctors came in to ask him questions, Bret finally shared about being on high doses of Oxy and trying to get off of them, so he'd just stopped.

I felt it again, the heaviness in my chest and the nausea in my gut. *I fucking knew it.* I sat there quietly, allowing him to share bits and pieces of his story with the doctor.

When they left the room, I just sat there, clenching my teeth as he dozed off, saying nothing to me. His pain seemed to ease up a bit, and he fell in and out of sleep, while I sat next to his hospital bed.

The buzz of his cell phone kept startling me as I sat there, reading everything I could find about withdrawing from opioids. *What an idiot to just stop,* I thought.

As his phone kept buzzing, my unconscious desire to open his phone and see what I could find consumed me. We've all been there, right? Tell me you've done that, too—seen the phone just calling to you, begging you to unlock it and scroll through to see what you can find.

I attempted to unlock his phone while he slept but was unsuccessful, he had changed his passcode. My heart rate started to rise.

Again, a call buzzed in from a number not saved in his contacts. Feeling annoyed, I answered, "Hello."

"Is Bret there?" a man asked.

"He's not available right now, but this is his wife. Can I help you with something?" Call ended. *Weird.*

The number called back, and when I answered, he hung up again. After several minutes, I guessed the unlock code for Bret's phone and quickly checked for any texts from the same number. Jackpot. Look at me—Sherlock Holmes.

I read through the conversation between Bret and the mystery man who didn't want to talk to me. I found several where they were planning meetups and pickups, but it felt like a code that I couldn't decipher.

When I scrolled through his emails, I found all kinds of weird conversations about "board shorts" and other random clothing items to random people on Craigslist. It all just felt weird, like a puzzle with missing pieces. *What in the hell was he up to, and what is really happening here?*

The number called again. I answered, "Hello. What do you want with my husband?"

"Tell him to call me. He owes me money," the man said firmly before hanging up. Red flags were falling from the sky.

I sat there next to the hospital bed, patiently waiting for Bret to wake up so I could confront him. I wanted the truth. I wanted to know why we were in the hospital right now. When Bret's eyes fluttered open, he looked over at me and I stared back at him.

"Hey," he said gently.

"I want to know the truth," I said firmly.

"What's going on? What do you mean? I told you and the doctors, I just tried to stop, and I guess I shouldn't have done that—"

"No," I interrupted. "I want the actual truth." I stared at him blankly.

He turned his face away from me, and I could see the emotion building up in his eyes, but I stayed firm, emotionless, and hard. I wasn't going to let him lie to me again. We were in the hospital, for fuck's sake. I kept staring at him, giving him time to work up the courage to talk.

"I fucked up," he spat. "I ran out of medication."

"What do you mean you ran out of medication?" I pushed for more.

He went on to explain that when his doctor told him she wouldn't prescribe to him anymore, he went to another doctor and another and another. At one point, he had multiple doctors prescribing him with opioids. One after the next started to cut him off, refusing to prescribe to him, so he ended up having to find more on Craigslist. He explained how you could find anything on Craigslist under code words, like "board shorts."

My face lit on fire.

The doctor walked in shortly after, to ask Bret more questions about his drug history and current usage. I insisted Bret tell him the truth, and when the doctor asked Bret how much he thought he was using daily, he replied it was over 300 MME per day. The recommended dose was no more than 50.

He told me that, for a couple of months, he'd been buying pain medicine online, because he couldn't find a doctor to prescribe to him anymore. He also shared how much money he had been spending on his addictions and gotten behind on paying some people he owed money to.

"Motherfucker." I blurted out. "I thought we were done with this. Past this. What in the hell, Bret? How is this happening?"

"I'm sorry," he cried. And it's all I got from him.

His machines started to beep then as his eyes rolled back in his head. The nurses ran in, asking me to step out of the room, and the alarm sounded overhead calling a "Code Blue." I'd worked in hospital settings for years and recognized Code Blue as "non-responsive." My stomach dropped, and I cried furious, frightened tears.

I got ahold of Bret's parents and explained the situation to them. They hopped on the first flight they could and made it to the hospital the next day. They weren't strangers to Bret's history, and after I explained what he'd shared, the disappointment oozed from them.

Bret's seizures didn't slow down. The next day, he was so bad, they moved him to the ICU to try to start titrating him off the drugs. Things started to get scarier when he was moved. His seizures convulsed his whole body. I ran to his side, helping to keep him on the bed, while talking to him and touching his face, letting him know I was there.

His body contorted, his arms and legs going in different directions. His mom and dad helped hold him, too. It felt like I was watching *The Exorcist*. I'd never seen a body bend and shake like his did, and it scared the shit out of me. Danelle recorded it one night, as we'd never seen anything like it, and his screams were horrifying.

The doctors had to give him more and more boluses of medication, because his body was responding wildly. As I stood by his bed after one of his seizures, on TV they reported how Prince had just died from an overdose of opioids. I turned to him and started to cry.

He was out of it, unable to see or hear me, and I just whispered, "I'm so fucking mad at you." I stood there, staring at him for what seemed like forever. Every memory I had of us flooded through my head. The good, the bad, the hard, the exciting—it all washed in and out, as I thought to myself, *My husband might die.*

I've never told anyone this, but there was a piece of me hoping it would happen. I stared at him, picturing what life without him would look like and how things could feel so much easier.

When the doctors walked into Bret's room the next day, they explained to both of us that they'd been able to get him down to about a quarter of the amount of Oxycontin he'd been on, but to have any chance of getting off the drugs, he'd need more support. They told him they would approve his discharge under the condition that he check into a detox facility, so he could be weaned off entirely with accountability.

They gave us a few suggestions of facilities in the area, and I spent the afternoon calling each of them to check their availability. The one we decided on was a thirty-day program that sounded perfect for him. The only catch was he would have *zero* contact with us while he was in the program. It felt like a no-brainer to me, but Bret struggled to commit.

Two days later, his parents and I dropped him off at the treatment center. I was a ball of emotions. It felt so hard to leave him, knowing I was going to be alone with the girls and have to answer all of their questions, while trying to work through all of the anger I had stuffed down. I drove home, sobbing as I strategized what the month ahead would look like.

Bret's parents had planned to stay in town for a few days, and I welcomed the help as we adjusted. I always loved having them around. They felt like my parents, after so many years being in their family. Bret's mom and I were very close; she called me her daughter-in-love, and I called her my mother-in-love. Bret's dad was always cool, calm, and collected, with a funny, dry sense of humor. We talked through Bret's situation together, and they always had the best advice. Still, I've always wondered how much they were enabling versus helping him grow.

Bret had been in the treatment center for a couple of days when we took the girls to the pier in Oceanside for dinner one evening. We walked all the way out to the end of the pier after dinner, to watch the sunset.

I got a call from an Unknown Number on my cell phone. I never answer these calls, but not knowing who would be trying to get ahold of us, I answered.

"Hey!" Bret said cheerfully when I answered.

Confused, I looked at Danelle and Jerry, mouthing, *It's Bret.* They looked at me with confusion.

"I'm out!" he said excitedly.

"What do you mean you're out? You're supposed to be in for thirty days."

"Yeah, well I checked myself out. I feel good. I'm not taking any more meds, and I just had to sign a paper, and they let me leave! Where are you guys?!" he asked, like nothing in the world was wrong.

"One second, okay?" I said, muting the phone to explain this to his parents.

"No!" Danelle said, worried. "He needs to stay in for the thirty days like they recommended!"

"I know, Danelle. What should I say to him?"

Jerry took the phone and walked down the pier for some privacy. When he walked back, he explained that Bret was out, coming home, and there wasn't much any of us could do about it.

My stomach dropped again, with a combination of defeat, resentment, frustration, and disgust. *How could he be so selfish to check himself out, knowing damn well he isn't ready. Will this always be a struggle? Will he always battle this?*

We drove home, where Bret was waiting for us, talking the entire way about what we would do and say and how we would support him going forward. I felt defeat to my core. I didn't know what else I could possibly do to motivate him to stay clean. I cried, wondering why his two beautiful daughters and our marriage, the life we'd built weren't enough to keep him happy. *Why was he so determined to numb out?*

He had always been such a smooth talker. He was the best at convincing anyone of anything, no matter what it was. This was part of the reason why he was always so good at his sales job. When we got home, we had a talk with his parents, and if you were a fly on the wall, listening to his side of the story, you'd have been convinced to step back, too. To support him and let him pursue the *clean* life he was determined to live.

All I could do was continue to focus on the things I knew I had control of: my wellness, my business, and my vision. And that's what I did. I also shared with my community on social media, as I had been doing to build my business, which helped me work through the complicated emotions around maintaining my focus.

———————— ·•●●⊙⑥⑥⑥⊙⑥●●•· ————————

INSTAGRAM POST: Sunday, May 8, 2016

What a week. It feels amazing to have my husband back in my arms and back to himself.

I know many of you didn't even know he was gone, but I know many of you were curious as to why my posts have slowed down.

Bret used to be an addict. Most of you know that about him. Cocaine, ecstasy, meth at times... His addictions were so strong and consumed him, nearly tearing our marriage and family apart.

God intervened about six years into our marriage and completely healed Bret of those addictions, sobering him up overnight. Literally.

It's been almost four years since he's used, and he hasn't had the desire.

In June-July last year, Bret was diagnosed with a Pars Defect (broken back), after they found a CSF leak near his neck.

That was chaos—two surgeries left him with a prescription of Oxycontin and Oxycodone.

After that, we learned one more surgery was needed, and the pain wasn't going away. He continued the use of Oxy for eight months, until his final surgery in March this year.

He had a spinal fusion at L4-5. This was a painful surgery that caused him to leave with an even bigger prescription for Oxy.

Week after week, Bret's tolerance grew, and the doctor kept increasing his allowance.

Last Saturday, April 30, Bret ran out of his last prescription with an intention of breaking this cycle and stopping his pain meds on his own.

He woke up in sweats, in pain, barely able to walk, and starting full-on withdrawal symptoms. I was terrified.

We took him to the ER around 9 a.m., and they ended up admitting him after he'd started having seizures and episodes from the withdrawals.

Sunday, he was having such severe withdrawal, they moved him up to the ICU to try to titrate him down. We were in the hospital until Thursday, May 5, and they were able to get him down to about a quarter of the Oxy he was originally taking. Safely.

They discharged Bret on the condition that he go immediately to a detox facility, to get the remaining drugs out of his system. He was 100% on board. We found a facility here in SoCal, and he checked in Thursday afternoon.

They were going to safely detox Bret from the opioids, and we had no contact with him for 72 hours. Those were the hardest two and a half days of my life.

Today, I got to hug my husband, pain-free, drug-free, and mentally ready to get back to the life we've built.

Bret didn't have an addiction to Oxy. His body did. The chemical reaction of this medication is terrifying, and I'm hellbent on getting the word out there.

Bret's body would not let him quit that medicine.

His heart rate was through the roof because of the withdrawals, because of the Oxy.

I don't know if he even wanted me to share all of this, but I just feel so much anger toward Big Pharma and the doctors who keep this medication rolling in... I'm lucky to have my husband here with me today. I'm lucky to be able to hug him and kiss him and tell him that I love him.

Someone dies every nineteen minutes from Oxy. Can you believe it? And most of the time, those people who develop their addiction had a legit injury, causing them to be on it.

I hope this helps someone, inspires someone, or speaks to someone at God's perfect moment. Kiss your family, love on your loved ones... and think about what you're putting in your body.

The truth was, I didn't even believe the words I was writing and sharing with the world. I was falling out of love with my husband more as each day passed. Yet, I didn't do anything about it, I had too much going on.

Instead, I stuffed down my anger, resentment, and frustration and kept my blinders on, so I could move forward.

At the end of June, Bret and I met up with the rest of the Top 10 in the company for our celebratory trip to Bora Bora. I had earned a first-class, all-expenses-paid trip, and I planned to leave every trouble, worry, and fear at the airport in Los Angeles. About twenty-five of us piled onto the plane, excited for the trip ahead. I knew almost everyone. The entire top 10, their spouses, a few people from corporate, and a photographer.

As we landed on the island, I let the sunshine and clear-blue water heal some pieces of me. I spent a week eating at the best restaurants with the best people, having the best conversations. But things felt weird with Bret.

It was like that feeling when you know you need to break up with someone, but you're kind of... stranded on an island with them. So, instead, you make it work. Meanwhile, every joke they make seems annoying, and every time they smile at you, you look away, acting like you didn't see them, so you don't have to reciprocate. I was avoiding him hard.

Years before, I'd talked to Bret's mom as I navigated through his drug use and series of affairs. I'd asked her, "How do I know when it's time to leave him? I just don't know if I can do it. I don't know if I'm ready."

She replied, "Honey, I think, when you know, you'll know. I think you'll feel it."

On this trip, I felt it. I felt the love I'd once had slipping away like water through my fingers, and I was unmotivated to try to save the drops.

I focused my energy on having the best time I possibly could on this once-in-a-lifetime trip. I linked arms with the other women and relaxed with them by the beach, talking about life and work.

I said yes to excursions and photo shoots, allowing myself to be free, present, and in the beautiful moment.

I swam in the ocean with sharks. I snorkeled in crystal-clear water with more fish than I felt comfortable with. I parasailed over the islands in awe and soaked up the sun while sipping cocktails. It was the best trip I'd ever been on.

On the flight home, reality started to sink in, and I wasn't ready for it. Bret passed out pretty quickly, and I couldn't sleep. My mind was racing. Every time I looked at him, it felt like I just wanted to hold a pillow over his face. I watched a couple of movies and glanced around the plane, bored and craving a distraction.

I caught the photographer, Mike's eye a few times. We exchanged glances and smiles while the rest of the plane dozed off.

We flew into Kansas City, to meet Bret's parents and pick up the girls. They'd had a week-long vacation with Grandma and Grandpa and probably didn't even want to go home. We decided to stay for a few days. I had the flexibility to work from anywhere, so we figured, why not? I always enjoyed being at their house. It was cozy and where we'd spent every single holiday since I was eighteen years old. Memories flooded the hallways.

Bret and Jerry started a conversation like they'd brainstormed and planned for it. At the time, we'd hired his dad to help us organize our finances and help us to save and invest. His dad had a job in the financial world, so I had overwhelming trust in him to help put us in a great position. When Bret asked if we could all talk, my stomach dropped. I was getting really fucking sick and tired of this feeling.

Bret started. "I think we should move."

"What? No," I snapped back, before he could even finish his sentence.

"Raina, we could be in such a better financial position if we weren't in California. The taxes are going to kill us," he responded.

"No. I make enough. It's why we're saving. I don't care. We can cut back and be smarter about our spending, Bret." Implying *his* excessive spending, I added, "There's been a lot of *careless* and *irresponsible* spending over the last year, don't you agree?"

Jerry chimed in, confirming that, with the high tax rate in California, it just didn't make sense to live there. They were very conservative and had lived in Missouri their entire life, so, of course, they wouldn't understand how badly I wanted this, how much I wanted to stay.

I started to cry. It felt like I was being ambushed, made to feel bad about the decision I had made, and punished for a debt I never created. Yet, I knew, if Bret wasn't in the picture, I wouldn't even be in this position.

He and Jerry went on to talk about all of the places we could look at moving.

I said, "I'm not moving back to Missouri or Kansas."

Bret threw out Colorado, reminding me of how beautiful I'd thought the state was, when we drove through it on our road trip to Vegas a couple of years before.

Defeated, I said, "Okay." Every piece of me was screaming, yet I didn't make a sound.

Bret and I decided to drive to Colorado on our way back to California. We'd try to make a fun little trip out of it, staying in hotels, so the girls could play in the pools, while we house-shopped and explored. We spent two days in Colorado, looking up homes to rent on Zillow and reaching out to realtors to set up appointments. It felt so similar to our trip out to California the year before. Again, I felt bummed that none of the spaces were what we really wanted—until the last home.

As we drove into Roxborough Park, I was in awe of the mountainous scene. We drove along winding roads lined with pine trees and herds of deer. We slowed down every hundred feet or so and rolled the windows down to say hi to the wildlife.

We pulled into the steep driveway of a beautiful mountain home. Again, I *gasped* when I saw the 180-degree view of red rocks and the city of Denver. Behind the house was a national forest, trails, and miles of mountains. If I had to leave the place that my soul called home, this would be an okay second option.

We signed a lease that day, agreeing to a three-year commitment in the home. Back in Encinitas, we put in our two-week notice and scheduled the moving trucks to carry all of my ocean-inspired furniture to the mountains.

I cried every single day, wishing that Bret would change his mind. He never did.

All I knew how to do was put on a tough face, tuck my feelings deep inside, and move forward. It didn't matter if I had to lie to the world while I did it.

Life #20

Colorado

Radically accepting the situation I was in, I settled into my new space. In typical Raina fashion, I unpacked the boxes as quickly as the movers had them unloaded. The house was a lot bigger than the one we'd moved from, so we took our time doing some extra shopping to fill the space comfortably. The girls enrolled in school, and we all settled into our new season.

Bret's little brother, Ty, moved to Denver within weeks of us. It was nice to have a little taste of family close by. He'd come over and go out on hikes with us. I even climbed my first Fourteener with him, becoming addicted to the feeling of that accomplishment. I have always thrived by testing my limits. I became a frequent hiker. Every time someone came visit us, I'd show them around my favorite trail that ran behind our house. When you reached the top, you could see mountains for miles. I often did this hike solo, just to think and have quiet time for myself.

My work continued to be my anchor. I was halfway through the year and pushing for Top 10 again for the second year in a row. I earned a trip with some of the other leaders on my team to spend a few days with Leslie at her home. I'd never been to Michigan before, so I was excited to get away and explore a new place. She'd just built a new home with a giant pool in the back yard that was calling my name.

We spent the first day of our trip downing margaritas by her pool and chatting about life and work, excited for the girls' time.

Everyone there had kids and a spouse they'd left behind. I think I was the only one trying to forget about the spouse I had back home. I'd gotten an email link to all of the photos from our Bora Bora trip that evening. I scrolled through all of the gorgeous images, time-traveling back to Tahiti.

I sent a message to Mike, the photographer, thanking him for capturing the perfect moments in such beautiful photos. He replied quickly, excited to chat about his work. We kept the conversation going and started to talk about all kinds of things, from photography to work and beyond. At 3:00 a.m., I could barely keep my eyes open but didn't want the conversation to stop. We said our goodnights and I dozed off, happy for the reconnection and the distraction.

The next day, Leslie rented a yacht for the group of us. We turned the music up, poured drinks, and coasted around Lake Michigan all day. *This is something I could get used to,* I thought.

Reality swooped back in when I headed home to Colorado. I'd had so much fun with those women, connecting and laughing, a foreign concept over the last few months. I reached out to some of my close girlfriends, and we decided to book an Airbnb in the mountains for a girls' weekend.

Within a month, we all met up in Denver and drove into Breckenridge for our little getaway, stocking up on essentials along the way. This lit me up: quality time with my best friends. We spent the weekend laughing, drinking, and hiking. We rode horses on trails, ate edibles, danced, and had hot tub dates.

This trip was the first time I ever said out loud, "I think I'm done with my marriage..." They group-hugged me, understanding completely.

The following month, I was preparing for our annual Leadership event, being held in Coronado, California. I was very excited about going back to the San Diego area and seeing all the coaches I loved and worked with. Bret always went with me to this event as my guest. We had our flights and hotel booked, and my mom was coming out to watch the girls.

Two nights before we were supposed to leave, I woke up in the middle of the night to rustling noises in my closet. The light was on, the door barely cracked. Bret wasn't beside me in bed.

What in the hell is he doing right now? It's so late, I thought as I quietly made my way to the closet. "Bret?" I said quietly. He was in the corner, behind the door. When I startled him, he dropped a backpack, and multiple pill bottles spilled out onto the floor.

I tried to look at him, but he wasn't even in there. His eyes were barely half-open. "What are you doing?" I asked "What *is* this?"

He couldn't even form a sentence to respond. I grabbed him by the arm and shoved him toward the bed.

"I am so fucking done with this, Bret. I'm *done!*" I yelled and began to cry.

He didn't say anything. He couldn't. He simply lay back down, leaving the pills behind, and forgot what had happened.

I turned my back toward him in the bed and cried myself to sleep. The next morning, he was awake, lying in bed next to me. When I turned to look at him, there it was: the feeling Danelle said I'd feel one day. I felt *nothing.*

I knew right then and there that I was done. I could feel the nothingness to my core.

"I'm sorry—" he began.

"Don't," I interrupted. "Bret, I've battled this addiction of yours for over a decade now, and I can't do it anymore. I'm tired of fighting something I can't beat. I've done everything I can to help you. I've been the wife I thought I needed to be, the mom I thought I needed to be. And even with all of that, it's still not enough for you to choose us," I continued. "I'm done. I want a divorce."

He started crying. I stood up out of bed and walked out.

I called my mom that morning in tears and explained what had happened. I told her I still wanted her to come, if she could, just to be here to be with the girls, because I had a work trip and I was still going.

I told Bret I wanted to go alone. He insisted that he attend.

"I don't want you there," I spat. "I'm going on a trip to be with the people I love, and I need you to not be there. I need time to think."

Since my mom was coming to stay with the kids and since we'd already booked two flights, he would fly to California and go do his own thing. I agreed, not caring how he decided to spend his time.

I landed in San Diego and took an Uber to Coronado Island for my event. Bret went in another direction. I still don't really know how he spent those few days, and there wasn't a single piece of me that cared.

I checked into my hotel room and threw myself on the bed, taking deep breaths. It was the first trip I'd been on by myself in a long time and in my very first without sharing a hotel room. This was me, only me, day and night. I needed it.

When I met a couple of my friends out by the pool, someone asked, "Where's Bret?"

Bret and Raina had been a team for the last few years, a duo everyone in the company expected. One was always with the other. In fact, he'd sort of earned the title of Instagram Husband, because he was always there with me at every event, cheering me on, taking photos, holding my bags—everything. We'd made such a good team. I started to grieve that.

"Oh, he met up with a few friends in San Diego this time. He may pop out here later on in the weekend, but it's just me!" I pasted on a smile, lying through my teeth.

I opened up to a couple of my friends that weekend, feeling I just needed someone to talk to. I was going to be filing for divorce, and I craved outside validation, the "Girl, you're doing the right thing," and I got that.

During my first day there, I decided I just needed to take this as a vacation. I wasn't going to attend a training or meeting. I would participate in the workouts and then spend the day by the pool, asking the bartender to *keep them coming*, before getting ready for whatever party or dinner of the night. I did just that.

It was one of the best trips I ever had with the company. In prior years, Bret would drag me out of the party around 10 p.m., because *he* was tired. I hadn't had the ability to let loose like I did this time. It felt amazing. I hopped on the plane home feeling empowered and able.

Two weeks later was a trip with some of the leaders on our team. I was scheduled to take four women and their spouses to Belize for a four-day, all-expenses-paid holiday. These were some of the highest paid and hardest working people on my team, and we wanted to treat them. The trip had been booked for months.

When we returned from California, I told Bret I didn't want him to go on that trip, either, even though we'd booked our flights. He again fought me on this, saying he *deserved* to go, too. That we could make it work, regardless of what was going on in our private life.

"I will not act like we're together, Bret," I told him. "I'm not going to hide anything we're going through. I'm not fucking happy. You've got a serious problem, and I'm done sugar-coating it to the world."

He accepted my terms, and we were on a plane together to Belize. We explored, sunbathed, snorkeled, did photo shoots, ate and drank. I had the best time with four of my closest friends and teammates. When the hotel room door closed at night, though, the smile dropped from my face. My hardened version returned. I slept on the edge of my bed, as far away from Bret as I could without sleeping on the floor.

My best friend at the time, Jen, knew everything that was going on. She and I had met while Bret was competing, and we reconnected when she wanted to sign up to work with me. We were inseparable, and she felt like a sister to me. During the entire weekend in Belize, she kept me going, cheering me up and holding space for me to vent while we wandered off to explore.

This was the trip when I started my series of travel tattoos. Our Airbnb was on a little island, so we had to access or leave it by boat. The man who drove our boat was the best: he hooked us up with the best restaurant suggestions and weed, and he even had a buddy who did tattoos. If I'd stopped to really think about it, I would have said *no thank you*, but when his friend offered to bring his needles and supplies to our Airbnb to give us tattoos, I said *yes!*

When he arrived, we pulled oversized bean bags into the kitchen, where he'd set up shop. I went first, getting a little tattoo on my left wrist, a symbol that means "be present," and Jen got one to match.

During this trip, I felt myself regress a bit in terms of my health. I frequently had to run to the nearest bathroom, with over ten diarrhea bathroom breaks a day.

One crazy thing: three of the four couples on this trip, including me, separated or divorced within months; the fourth divorced a few years later. Jen and I laugh that this trip cursed all our relationships. But in reality, I think it woke a lot of us up.

Chapter #21

Divorce

After Belize, it felt like game time. Like reality had set in. Bret and I had no more trips to go on, and I needed to file for divorce. I found an attorney, paid my retainer, and started the process. After I left his office, I paused to appreciate this situation, even though it was hard.

Years before, I'd had to ask my dad for the money for a divorce. I had mere pennies to my name, but I wanted to start over. During this current season of my life, I felt financially secure and stable enough to say, *I'm done,* and I could live my life with confidence. Had it not been for the years I'd put into entrepreneurship, I don't know if I ever would have left.

I told both of my parents about the decision I'd made, and they both were extremely supportive. My dad still jokes about a time when he visited Colorado and went hiking with Bret.

"You know, there was a moment at the top of that mountain, where Bret was looking over the edge, and I thought about pushing him… I should have pushed him!" he jokes.

I laugh so hard at that. That's my father.

We told Danelle and Jerry, too, who were a little more hurt and emotional about the news. In a private conversation with them both, I held nothing back. We cried together as Danelle said, "Raina, you've literally done everything you can do. You have to do this. You have to leave him."

After I moved forward with my decision, Bret accepted it, and we were able to have civil conversations. Thanksgiving was coming up in a few weeks, and he asked if he could stay in the house until then. After the holiday, we'd tell the girls what was going on, and he'd move out. His parents would be with us then, so he'd have some help moving his things. I agreed.

Thanksgiving rolled around, and my anxiety skyrocketed. Bret and I had been sleeping in different beds, him downstairs in the guest room and me in the master bedroom, and you could have cut the tension with a knife. The girls were so young and seemed to have no idea what was going on, but I hated feeling like this was going to ruin their holiday.

When Danelle and Jerry got into town, things started to feel real. We had deep conversations and strategizing. Jerry still had his hands in our finances, so I asked him to sit down with Bret and me to talk through what the separation would look like, financially.

"So, what do you think, Jerry?" I asked. "Knowing the position we're in, what are your thoughts before we start?"

He looked at me, confused. "I honestly don't know." He started up his computer. "It's been a while since I've looked at where you guys are at."

I looked at Bret and raised my eyebrows. "What do you mean, Jerry? I thought you were helping Bret with taxes, a budget—all of that."

"Raina, I haven't been helping with all of that for a long time now," he told me, looking between me and Bret.

I snapped my neck to Bret. "That's not what I was told. It would have been really nice to know that." My voice was full of resentment and frustration.

"Bret asked to take back over, changed all the login info, and said he didn't want my help anymore," Jerry explained.

The hardness returned to my face as tears rolled down my cheeks. *There's no telling what kind of financial mess we are in*, I thought. Hindsight being 20/20, I feel like such an idiot for trusting my husband, the ex-drug addict with a spending problem, and the people who always had *his* back and not mine, to take over our finances. In my mind and inherited thoughts, *my husband should handle the finances and make sure the family is taken care of. Surely, he'll do taxes, keep up with bills, save, and invest in a way that sets us up for success...* At least, that was what he was telling me to my face. So silly of me to trust.

Jerry nudged his computer toward Bret, asking him to log into the banks and investment sites, so we could start talking about moving forward.

With sad eyes after studying the screen, Jerry asked, "Where is everything?" Bret just stayed quiet. "Bret?"

"That's it. That's all there is," Bret said, embarrassed.

Jerry looked back at me and shrugged. "It's gone."

Bret hadn't maintained much of a balance in our account for *months*. Transfers in and out, ATM withdrawals for cash, transfers that no one had recognized. At the time we'd filed for divorce, I was making an income in the high-to-top six-figures, and I had nothing to show for it.

"How could you do that?" Danelle snapped at Bret.

Defensively, Bret retorted how expensive this and that had been, how much it cost to move us from California, and he threw out a hundred other scenarios that didn't make sense.

Like my money, any love I'd had left for Bret was gone. I felt betrayed, screwed over, and empty. He got up from the table and walked out of the kitchen, while I just stared at Jerry with tears in my eyes.

"Raina, you make enough every week to be able to recover from this with time. If you want me to, I'll help you," he said.

Through my tears, I replied, "I would appreciate that."

After a couple of hours, Jerry and I looked up from the table with a plan in place and goals set. "You've got options," he told me. "You don't have to worry when you have options. You only get to worry when you have no options." That advice has stuck with me every year since that conversation.

Bret and I sat the girls down together that night and told them we were going to get a divorce. I flashed back to little Raina and her brother Mark, when my mom and dad told us they were getting a divorce.

Kenzie cried and asked a hundred questions, and Ella just sat there like it was the most boring conversation she'd ever had. Later that night, I told them both goodnight, that I loved them, and I promised that the three of us were going to be *just fine.*

Thanksgiving Day, I helped Danelle cook, channeling our familiar holiday energy together. I wanted normalcy for the kids. I had to excuse myself several times during dinner to run to the bathroom, though, and returning to the table each time a bit more drained.

We decided to go Black Friday shopping, a pastime we all had enjoyed for years, but I barely made it through each store, I was in so much pain. It was hard to walk and embarrassing to have to excuse myself every fifteen minutes to find the bathroom. After only a couple of hours, I headed home to rest. There were more painful shifts in my body every day.

With a new budget and plan in place, I paid my attorney and moved forward with my divorce with no regrets or hesitations. I also had to meet with a bankruptcy lawyer, because I wanted to separate our debt. In that meeting, he explained how much of the debt was in my name, and because it was filed in Missouri, I'd have to refile in Colorado. The amount of debt I was left with and been unaware of sickened my stomach. I left his office with a new monthly bill of $5,000 for a Chapter 13 bankruptcy, to pay off the debt Bret had accumulated in my name while we were married.

While he went back and forth with our attorneys, Bret had toyed with the idea of pushing to receive child support and/or alimony. We'd been together long enough, and because he didn't have a job, he'd potentially qualify for both. This still makes my blood boil to think about.

I looked him in the eyes one day after he mentioned this to me, staring into his soul, and hoped, if I stared hard enough, he'd feel it like daggers in his gut.

"Bret, if you try to take any more money, I will literally fight till the death of me. You took it all. You took everything. You don't deserve anything more," I spat at him and then turned to leave before I burst into tears. I couldn't let him see me weak like that.

This event left me with deep trauma around money, debt, and taxes. Not a month went by that I didn't think about what happened and how naive I was, to trust another human being with such a big responsibility.

Bret moved out that weekend and into an apartment twenty minutes away. I welcomed the next season of my life. I had no idea what it was going to look like, and I honestly didn't care. It had to be better than this one.

My business felt like my anchor at this time. It didn't matter what went on during the day, this was my constant. I truly loved showing up on social media, sharing my day and my thoughts, and working with the women on my team. I didn't share about my divorce immediately. Instead, I just slowly faded Bret out of my stories, posts, and conversations. I worked with my team while the girls were at school, and I turned on mom mode when they were home. After they went to bed, I'd pour myself a glass of wine, turn on reality TV, and start working my way through emails.

The photographer, Mike, and I stayed connected through all of the ups and downs during these couple of months. He was actually the first person I told about filing for divorce. I didn't know what would happen with Mike, a relationship or just a friendship, but he was the first person I felt able to truly open up with. I shared my feelings, frustrations, and fears. We laughed and talked some evenings until 2 a.m., while I worked on my emails, only stopping because neither of us could keep our eyes open.

I fell in love with who he was and his ability to help me *feel* something again. He had a way of motivating me to keep going and to push through the hard days like no one else. When work felt hard, he insisted I set my goals bigger, and he inspired me to continue pushing for the Top 10 again that year, even though time was running out.

I'd sit and work while he shared about his day. This became one of my favorite times of the day, while things felt so hard. He was my best friend at the time, which maybe he didn't even know.

My mind felt strong, and I felt supported and encouraged by the community I had, but my body was really struggling.

Life #22

Gutted

IG POST: Saturday, December 17, 2016

It's killing me to not be on here, sharing workouts, lip-syncing, and just being energetic. I think, too often, we take our health for granted.

Not realizing how blessed we are until something changes.

I'm still in a full-on flare with my #UlcerativeColitis - I've had no relief yet with prednisone or Lialda.

I'm noticing no changes in my flare from adjusting my diet to very basic and bland.

I'm knocked on my ass during the day and kept up at night.

No energy. My body literally aches.

I've dropped 10 pounds since Thanksgiving, because my body holds onto nothing.

Wait - this will be a positive post, I promise.

You see, we all have life events that slow us down, discourage us, derail us, even change our mindset. I've gotten messages from my dad nearly every day, "Don't give up."

DON'T GIVE UP.

Giving up hasn't crossed my mind. I'm not that person.

However, I could see how easily someone could choose to give up, when they're thrown so far off course.

I AM ALIVE. I AM STILL STANDING.

I am SURROUNDED by kind words of encouragement of complete strangers.

I am REMINDED of all the people I am silently fighting for.

I am not wired to give up.

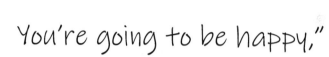

You're going to be happy," said life. "But first, I'll make you strong."

I ended 2016 celebrating the fact that I had, once again, locked in the title of Top-10 Coach, landing at #9 in the company. I had earned my second all-inclusive trip for two, this one to the Amalfi Coast in Italy, and I asked Jen if she'd be my plus one. I was excited to explore Italy with my best friend. I was also so freaking proud of my team and what we had accomplished, all while so few people knew about the shit-storm that was my personal life.

I announced my divorce and started to share honestly about the health crisis I found myself in, leaning on the support of my community on social media. It was easy to share there, in a safe space I'd created.

I started to decline very quickly. By January 2017, I weighed barely a hundred pounds and felt like I was slowly dying. When

I looked in the mirror, I barely recognized myself. None of my clothes fit, just hung over my body.

IG POST: Friday, January 6, 2017

Still in a "severe" ulcerative colitis flare, the doctor said.

I got labs done today, so I can begin Remicade infusions.

It will still be a couple of weeks to a month before I can start this medication, but they are saying I should have relief after my first couple of treatments.

It's going to be a long month or two, as I continue to try to just take care of my body and rest.

I'm dying to push play again, eat tacos, and just live my life.

Thank you, guys, for the continued prayers and thoughts. It means the world.

By the time I made it back to Colorado after the holiday, I had to wear Depends adult diapers, because I couldn't control my bowels. When I woke up in the mornings, I could only drink water, nothing else, or I'd be in the bathroom even more. I missed coffee. I'd send the kids off to school and lie down on the couch with hot water and lemon, trying to do some work on my laptop. Every thirty minutes, I'd have to clench my butt, try to stand up, and shuffle to the bathroom twenty feet down the hall. Ninety percent of the time, I wouldn't make it and would have to stand in the middle of the hallway, scrunched over in pain, shitting myself. I couldn't do anything but let it happen.

Then, I shuffled to the bathroom to change my diaper and attempted to work another thirty minutes without an accident. The diaper accidents made me sob, at first, I was so embarrassed.

But after several days, I numbed out. Just let my bowels release, unbothered and checked out.

I made Cream of Rice for breakfast and lunch, about the only thing I could eat that wasn't out of my body within minutes.

Attempting to be the single, strong woman people write songs about, I'd head out to the grocery store, trying to negotiate with my health. "Just make it through the grocery store. Twenty minutes. We'll be fine," I said to myself as I got out of my car. I went to the bathroom as soon as I got inside, hoping to prevent any accidents as I stocked up for the week.

Once, I was in the cereal aisle when I felt the burn. I clenched, leaving the cart right where it was, and began to speed walk awkwardly toward the bathroom. *Fuck, fuck, fuck,* I silently mumbled, as I felt it in my underwear. I got into the stall, locked myself inside, and just cried. When I ran out of tears, I called Bret, told him what had happened, and asked if he'd meet me there with new underwear and pants. He was there within fifteen minutes.

After that, he offered to help me with errands. I was so grateful for that. I hated him for the husband and dad he was, but I appreciated the friend he turned into.

We had the girls in the backseat of the truck one afternoon, after picking them up from school, when he was taking me to pick up a medication refill and more Depends. Bret ran inside Walgreens to grab the goods, while I caught up with the girls on how their school day was.

Fuck fuck fuck fuck... I silently panicked. My face tensed, and Mckenzie asked what was wrong.

I replied, "I'm pooping my pants. I can't hold it." Laughing with the girls as I lifted my hip, I added, "I can't get it in your dad's air-conditioned seat!" They thought it was so funny, I couldn't help but laugh with them.

A few days later, I got a text from Bret asking if he could pick the girls up from school, which was always a help. When he got to the house, he found me lying on the couch. I don't know what my face looked like but my body was so frail, and he could tell I'd been crying.

"I can't get up," I told him.

"I'm taking you to the hospital," he insisted. I had no fight in me, so I allowed him to help me up. We all loaded into his truck and went straight to the hospital.

IG POST: Friday, January 20, 2017

Waking up today after finishing my infusion last night, I feel weak and tired and like a granny.

Bret picked up some sweats for me yesterday, size small. I haven't been a size small since high school.

I'm motivated today. Motivated to get back to ME. Motivated to bounce back from another rock-bottom and prove to you guys that it can be done - in a healthy way.

Never, ever, ever take your health for granted.

You never know when you'll need that health on your side, and trust me, it's cheaper than medication.

Without insurance, the medication I had received had a price tag of $50,000. I couldn't believe how expensive it was. *What do people do without insurance?* I thought. I guess they just live in pain.

I spent a few days in the hospital after receiving my first infusion of Remicade, a biologic medication given through an IV. I was hopeful after that, which released some of my fear and resentment toward medication. I knew it was something I would take *for now,* in order to heal, and when I was done with it, I'd be done with it. I would need a couple of infusions before I'd be able to see if it was working or not, so I braced myself for the weeks to come.

When I was released from the hospital, Bret took me to iHop, because, after a week of liquids and hospital Jello, I craved pancakes. I could only eat a couple of bites, but I savored them. Once I was home, I made a plan to start slowly incorporating normal food back into my diet, hoping I could gain a little bit of weight. I added daily green juices, ready to return to some normality.

My thirtieth birthday was approaching. Two of my friends asked if we could plan something. They knew Bret and I had split up and were there through the separation. I'd grown really close to my friends, Jen and Keisha, and I enjoyed their energy. We were always laughing, always exploring, and I really needed that vibe right now.

I told them I was down for whatever, but I had to be back in two weeks for my next Remicade infusion. I also warned them that I wasn't yet 100%, so whatever we did, I needed access to bathrooms just in case.

Bret stayed at the house with the kids while I hopped on a flight with Jen to Los Angeles. We'd decided to meet Keisha there and then drive her car up the coast to Portland, Oregon, taking our time and exploring everything that the Pacific Northwest had to offer.

IG POST: Thursday, February 9, 2017

Today, I'm heading out on my first trip FOR ME.

Not for work, not for family. For ME.

I turn 30 tomorrow, and you see, I've decided that this is the year I'm going to be a little selfish.

With so many changes going on right now, my health, stress, personal life, etc., I decided to head out on a road trip with my favorite people to explore the Pacific Northwest.

Disconnecting with people that build me up, nature, and a little fun to go with it!

ARE YOU READY?!
#THISis30 #ThelmaandLouise

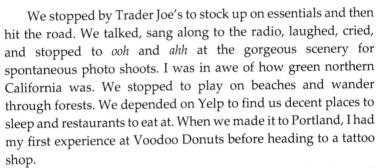

We stopped by Trader Joe's to stock up on essentials and then hit the road. We talked, sang along to the radio, laughed, cried, and stopped to *ooh* and *ahh* at the gorgeous scenery for spontaneous photo shoots. I was in awe of how green northern California was. We stopped to play on beaches and wander through forests. We depended on Yelp to find us decent places to sleep and restaurants to eat at. When we made it to Portland, I had my first experience at Voodoo Donuts before heading to a tattoo shop.

"I think I want to start getting tattoos every time I travel now," I told the girls. They loved the idea and encouraged me.

When I was married to Bret, I only had a few tattoos. I got my first tattoo with Carol when I was eighteen. Then, in 2010, I had the girls' names tattooed on my forearms.

I got another on my shoulder the day I left Bret and filed for divorce (the first time). I'd been out drinking with coworkers, and one of them had a friend who could get us a deal on a tattoo. I put a beautiful flower on my shoulder with the words: *my fairy tale.* That one always pissed Bret off. I then got a feather on the back of my arm during a trip to Vegas with some of our new friends at the church in 2012. Around the feather is the quote: *Do not tremble; the battle is not yours.* Then, the little one I got in Belize.

I had always begged Bret to let me get more tattoos. I had a giant crush on one of the coaches in my company who was covered in tattoos: she had blonde beach waves, a tan, and the coolest ink I'd ever seen. Bret said it was trashy and wasn't a good look for me. I believed him, like I did a lot of things. Tattoos became a safe way to start telling my story, on my terms.

In Portland, I got an outline of a compass overlaying a globe. Around it, I put the coordinates to Encinitas, the place that would forever have my heart.

We took our time heading back toward California, stopping at beautiful beaches along the Oregon Coast and hiking through trails in Muir Woods National Park. By the time we returned to Los Angeles, I felt so recharged and grateful for the community of people I had chosen to surround myself with. These women, no matter how long they would be in my life, played a huge role in my evolution during that season.

I made it home just in time for my second Remicade infusion, and I started to feel better already. My symptoms had not disappeared, but I was able to wear regular underwear again without fear of accidents, and my weight slowly but surely started to increase.

I took another trip out to California with Jen for a long weekend at the end of the month, feeling like I'd gotten so much of my energy back. I missed the coast, the water, the palm trees. Jen had a daughter who lived outside of Los Angeles, so she invited me out with her, knowing it would fuel my soul. We looked around at houses over that weekend, daydreaming about getting a place together, just to get back to the coast.

I started hiking again and even doing some of my workout programs slowly, and I kept up with my juicing regime. I really think that helped to put some healthy weight back on. The next couple of months felt like I was getting back to reality.

I went to Tulsa to speak at an event about overcoming adversity. I went with a small group of my friends, and we made a weekend out of it. I also went back to Missouri for a work event, stopping to see my family and my friend from high school, Carol. It had been so long since I'd seen her.

When we saw each other, she hugged me and said, "I feel like I owe you an apology for introducing you to Bret." We laughed afterward, not regretting how life had ended up. I got a new tattoo on both trips, keeping up with my promise to fill my body with souvenirs and memories.

In late March was my annual company trip to Punta Cana. I'd never gone on my own before, so it was exciting, being there with all of my favorite people. My love for traveling only grew as I explored solo, choosing who I spent my time with. There is nothing like the freedom I felt in these new places, after being sick for so long.

Toward the end of my Punta Cana adventure, my stomach began to hurt again, so I spent the last twenty-four hours close to a bathroom, hoping it was just something I'd eaten, but knowing it wasn't.

Unfortunately, things continued to spiral. I went into the doctor, and after another biologic and steroids, he was concerned that the medication might not be working like he'd hoped it would. He told me to rest, to try to keep a close eye on the food I ate, and see if it improved over the next month or so. If not, I had the option of scheduling a total colectomy or continuing my medication journey.

"I just don't know if these are going to work for you, given how diseased your intestines are currently," he told me. I gave it time like he suggested.

To be real, half of me was ready to just have surgery and find some relief. But the other half of me had a life she wanted to live, including a trip to the Amalfi Coast. I already carried a sadness for things I was going to miss out on, if I'd decided to have the surgery. This war between two parts of myself felt unfair.

After spending another month in Depends, I walked into a follow-up with my doctor, ready to chat about my other options. I wasn't one to give up, but I had begun to run out of fight. Still, I remained positive with my social media community.

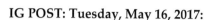

IG POST: Tuesday, May 16, 2017:

I'm so sorry I've been MIA guys.

I went to the ER on Sunday (Happy Mother's Day to me) after just not really being able to control myself, eat, hold food down, extreme fatigue and a nearly 15 pound weight loss in 2 weeks.

They admitted me to the hospital shortly after, so I could speed up the process to get my colectomy.

I was originally pushing the surgery off till July, because I selfishly didn't want to miss any trips I had coming up.

The Universe had other plans…

So here I am—fluids, steroids, some pain relief. I just got a PICC line started, so I can begin IV nutrition until my surgery on Thursday morning and possibly for a while after.

I'm comfortable. I'm at peace with the situation and the surgery. And I'm just ready to get my life back. Thank you for letting me vent.

#FUCKUlcerativeColitis

I woke up on May 18 after my first surgery, a total colectomy, feeling an immediate difference. They had removed my large intestine and parts of my small intestine.

"There was a lot more diseased intestine than we'd originally thought," my doctor told me that day. But I didn't care how much they'd taken from me. I felt fucking incredible already.

Life #23

Healing

I was completely pain-free. I lifted my hospital gown to look down at the ileostomy they had placed on my stomach. Just below my belly button was an inch of my small intestine, sticking out from my stomach. My ostomy bag was clear, so I could see it, moving and pulsing. It was the craziest thing I'd ever seen.

"You can touch it. You won't even really feel it," the nurse told me, as I put my hand on my stoma. It was warm to touch. *This is too crazy,* I thought.

I spent a few days working with my ostomy nurses, learning how to clean and change my ostomy bag myself. Other nurses gave me my IV nutrition through my PICC line and taught me how to care for that, as well. I went home to heal, while an ostomy nurse came out to the house every week, to check on me and help with my IV nutrition.

The plan was to have two surgeries, total. The first one had removed the diseased intestines and place my temporary ileostomy. The second phase was scheduled for the next month, when they would remove my ileostomy and create a "J-pouch." This pouch, made from my small intestine, would act as a colon, allowing me to have nothing outside of my body and to use my bowels like a normal human again—just with some rewiring on the inside.

Step one was done, and I was so happy about it.

At home a few days later, I was walking up the stairs and saw Danelle standing in my kitchen. She'd flown in to stay with the kids while I was in the hospital. I was so grateful for her help, I started to cry. I couldn't stand up straight yet: the nine incisions in my abdomen were still pretty painful, so I was walking hunched over a bit. When I made eye contact with Danelle, she, too, started crying, and she hugged me.

"Raina, I'm so glad you're okay. Honey, you had to leave him, or he would have killed you. Look at you. I'm so glad you're okay!"

You had to leave him or he would have killed you. I repeated those words in my head. She was right. The stress that had consumed me over the couple of years had nearly killed me. The truth was, the stress over the last *decade* had piled on so high, if I hadn't left, I don't know what would have happened. I think that thought haunted her more than it did me. I was prepared to move forward and end the cycle.

The ostomy nurse came to my house every week, along with a nurse who changed and cleaned my PICC line. Danelle stayed with me for a month, helping me do my IV nutrition and medication each day. She was a saint.

Bret had decided to move to Austin, Texas right after my surgery, to live with his new girlfriend. Danelle was all I had at that time, and I didn't take it for granted. She was an angel, helping me recover and taking care of the kids, who managed well enough with all of the changes. *We're all going to need to be in therapy before long,* I told myself.

In just a week, I felt as if I had gotten my life back. While I was sad to miss out on my trip of a lifetime, after giving up my spot on the Top 10 trip, I could already eat full meals and food I hadn't been able to eat in months. I learned quickly what my body could digest and what it wasn't able to.

I healed well, and I got into a good routine. People from social media sent me the cutest ostomy bag covers, and I wore a different pattern every day. I fell into a beautiful flow with my new temporary body.

Temporary. That is why I was able to adjust so quickly. I knew I could do anything, if it wasn't forever.

Jen came out to visit me several times. We went out on the town for donuts and matching tattoos. I got a unicorn horn on my middle finger, along with some other fun ones, like mermaid scales on my leg and thigh, which channeled all of my warm ocean energy.

One evening, after Danelle made us all dinner, we were sitting out on the balcony, drinking wine, when Jen reluctantly told us something I could tell she didn't want to say.

"I want to talk to you about something," she began. "I think I'm going to leave the company."

My heart sank. "What? Why?" I wondered if I had done something to upset her.

"I just need to do what's best for my family. I found a new company, and the compensation plan is better." She explained how people she knew had left for the competing company and were making more money soon after their move.

On one hand, I understood. If I were in her position, I possibly would have done the same thing, chasing the money. On the other hand, she was my best friend, my partner in crime. We'd attended every event together and built such a beautiful community together that, without her, it wouldn't be the same.

I started to cry immediately, knowing I couldn't change her mind and this would be the end of what we'd had, because my job had to come first. She felt the same way. Jen walked out of my house, leaving samples of a drink from the competing company, and I never saw her again. I later heard she was dating a bigwig at the company, but we never spoke after that day.

It took me a long time to heal from the loss of that friendship. I also knew, for whatever reason, this was a part of my journey. Right then, I needed to allow my body to heal.

My doctor approved me to attend our annual company conference at the end of June in New Orleans, so long as I promised to rest. I needed to reach a certain weight by then, eat without problems, care for my PICC line, and feel like I could handle the trip. My attendance was non-negotiable for me: I had been asked to speak on stage at the event and would be recognized for the second time as a Top 10 coach. I felt, if I had any control over it, I needed to make it work.

My friend Kari had been a full-time nurse before starting to coach with me. I planned for her to help me at my hotel room each day. At our event in New Orleans, I had the time of my life. Everyone was so supportive, checking in with me on my emotional and physical health. When I stood on stage to speak and to receive my recognition as Top 10, with my ileostomy and my PICC line exposed on my arm, I didn't feel ashamed of my body at all. I didn't want or need any pity. I felt like a fucking warrior.

My second surgery was planned for the Monday after our conference.

"Who's going to be there to help you?" Kari asked as we were checking out of the hotel.

"No one," I said. "Danelle had to head back home, but my dad will be out in a few days. I'll have a lot of help with the nurses and everyone at the hospital. I'll be fine."

"*Ummm*, no. I'm not letting you go home and take yourself to the hospital, waking up after surgery with no one there," she insisted.

"Girl, you don't have to—"

But she interrupted, stopping me with her hand. Immediately, she called her husband and changed her flight to Denver.

Kari and I flew home, and hers was the first smiling face I saw after my second surgery. She was a retired nurse with the biggest heart, so the exact person I needed by my side.

Kari had me up and walking every couple of hours, so I would not need heparin shots after surgery, which were really painful the first time. As she did her daily workouts in my hospital room, I cheered her on, feeling so motivated by her and hopeful for my quick recovery.

IG POST: Monday, July 17, 2017

Out of surgery and officially BAGLESS.

I'm on my feet for the first time, not a lot of pain... but a lot of gratitude.

This has been one of the hardest things I've ever gone through, physically and emotionally.

As I walked into the hospital today, I almost teared up, thinking about removing my ileostomy bag.

That sounds crazy, right? Let me explain.

THAT BAG SAVED MY LIFE.

THAT BAG gave me my life BACK.

THAT BAG took away pain and discomfort.

I kept reminding myself how shitty (pun intended) I felt without a bag and thought to myself: I would be willing to wear that bag for the rest of my life, if it meant feeling as good as I do now.

I am a warrior. And now... healthy from the inside out.

I can't wait to begin this new and improved chapter.

When I got out of the hospital, it truly felt like a new chapter.

My kids had spent the last month with my mom in Missouri, and I'd missed them so much. Dexter and I made the nine-hour drive to Missouri and then decided to stay for a week, as I was still healing. The hole from my ostomy had been sewn up but had barely scabbed over yet.

When I pulled into my mom's house, the girls ran up to me and squeezed me harder than they ever had. I cried, unable to contain all my emotions. I walked with them to the creek and watched them play in the water, catch crawdads with my mom, and ride the four-wheeler. I was so thankful to the universe and any God that I could be there and experience this life with the two most important people to me.

I went a little tattoo heavy for a little while. I got my next couple of tattoos on my trip back down to Missouri, and this is before my *Year of Traveling,* when the tattoo project really took off.

I went by myself to get two black crows tattooed on each shoulder blade. The crow represents death and rebirth, which fit, seeing as I felt I'd left a version of myself in the hospital bed.

Once my PICC line was removed, it left a little indention in my arm and I decided to get that shape tattooed, mimicking the PICC line. In the middle, it says, *did I live?*

When the girls and I returned home to Colorado, I craved some normalcy yet had no idea what my new normal would look like. It was the first time I'd been home, divorced, recovered, and looking forward to my next season of life.

Life #24

Temporary

I started doing acupuncture to help heal my body and lower my stress. I enjoyed being able to eat food again, though it wasn't as easy as when I had my bag. I went to biweekly check-ins with my doctor, so he could monitor how my body was adjusting. I felt good; I felt okay. Still, not as good as when I'd had my bag. My body had a hard time adjusting to the new wiring, as if my sphincter muscles hadn't yet remembered how to work. If I left the house, I threw on a Depends, just to be safe.

That fall, I took a trip with a group of women from my team for an event with Brendan Bruchard. He is like the *entrepreneurship guru*, and it was so fun to be there, moving our minds and businesses forward. I flew into Los Angeles by myself, rented a convertible, and drove down to San Diego to the meeting, reminiscing about and mourning my old life as the wind tossed my hair.

When I arrived, we went straight to the tattoo shop, and I returned home with three new tattoos: little arrows on my finger symbolize "moving forward"; a quote across my bicep that says, *I'm the hero of this story, I don't need to be saved;* and, in honor of something Brendan said during one of his talks, *Honor the struggle,* across the top of my shoulders on my back.

While tattooing one of my fingers, the tattoo artist looked at me and said, "You kind of have this Jekyll-and-Hyde thing going on." He'd noticed how I had stacked 99% of my tattoos on my right side by that point.

I smiled. "Yes, I love that actually."

It fit. I had long felt like there were two versions of me: the angel and the devil. The good girl, and the one living life. Sara and Jane. This felt like the perfect representation of me in my tattoos. I decided I would keep that up, only tattooing the right side of my body.

That was a hard weekend for me. I felt weaker than I had in a long time. I took more bathroom breaks and stuck to smoothies and acai bowls, because they felt the easiest to digest.

Something felt off. I could feel that. I had so much self-awareness about my body at this point, I could sense when something wasn't right. *My body doesn't like this J-pouch,* I thought to myself almost every day.

I wish I had known about the power of our thoughts back then, in the ways I do now. Everything happens for a reason, but I wonder, if I had changed my thought patterns around my illness, things would have ended up differently.

Hindsight.

When I arrived home, I hit recovery mode hard. I had a trip to London booked with some women from my team, because our business was about to expand overseas. I did my acupuncture, juice, and bananas, and I rested like my life depended on it until the day I got on my flight to Heathrow Airport.

It was my first time in London, and I fell in love. To this day, it's one of my favorite places to travel for many reasons. We were all jetlagged, so we took it easy on day one. When my friends asked how I was doing, I was brutally honest, sharing that I didn't feel great. I missed my bag, but I was excited for the week and hopeful my body would adjust soon.

I rallied. We tore up the town. We played tourist for a few days, stopping to take pictures in the big red phone booths and posing as a group outside of Buckingham Palace. When we found a tattoo shop, most of us decided to get tattooed. I got a beautiful vine that wraps around my hand and wrist, still one of my favorites to this day. Another day, we got three passport stamps tattooed, carbon copies of the actual ones in our passports.

That night at dinner, Kari sent photos of her tattoo to her husband. Then I saw the anger in her face, and I'm pretty sure she said "fuck" out loud.

"Were they supposed to spell Heathrow wrong?" he'd asked her, nonchalantly.

She looked up at me wide-eyed. "Let me see your tattoo!" I lifted up the protective wrap and bent my arm in her direction.

"They spelled our fucking tattoos wrong!" she shouted in the middle of the restaurant. All heads turned toward us.

I looked at my arm. *Heatrow*, it read. Like "death row" in a prison.

"Hahaha—ohmygod," I said, shocked that no one noticed that. The artist lived in London, for God's sake. I couldn't believe that had happened and couldn't stop laughing about it.

Kari, on the other hand, was not as entertained by it as I was. We talked about how to get it fixed, though I would have left it, then went back the next day. The artist was humiliated. She apologized and strategized with us on how she'd fix it. Eventually, she covered they typo with a thick, black line and then rewrote *Heathrow* above the shaded error. You'd never know if you saw it that it was an error. But I still smirk every time I look at that tattoo.

When we went out for drinks the next night, we found a dark bar with a great DJ in the back, who played the best music we all knew every word to. When I spotted the insanely-attractive man behind the turntable, I quickly told the girls, "Oh my god, he's hot."

"*Who?*" They all excited to hear me say those words. I was the only single girl in the group, and even though I'd only been divorced for several months, I was ready to move on. They knew this.

I had mourned the loss of my marriage while I was still in it, so I felt ready to move on sooner than I admitted. The photographer, Mike, and I had stayed in contact, too, and we had been talking almost daily, but I knew deep-down we'd never be able to take the next step. We lived two different lives.

"We should get his name and number for Raina!" my friend Brie said, elbowing two others. Before I could argue, they had slid out of the booth and were navigating their way to the back of the bar. I palmed my face, nervous, because I had absolutely no game. I just wished I had a couple shots in front of me.

"*He's single!*" they screamed as they jumped back into the booth. "He DJs part-time and teaches at the university full-time! Wait till you hear his voice!" They laughed.

There's no way I could have a fling with someone in another country, I thought.

I felt like I'd missed out on the wild college days a lot of women my age had. You know, you graduate high school, attend college, then have mindless sex and one-night stands, not remembering the names of most of them. Maybe, after five to ten years of that, you finally settle down and have kids. I did it all backward. Maybe my thirties would be my adventurous decade, I thought... Doubtful.

We ordered shots, and I downed my drink, hoping the liquid courage in my veins would grow me some balls and allow me to carry on a conversation with this random, hot human. By this time, I'd also not had sex with anyone in what felt like ages.

I snapped off the chatter in my head, stood up, and walked over to the hot DJ. He was tall, over six feet, with messy, light-brown hair and the biggest smile that made me stumble over my feet.

"Hi, I'm Raina," I said, smiling.

"I'm Tom. You must be the single lady your friends said I *had* to meet," he replied with the sexiest accent, smiling from ear to ear. *Oh, dear God.*

Tom put on a song and said he could let that play for a couple of minutes, so we could talk. We stepped a couple feet back from the DJ booth and talked about life. I told him why I was in London and the plans we had for the next couple of days. He shared a little about his life in and outside of DJing.

"I'm going to be playing at a fun little bar tomorrow night. You should come out," he insisted.

We exchanged numbers, and I told him we'd be there. I walked back to the girls with a little pep in my step. They all turned in the booth to watch, and I couldn't stop laughing as they cheered loudly.

The next night, we all got dressed up and made our way out to a cute little bar in London. It had a bar along the right wall and a big dance floor in the rest of the space, including a DJ area. We didn't see Tom when we walked in, so the girls and I sat at the bar and grabbed a drink or two. Immediately, the place passed the vibe check. We had many fun conversations with random people, laughing and connecting. Then, I saw Tom walk through the door. We made eye contact. He smiled and came to give me a hug.

"Come with me," he said. I stood before he even finished the sentence and followed him to his area, where he pulled up a seat for me next to his, behind the booth, and I sat with him the entire night.

My friends kept refilling my drink while they danced, and we sang along to every song Tom played. Every once in a while, he put on something prerecorded, so he could sit down next to me to talk and laugh. It felt like we were in a bubble no one could penetrate, our own little world.

I said my goodbye *for now* to Tom, and we went back to the house, unable to stop smiling. I spent the next two days sightseeing and playing tourist before we caught our flights back to the United States. Every once in a while, I looked around me at the airport waiting to spot Tom running through the crowd, yelling my name, asking me to stay, and declaring his love for me… I think I've watched too many romantic movies.

I made it home safely, happy to be back in my bed with my dog and my babies. I missed them deeply when I traveled but felt very confident about the people helping me take care of them. The girls loved the time with their grandparents, and I was beginning to realize that, with each trip I took, I returned home a different, new version of myself. Traveling, exploring, and meeting new people all expanded who I was as a person.

Even though Bret and I were officially divorced, we decided to continue our holiday traditions with the girls for as long as we could. We spent Christmas Eve and Christmas Day with Jerry and Danelle, like we had every year before, and then drove down to my hometown, to spend a few days with my family.

It was always hard to go home. Ever since I graduated and left home, it felt like there was a wall between me and my family. This year especially, I pushed through that feeling and tried to make my girls feel as comfortable as possible, attempting not to put my baggage or resentment on them.

While I was home, I scheduled an appointment to get a tattoo around my scar, now that my ostomy had healed. A tree of life. It would honor my journey with my ostomy and my feelings about how it gave me my life back. I envisioned dead branches on one side of the tree and vibrant-green leaves on the other. Around my ostomy scar, the artist created a tree stump.

It is large, on my stomach from my panty line all the way up to my bra line and around my side. To this day, it is the most painful tattoo I ever got. The vibrations radiating through my sternum literally took my breath away. I was in love with it, though.

My photographer friend, Mike, whom I'd talked to pretty much every day since before my divorce, invited me out to Los Angeles for New Year's Eve a few days away, and I jumped at the chance. I hadn't seen him since the prior summer, and I was excited to hang out with him outside of work.

While the girls stayed with my mom, I hopped on an early flight that day, feeling incredibly nervous, because, while I felt Mike had me in full friend-zone, I had developed feelings for him. I wasn't sure how everything was going to work out.

I Ubered to his address from LAX and let myself into his apartment. It was so *Mike*. Clean, white, mid-century modern, with beautiful art everywhere.

He is one of the most talented photographers I've ever met, and it made me smile to see his flavor around the apartment. I should have snooped through drawers and cabinets, but I kept my inner psycho chill. Just lying down on the couch to wait for him to get home from work.

When he walked through the door, it was like seeing my best friend arrive. I smiled, he smiled, we hugged, and thus started our forty-eight-hour adventure.

That night, he had made reservations with a group of his friends, so we headed out to dinner. After that, the entire night was winged! We ventured to a club before snagging tickets to see David Spade. We sat at the back of the comedy club, laughing and drinking until 3 a.m. when we went to a twenty-four-hour restaurant and filled our bellies.

We got back to Mike's apartment just before sunrise, and I prayed I could sleep till 10 a.m. I put on my pj's, and we awkwardly slipped into bed, facing each other, smirks on our faces. It was wild, lying in bed next to the man I'd talked to on the phone every day for the last year and a half. I knew so much about him, and he about me. It felt so comfortable as we both drifted off to sleep.

We woke up around 10 a.m. Knowing I would be flying home that evening, he took me to grab a juice, and we headed to the ocean with his surfboard in tow. I sat on the beach, watching him like I'd used to watch the surfers outside of my window in Encinitas. I dug my feet into the sand, remembering life back then. Missing life back then.

We watched the waves together for a little while before I had to go pack my bags. I hugged him goodbye, missing him before I had even left.

Life #25

Permanent

IG STORY: Tuesday, January 2, 2018

2018: my year of traveling, taking chances, holding nothing back, and giving zero fucks about anything that doesn't fill me up.

Starting the year, I felt so optimistic about what was to come. I had ended 2017 feeling like a different woman, after all of the trips I'd been on. And I told myself that 2018 would be my year of traveling. I needed my own little *Eat, Pray, Love* experience, I needed to rediscover who Raina was. I would say *yes* to every trip, every travel opportunity presented to me.

Danelle encouraged me, saying she'd help with the girls as much as I wanted. I appreciated the support, and the girls loved when Grandma slept over.

Even though my body wasn't 100%, I did my best to stay consistent with the things that had always made me feel good. I was back to working out and eating the food I knew my body liked, hopeful that, with time, my J-pouch would settle into my body. I scheduled weekly acupuncture appointments, which really helped, too.

My friend Kari came out to spend a few days with the girls and me in February, to celebrate my birthday. My energy had been so insanely low before she arrived, and I'd seemed to be dropping weight quickly, like I had the year before.

We worked out together, grabbed a quick tattoo, and she made me the biggest stack of gluten-free birthday pancakes with a candle on top. The girls sang as I blew out the candle and wished I would start to feel better soon.

After Kari went home, I decided to do my best to rest and recharge. I didn't have a lot on my travel calendar yet, so if I was going to slow down to heal, this was really the time to do it. I'd always had a hard time slowing down. The word *mindfulness* was never in my vocabulary: I had kids to raise, a business to build, and a world to explore. Where would *pausing* fit into my schedule?

I carried on, working out, working from the couch, struggling to make it to the bathroom, and I started to reset my diet with bland options. When I stepped on the scale and it read 107 pounds, I felt so disappointed. I closed my eyes and counted how many times I'd had to run to the bathroom that day.

I loved my acupuncture appointments. I was fascinated by the process and always welcomed the relief. Each week, she always sat me down and asked how I was doing with my health, stress, relationships—all of it. Then she placed the acupuncture needles based on how I felt, in the areas of my body where I needed most relief. I even kept permanent needles in my ears, to promote stress reduction as I continued to work my way up in business and refill my bank account.

Whenever I lay on the table, I held a little panic button in my hand, in case shit hit the fan. I'd never had to push it, but it helped me feel safe.

Then one day, I felt it, the rumble in my stomach and the accompanying cramps. I clenched my butt, nervous to move even an inch, and I started to pray. I began to sweat, thinking, *I wonder how long I've been lying here. How much longer do I have? I wish she had a clock in here. Fuck, my stomach hurts. Ugh, it burns. I don't know*

if I'm going to be able to hold it. Raina, you have to hold it. What would
happen if you shit your pants on the table? What would you actually do,
Raina? Hold it. Fuck fuck fuck fuck…

It slipped. I could feel the warmth and knew I wouldn't be
able to save myself. I hit the panic button several times hoping it
would get her there faster.. I sighed, emotions running through
me faster than I could even label them, and then I just started to
cry.

When my doctor walked into the room, I started apologizing.
"I'm so, so sorry. I have to get up. I have to get out of here. I think
I had an accident on your table. I'm so sorry!" I cried.

"Oh, honey…" She tried to comfort me as she pulled the
needles out of my skin, one by one. "Please stop apologizing.
What can I get you? What do you need?"

"I just need to leave," I cried. "I think I need to go to the
hospital."

I got into my car and just melted down. I cried until I had no
more tears left to cry, then I called my family for reinforcements.
I called my mom and asked if she could come to Colorado,
explaining the situation and telling her I was going to check
myself into the hospital. I called my ex-brother-in-law, and he
offered to come stay with the kids until my mom got there,
Danelle was also on her way, with my dad coming out a few days
later to relieve my mom.

I checked into the hospital, and they admitted me
immediately, calling my surgeon, who was on call. I felt defeated,
being back in the hospital, yet I knew, deep-down, after this visit,
I'd start to feel better. My surgeon said, based on the tests run, my
J-pouch was failing and covered in abscesses. He explained the
surgical options and medication options.

When I asked him how well *he felt* these options would work,
he didn't seem confident. I knew in my gut that I needed to go
back to my ostomy bag.

"Raina, I need you to understand, if we remove the J-pouch,
your ostomy will be permanent," he explained. "You had so much
disease in your small intestine that we took as much as we

possibly could, while still being able to create the pouch. With that much gone, we won't be able to create another pouch."

I closed my eyes, mentally removing everyone from the room. In seconds, I flashed back to life with my bag. While it was temporary, it was the best I'd felt in years. I'd felt like a superhero, like I'd gotten my life back—truly, I felt no pain. I could eat, I could drink, I could walk, I could play.

I opened my eyes and told him, "I'd like to have the surgery."

He scheduled me for the next morning. The doctors and nurses left the room, and my mom went downstairs to get some food, leaving me alone in my room for a moment. I took a deep breath, knowing I was making the right choice. I grabbed my phone, opened Instagram, and started a *live* video stream to share an update on what was going on.

I realize now how wild it must sound, that going live on Instagram was my first action after finding out my body would never function or look the same again. Truth is, I'd found such safety in the community I'd built on social media. I'd brought them through so many different phases of my life, from parenting to entrepreneurship. They celebrated with me when I hit Top 10, *twice*, in my business. They cried with me when I filed for divorce. They traveled with me as I began to explore the world, and they mourned with me as my illness began to put up a bigger fight.

On my live video, I cried, explaining the situation I was in and the decision I had just made. A *Top IG Live* notification popped up on my phone, as I watched hundreds of people join, commenting on my stream, and sharing how inspired they were because of my vulnerability. They mourned with me as I said goodbye to a version of myself and welcomed a new one in this new season of my life.

The next morning, a core memory was ingrained as I prepared mentally for surgery and chatted with my mom. Together, we watched *My 600 Pound Life, Hoarders,* and whatever junk TV we could find. A knock on the door snapped us out of our trance.

I was expecting the doctor or a nurse with updates and instead, the fluffiest golden retriever peeked his head around the corner into my room.

"Hi! Would you like to meet our therapy dog?" a voice called through our door. I was already halfway off the bed to greet the good boy.

"I definitely would!" I scooted close so I could soak in as many puppy cuddles and smells as I was allowed. It made my day, caressing the face of the best-behaved dog I'd ever met. He sat there, panting, a smile on his face, while I whispered sweet nothings to him, thanking him for being there and making my day better.

I had no idea that therapy dogs were even a thing, but this was the medicine I didn't know I needed until that very moment. Part of me will never forget this.

I was wheeled back into the operating room around 5:30 p.m. My hunger pains after no food for three days had faded, replaced with anticipation. They would be removing my J-pouch, along with any abscess or diseased parts they found, and then reconnecting my ileostomy. In addition, because this was going to be permanent, they were going to remove my anus and sew up my butt hole. It was a big operation, and it would take me a while to recover, they said, but I had never been more ready.

IG POST: Saturday, February 17, 2018

Sorry for the lack of updates! I'm still here, 2 days post-op, and recovering well, and I'll probably be here for a few more days. I still have 3 drains connected now and a lot of abdominal pain, but I've been able to stand up twice. It's a good feeling, trust me.

We did a little ileostomy shopping, so I made Kenzie try on a bag. Thank you, guys, again for all of your support! Xx

I was laughing in the photo I posted with that caption. Kenzie and Ella were visiting me in my hospital room when the ostomy nurse came in to have me look at some bag options. Kenzie took the protective layer off of the adhesive and stuck it to her stomach, thinking it was so funny.

I felt immediate relief when I woke up from surgery. I know it must sound crazy to hear that, but it's true. I knew in my gut immediately that I had made the right decision to go back to my bag. I'd always felt something like rejection from my J-pouch. With the bag, I was given permission to live.

This recovery, however, was the most painful. I had the hardest time sitting up, because, one, my butt hurt so bad from being sewn up that I couldn't sit flat, and two, my abdomen pain from my incisions and drains were incredibly painful, as well. I had asked the surgeon if he could put my ostomy in the exact same place as before, so the stump on my Tree of Life would now be my stoma. He laughed, saying he would do his best. He did: it's perfectly placed.

Each day, I started to feel better, regaining my strength. When the nurse came to explain they would remove my subcutaneous drains today, I got nervous. They had described how long the tubes were, going into my stomach and down to my bowel area. As we prepared to take out the first drain, they gave me a bonus dose of pain medication. *Red flag: this isn't going to feel good,* I thought.

They asked me to close my eyes and take a deep breath as they removed the tape holding my tubes in place. As I took another deep breath, they tugged on the tube, pulling it from my abdomen. As it slid through my body, I swear I could feel the end of the tube gliding through my insides, getting caught at random spots, so they had to tug a little harder.

I started crying plus hysterically groaning at the pain as the end of the tube left my body. *Holy fuck.* I had never felt that much physical pain before in my life.

My mom put her hand on my head, asking over and over if I was okay, but I couldn't even talk. Two more drains to go.

I swore to the nurses it felt as if the tubes had adhered around some of my insides, and when they pulled, it was like ripping off a scab inside my body along my organs. I could feel the tearing, the most excruciating pain.

Before attempting to remove the other two tubes, they gave me a break and another big dose of morphine, to borderline knock me out for the last two tubes. Thank God they did because I cried through them both, feeling like I was being ripped apart by a zombie. I've probably watched too much *Walking Dead*.

A few days later, I was home and, this time for real, ready to settle into my new body and life. My mom and dad both took turns staying with me for the first month, post-surgery. It was insanely hard to walk around, and sitting was even worse. I had to carry a little blow-up donut, if I wanted to sit anywhere. I struggled with hydration and would get really lightheaded if I was up too much, occasionally passing out.

Yet, I adjusted, I expanded, and I evolved.

I could eat.

I could move.

I could do it all with no pain, and I had no regrets. Given the choice, I'd go back to the bag every time, no matter what my body looked like from the outside. It was loving me on the inside.

"Everything you're going through is preparing you for what you asked for..."

Life #26

Alive

It felt like the beginning of a new season. I moved forward with my new normal, picking up where I'd left off with my daily routine. I needed at least six to eight weeks before being released to work out and weeks more before I could lift even five pounds, so I took it slow and focused on my business. I hadn't really taken time off: my business had grown to the point where I could do ninety-nine percent of it from my phone.

I spent those boring days in the hospital connecting with my team and vulnerably sharing my journey. One of my new coaches and soon-to-be best friend, Linzy, signed up with me while I was in the hospital, because, "Your vulnerability was inspiring," she said. She, too, struggled with the same disease and had decided not to let it control her life.

Between sitting on my balcony while I worked, soaking up the sun, and *actively* being a mom again, I got daily IV vitamin infusions and worked on the mindset needed to heal my body in a way that aided longevity. Dexter was my only constant; the kids came in and out from school and with friends. He and I spent hours out on the balcony, sunbathing and watching the sun rise and set.

Dexter and I had grown closer since we moved to Colorado. While I was angry, sad, sick, and healing, he was always by my side. He was always the kids' dog, but I'll remember his connection with me forever.

Once Dexter arrived as a puppy, I'd no longer had the burden of feeling like it was only *me* who kept the family together. He played a big role in keeping me together, too, through many seasons, especially when I felt like I was about to fall apart.

He would be in my lap while I built a business.

When I moved my family to California, I got to watch him run his little heart out every day on the beach.

I held him in the car as we left California, Denver-bound, tears rolling down my face.

He was in the room when I told my husband I wanted a divorce.

He lay in my lap, watching movies with me, while the kids were in school and I battled the loneliness.

He was in my bed when I became ill and as I recovered from my surgeries.

He sat out on the balcony with me to sunbathe as I regained my strength.

He approved partners as I dated and grieved with me as relationships ended.

He watched our girls grow, year after year, probably in as much awe as I was.

I'd had animals growing up. Though none of them were around consistently, I'd learned how much love an animal can share. None of those compared to the unconditional love and joy I felt with Dex.

At my six-week follow up, my doctor looked at me, completely weaned off of every medication possible, and said, "Wow, you really didn't mess around in this healing process."

No, I didn't. I was ready to regain my life and get back to the flow, where I knew I felt good. I was released and ready to move my new body.

Everyone I knew told me to start slow, but I knew me, I knew my body, and I knew what she was capable of. I started doing an advanced eighty-day program from home that I knew I'd love. That's always been key for me: if it wasn't something I enjoyed, I'd find myself procrastinating more than anything else.

I took a photo of myself in my workout clothes with my ostomy bag hanging out. *Day one!* I wrote, excited to continue writing my story. I had told myself this was going to be my year of traveling, and I was determined to keep that promise. I wanted to continue to fill my body with tattoos, commemorating my life.

My little brother, Ivan, had sort of followed in my footsteps over the past several years. He'd beefed up quite a bit and started to compete in physique competitions. He had asked for my help through some of it and invited me to travel to St. Louis, to stay with him, help him prepare, and just be there to support him. I said hell yes, excited for the thrill of what that world had to offer.

I was just a couple of months post-op, so I was still taking it slow. I had a pretty good idea of what I could eat and what kinds of movement my body liked, so I stuck to that, working from the airplane and hotel room in between working with my brother.

While I was in St. Louis, I got a text from someone that sent butterflies loose in my stomach, a blast from the past. I had met Adam in 2006, while I was working in my call-center job, stuck in my cubicle, counting down the minutes until my next break. I'd seen a new hire, tall, dark, and handsome, walk in and plant himself nearby. I had just given birth to Mckenzie and was with Bret, hanging on by a thread in the midst of our ups and downs, when this man caught my eye.

For a while, I tried not to make direct eye contact, but at work, everyone chatted and got along, so the conversation began to flow with ease. Before long, we were seated catty-corner to each other, taking turns writing notes and tossing them back and forth. We talked about everything and nothing all at once. But I was honest with Adam and shared openly about my life.

Understandably, he hated Bret and often told me to leave him. "I don't care if you have a kid, Raina," he said, making my heart sink. I was torn between staying with the father of my children or taking a chance.

I didn't take chances at that point in my life. I needed safety. Adam and I eventually lost touch. He got another job months after, as did I, and he became a distant "what if" memory hidden in my mind.

I got a text from him in 2010, when I had just filed for divorce. My girlfriends threw me a "divorce party," and one of them had connections with him. Adam and I talked for a few days but never really pursued anything. It was just good to be able to talk to him again.

When I landed in St. Louis, I don't remember how we connected again, but we did. Adam was now living in St. Louis and also in the competition world, attending the show I was going to with my brother. He messaged, asking if I'd be interested in grabbing lunch, and I said yes, butterflies back in my stomach.

"Have you ever had a sushi burrito?" he asked.

"No! But I'm in!" I replied.

He pulled up to my hotel, and I hopped in the car. We both were smiling from ear to ear. I'd missed him: his presence, his soul. We caught up over dinner. He was now covered in tattoos and had two little boys of his own. Life had happened to him, too.

After hours of reminiscing over cocktails, he blurted out, "We should go get tattoos."

"Oh my god, can we?" I knew in a heartbeat I'd get a tattoo with him. He was someone in my life I didn't want to forget.

We each got a long-stemmed rose on the outside of our right hands, with leaves down our pinky fingers. At the end of my pinky, I got an "A" and he got an "R." It's still on my finger, a reminder of our tipsy adventure.

He dropped me back off at the hotel and asked if he could join me at the show the next day.

"Of course! But my dad will be coming, so you may have to meet him," I said, smiling.

"I'd love to," Adam replied.

The next morning, I helped my little brother prepare for his first big show. He looked so good. So many memories popped back into my head from that earlier season of my own life. I missed the thrill of it but decided that a sushi burrito was better than a competition trophy.

Adam met me at the hotel, and we walked over together, spotting my dad near the convention center entrance. I introduced them.

"Wow, you're a big boy," Dad said, laughing.

Adam definitely towered over us, at 6 '4" and weighing around 250 pounds, all solid muscle. My dad smiled as though thinking, *Raina, this guy can take care of you.* He'd always thought Bret was a scrawny, pretty boy. I smiled reading his mind.

I was scheduled to fly out that evening after the show, and Adam offered to take me to the airport. We held hands as we drove, and my mind raced, thinking about how different my life might have looked, had I made the choice to be with him all of those years ago. Who really knows, though, right?

I basked in the daydream until we got to the airport. He opened my door, grabbed my bags, and hugged me, swallowing my whole body. I looked up at him, he looked down at me, and we kissed. Just one kiss.

"Call me," he ordered.

"I will," I replied, a stupid smile across my face.

"I'm choosing happiness over suffering. I know I am. I'm making space for the unknown future to fill up my life with yet-to-come surprises."

—Elizabeth Gilbert, *Eat, Pray, Love*

Adam and I kept in touch, texting here and there, while I kept living the life I'd created. In March, I was asked to speak at a work event in Pittsburg, so I hopped on a flight ready to explore a new city. I'd had a lot of speaking opportunities over the last several years, which took me to all kinds of places to share my story and business evolution, letting me inspire other entrepreneurs to grow the business of their dreams.

When I got home from Pittsburg, I hopped on a flight with my childhood friend, Carol, my plus one for our annual trip in Riviera Maya. Carol had never been out of the country before. We had so much fun, exploring, drinking, laughing, dancing, and playing in the ocean for a week. These trips were always so much play and a little work, meeting groups of friends for dinner and cocktails each evening.

I always needed a massive recharge afterwards, but this time, I decided to extend my trip by a couple of days. Carol flew back into Missouri, so I decided to join her and stay in St. Louis for forty-eight hours. I texted Adam a heads-up, and we made plans to have a date night.

I checked into a hotel when I landed, put on pj's, ordered a semi-normal meal from room service after five days of Mexican food, and soaked in the tub, allowing myself an evening to catch my breath between trips.

With an ileostomy, the food I eat typically goes through my system within thirty minutes. So, the dinner I ate that evening before should have released into my bag throughout the night. But when I woke up, my bag was empty, which was not typical for me, even if I hadn't eaten right before bed. I began to massage my stomach gently and felt kind of crampy which was also not typical.

I did a light workout in my hotel room and got dressed for the day, then headed down to the hotel lobby to do some work while I waited for Adam. I loved being able to work from anywhere. As long as I had my computer and/or phone, I could make money. I'd become quite the little hustler on-the-go.

My stomach cramps didn't go away, and I started to get a little nervous about what the lack of output and cramping meant. It could potentially be a blockage, I learned, reading about how to watch for signs, like cramping, low to no output, nausea, etc. Stomach massage and drinking carbonated drinks was recommended, to help push through anything being blocked. I went nearly the entire day with no output and started to get nervous.

I met Adam for sushi and a movie, enduring insane discomfort in my stomach but nervous to tell him what might be going on. When we headed back to his house after the movie, he kept asking, "Are you okay?" as if my amazing job hiding my pain wasn't really convincing.

We lay down on the couch, snuggling and watching TV. But when he fell asleep, the pain in my stomach got worse and worse. I started to sweat while lying there and my heart raced, knowing that what my body was doing wasn't normal.

After an hour or so of waiting and wishing for it all to go away, I nudged Adam awake and said, "I'm so sorry to do this, but I need you to take me to the ER."

He jumped up, helped me into the car, and we checked into the emergency room down the road. As I was sitting in the exam room, Adam by my side, it hit: symptom number three. Nausea. I started to break out into another sweat as the vomit came up.

I grabbed the trash can as vomit ripped out of my body. I saw Adam stand up quickly and leave the room, which made me giggle, despite the pain. He didn't have a very strong stomach.

They admitted me shortly after and gave me some meds and fluids to ease my pain. Adam called my mom, who lived just a few hours away, and she insisted on coming up to stay with me. A couple of nurses came into the room and explained I did, in fact, have a blockage. They needed to place an NG tube in my nose, to help clear it, which was excruciatingly painful and made blood drip from my nose. I couldn't stop crying.

Adam walked in at one point, only to turn around and leave when he saw my blood-soaked gown. When they finally gave up on placing the tube, I noticed some output in my bag, which was a great sign. I don't know if it was the stress of placing the tube, the vomiting, or the pain meds relaxing my body, but *something* had allowed the blockage to clear, and my body released what it needed to.

The doctor came in, asking if my surgeon had told me anything about what I should avoid eating, with an ostomy. It wasn't much other than popcorn and small seeds, to my recollection. He handed me a pamphlet of ostomy tips and advice. On the *what not to eat* list was raw vegetables, leafy vegetables, beans, sprouts, potato skins—the list went on and on. I looked at my mom kind of in shock at the length of the list. *So, vegetables are out, I suppose.* I didn't think a vegetable medley from room service would almost kill me, but it did.

They insisted on keeping me for a day to monitor me. Mom arrived and I prepared to stay the night, so we released Adam of his duties, sending him home to get some sleep. When I was released, Mom took me over to Adam's house to rest for a while before I caught my flight that evening.

When I walked into his house, Adam just hugged me. Looking back, the entire experience had to have freaked him out, not in a weird way but in a fearful way. I had never had a blockage before, so it freaked me out a bit, too. That experience has definitely changed how I eat and drink to this day, but I think it also left a mark on Adam. When he drove me to the airport, we kissed, but not a *see you soon* kiss, more like a *goodbye* kiss, and I flew home.

After texting for another month or so, we decided that perhaps our story stopped there. He had two little boys and lived in Missouri. I had two daughters and had no desire ever to step foot in Missouri again, let alone move back there. It all just felt too misaligned, so we said our goodbyes and moved forward with our lives.

Over the summer, the girls and I decided to take a trip to California, just the three of us. We flew into Los Angeles and spent a few days at Disneyland and then took the train down to

Encinitas to spend the week. It felt so good, being back there, just wandering through the town with the girls and seeing what they remembered and what they didn't. We ate at our favorite restaurants, lay out at our favorite beach, and soaked in the palm-tree energy we'd all been missing for years.

We walked up to the lookout where we'd often hiked, and I wasn't sure if the girls would remember it. Kenzie and I stood at the fence at the top, overlooking the Pacific and crying as the memories flooded back in. California represented such a beautiful time for all of us, yet there was so much darkness in it, too, although we didn't recognize that until we were out of it.

I always spent a week or two at home after each trip, falling back into a flow, while focusing on work and being a mom. Work felt so easy at this time. I'd spent so many years building a team of people under me and establishing myself as the influencer to trust, all I really had to do was keep going.

I'd schedule calls with my team to mentor and encourage them, still sprinkling in the tough love I was known for. The other half of my day was literally showing up and sharing my life on social media. I shared my workouts, a food choice or two, a transformation or progress picture, since I was focused on regaining my health and weight, and maybe a tattoo or a funny quote. This became the easy part.

The hard part was softening my heart. This began with a process of identifying the two distinct parts of myself, both Sara and Jane. I believe I had had a healthy balance between the two of them, at times. Now, however, I was seeing how life had started to harden me.

This really hit me post-divorce, when I had to mourn a version of me who was no longer aligned with the life I needed to live. I'd always had a strong work ethic and a drive for more, followed by what felt like a devil and an angel on each shoulder.

On one hand, I was Sara. I felt the deep need to please people and make sure everyone liked me. I'd gone through most of my early twenties being the wife who spoke only when spoken to and doing the Christ-like things accepted by my friends and family at the time. I'd behave because of a voice in the back of my mind telling me I'd be on the fast track to *hell* if I didn't.

On the other hand, a *fuck-you* mentality started to consume me. I call this Shadow Jane. My *fuck-you* attitude started to dominate the other version of me. *Fuck you,* if you don't like what I say, if you don't like what I believe, and if you don't like what I do. I should have tattooed "IDGAF" on my body, though I never did. This part of me would steamroll right over anyone who tried to stop me from saying what I wanted to say and living the life I wanted to live.

In the midst of this internal war with myself, I was healing from a divorce, mourning the loss of my prior body, trying to show love to and heal my new body, and navigating parenting by myself. Bret had long been out of the picture and was now living with another new girlfriend in Missouri who had a child of her own. *Really, you're going to just jump ship and leave your family to take care of another?* I felt so angry about that, mostly for my kids' sake.

After our trip to Los Angeles, I dropped the girls off with my parents and went on to Indianapolis for a work event. I don't even like racing, but because we were there, I got a checkered-flag tattoo under my whole right bicep. After a few days in Kansas City, I headed north to speak at an event in Vancouver, Canada.

I needed to try to listen to my own voice: I didn't even know what she sounded like or what she had to say. I decided to make this a trip I'd never forget, finding myself again.

When I shared on social media that I would be going, a few people reached out and asked if they could show me around when I got there. I did not generally hang out with random people, but something in me said yes. This was my year to be adventurous, so I jumped on any opportunity.

I'd booked an Airbnb over on Victoria Island, B.C., a little one-room treehouse that looked *perfect*. Everything compact but just fine for a few days. The tree house was in the middle of the woods, beside a little trail down to the rocky coast.

I navigated to the ferry over to the island, where I rented a car and drove into the wilderness to my tree house. Once I'd dropped my bags, I headed to the water, where I sat on a rock, looking out over the water, and just let myself cry.

I released it all, sobbing and grateful no one was around for miles. In an effort to birth Healed Jane, I released old versions of myself, old visions I'd been clinging onto, and beliefs that no longer aligned with the woman I wanted and needed to be. And I mourned the loss of it all, ready to figure out what the next season of my life could really look like.

I felt so lucky in so many ways. I had worked for years to build a business that provided me with financial freedom, so I could leave a marriage that was never going to work for me. I'd created a foundation for my children and myself, and I knew we could go in any direction we wanted to, just the three of us. I felt so lucky to have my life as Healed Jane, to be able to walk down that path to the water and be healthy enough to enjoy it. I was adjusting, still, but so grateful for the choices I'd made.

I stayed in the tree house for three days, taking my car into the little town for breakfast and then navigating to a hike or trail. I sat in beautiful streams, closed my eyes, and listened to the birds, while the water moved effortlessly around me. I sat by myself in little restaurants and cafés, watching the local people live their lives, curious about their stories.

When I packed up my bags, I said, "See you later" to the ocean and was about to head back across the water to Vancouver, when I slammed the door in front of me.

"Oh *fuck!*" I screamed. Peeking out the window, I caught a glimpse of two little bears running off my porch and back into the woods, their little fluffy butts wiggling as they ran away.

Ha! I just nearly ran into two bears! That was insane, I thought, although I wondered if their momma would be close behind them. I nervously waited in the treehouse for thirty more minutes before cautiously walking as fast as I could to my car, towing my two bags behind me, and jumping inside. My heart raced, while my intrusive thoughts imagined me, Goldilocks, being mauled by the three bears.

When I shared what had happened on social media, a few people sent me messages saying that bears were symbolic of strength, courage, and protection. What a beautiful message to receive!

My hotel in Vancouver had lovely clean sheets and a luxurious oversized bathtub to soak in. The next morning, I went to the event to share my story yet again. I always included what people requested: the hardships I'd gone through plus the growth of my business and how I'd maintained its consistency. I found it as inspiring to talk about as it had been to live it and then make it to the other side.

The event went well. I met a couple of women I'd only known from social media, and we all went to lunch after. I invited one of the girls, Amanda, to hang out later that day and possibly hike with me before I finished my trip. Amanda had purple hair and a magnetic energy I knew I wanted around me.

Before getting my tattoo, I met one of my unofficial Internet tour guides for coffee, and we connected the dots for many life similarities we shared. Her name was Caitlin, and she lived in Vancouver with her boyfriend and two dogs. We just clicked, two souls destined to meet.

As we walked over to the tattoo shop, I mentioned how another social media acquaintance had offered to meet me there and hang out after.

"I'm nervous to meet this person," I said with a laugh. "Ali" had reached out on social media and offered to show me around, but I had hesitated because she had no profile photo. I figured, if we met in a public place, it would diminish the possibility of my being kidnapped and chopped up.

Ali walked in with the biggest smile and curly red hair to match her energy. She and Amanda and I hit it off, laughing and excited to get to know one another more. I ended up getting a bear tattooed on my back (naturally!) In addition, I had a little red Canadian maple leaf tattooed on my elbow.

The three of us wandered to a taco spot in the Gastown area after, where we ate and talked about life. I loved them instantly and knew I'd have lifelong friendships with each of them.

Ali was a high school teacher and not yet out of school, so the next morning, Amanda and Caitlin and I met to do a hike in an area called Deep Cove. Oh, it was insanely gorgeous: the most beautiful trees, with water and mountains kissing in the background. It felt like heaven on Earth. Then, we met up again with Ali to hop around a few bars and eat poutine. Our goodbye was a four-way hug, a beautiful soul connection I am so grateful to have experienced.

When I hopped on my flight back home the following morning, I felt like I was leaving an old version of myself behind. The woman who flew out to Vancouver was not the same one going home to Denver. She had shifted, released, grown, and transformed, and I felt so proud of her.

Life #27

International

On my quest to continue saying yes, I felt ready for the next trip. Ready to continue to expand, explore, and get outside of my bubble as I healed.

My little sister, Bobbi, was turning eighteen. As a graduation present, my dad organized a trip for her and me to Spain and France. I still don't know how this happened or where it came from! We'd never had money growing up, and while I did pay my own way, a trip to Spain and France was way more than I'd received for graduating high school.

I let the judgment slide, allowing myself to set aside the feeling of being unworthy, and agreed to join her on the trip, excited for the adventure.

My dad had hosted two foreign exchange kids recently: a girl from Spain, Maria, and a boy from France, Victor. My little sister had grown really close to both of them and their families, so they agreed to let us stay with them on our trip. We had housing covered and people to show us around, which was a huge help in a new country we'd never explored.

I asked Bobbi if she had any interest in going to see London also, since we'd be so close. We could take the train over and play tourists for a while.

And I could see Tom.

I messaged him, letting him know I was making the trip out and hoping to see him. He responded quickly, excited, it seemed, for the ability to reconnect. I felt giddy with excitement at the possibility of seeing him again.

We hopped on our flights out of Denver and landed in Spain, adjusting to the time change and jetlag to the best of our ability. We first met Maria and her family—her little brother, mom, and aunt. It was fun to see Maria again. Her family was very warm and welcoming, excited to host us for a few days.

As our tour guides, they showed us all around their hometown of Seville. We spent a day at the beach, eating ceviche, playing paddle ball in the water, and soaking up the bright sun. We explored every tourist spot, even the Plaza de Toros Seville, where I took photos standing in the middle of the enormous bullfighting arena. We spent another day at an outdoor pool club with incredible "people watching."

On the final night, Maria's mom and aunt took me out to the clubs. I was not sure what to expect. Bobbi and Maria stayed home with her little brother, and I prepared by taking a good nap. Siesta is a serious thing in Spain, and I gladly participated. Around 10 p.m., we went into their closet to find an outfit for me, as I had not packed any appropriate club attire.

With my cleavage out and borrowed stilettos on, around midnight we headed out to the first bar for some drinks. We stopped into three different spots that night, drinking and dancing to the most fun music, surrounded by incredible energy. Very few people spoke English, which I didn't mind. I felt immersed in the culture and along for the ride. You've never partied until you've partied in Spain. I'll never forget it. We wandered home as the sun was about to come up, and I got a few hours of sleep in before we woke up for our last day in Seville.

Before we went to catch our short flight to London, we found a little tattoo shop that fit me in, and I got a bull's head tattooed above my elbow, representing the trip and our beautiful little adventure.

When we landed in London that day, my stomach was full of butterflies. Bobbi was very tired and didn't want to do much, so we grabbed burgers at a local restaurant and called it an early night. I think we both craved a full night's sleep. The next day, we visited the tattoo artist who did my work when I was in London before, after grabbing lattes and pastries. While Bobbi got her first tattoo, I lay down on the table, ready for my own.

Before we'd left for the trip, I'd asked my dad to write out the lyrics to "Sweet Child o' Mine" by Guns N' Roses. I handed the artist the photo of them; she expanded it to fit the length of my back. From my shoulder blade down to my butt, she copied the lyrics in my dad's handwriting. It is still one of my favorite tattoos to this day.

While I waited for Bobbi to finish up, I randomly asked if they had any openings for piercings. They did, and I got my nose pierced, my first since my belly button years ago. It all felt kind of rebellious again, but I loved it. With a new piercing and new tattoos, we headed out to play tourist all around London, and I showed Bobbi many of my favorite spots from the prior trip.

Once we returned to the Airbnb, Bobbi was exhausted, so she opted to stay in the room to catch up on her sleep. I, on the other hand, had made plans to meet Tom and hang out for a while.

I felt so nervous, waiting for him. *Will he still like me?* I wondered. *Will he remember me? Will it be awkward? What in the fuck are we going to talk about? Wait, what am I doing?* I almost had to talk myself out of turning around and heading in any other direction.

When I made eye contact with him, though, every hesitation vanished and the butterflies settled down. When we hugged, it felt like I fit perfectly under his arms.

We grabbed some gelato and wandered around London, over the Waterloo Bridge and the South Bank area. We caught each other up on how the last year had played out, from illness to relationships to life... everything that mattered. We had lunch at a local taco spot, like he knew my love language, and enjoyed a couple of drinks together. We snapped selfies that still put a smile on my face, when I see them.

Eventually we landed at a local bar and were listening to music and talking when his mom texted him.

I said, "Tell her to come out!" He laughed and texted her the invite.

When she, the sweetest woman, arrived, we hugged, introduced ourselves, and chatted until dinnertime. We all went to another taco spot, where we got to know one another, ate, and enjoyed some drinks.

His mom was so lovely, I could easily see where Tom got his charm. I found myself wishing the Atlantic Ocean didn't exist. It would be so easy to fall in love with him, and I found myself purposefully trying *not* to, since we were separated by worlds.

We said goodbye to his mom, and then Tom and I wandered off along the path that runs parallel to the River Thames, holding hands. We sat on a bench overlooking the river as the sun set and time quite literally stopped. And we just sat there, my legs draped over his, my head resting on his shoulder, watching people as they walked by.

The next moment, we were kissing, consumed by each other. It felt like we couldn't stop or maybe we didn't want to. Like teenagers, we sat there, making out on the park bench in our own little bubble, unaware of humanity around us.

"I wish things were different," I said as he agreed, kissing me in between sentences. *I wish you lived closer. I wish you could come home with me. I wish distance didn't exist.*

And, I was saddened by the circumstances that were out of my control. We kissed until we couldn't kiss anymore, and then Tom walked me back to my Airbnb, kissing me for the last time. I watched as he faded into the dark of the night, swallowing my tears before they could escape.

The next morning, I woke up and thanked London for being amazing as always. I refused to let a tear slip from my eye as we hopped on our train bound for France.

One of Bret's cousins had a home in Paris, so I'd reached out about staying there, and he'd gladly offered up the space for two days, until we met up with Victor and his family. It was a beautiful home on the third floor of a building overlooking an adorable park. *I could totally live here,* I thought, like I did about pretty much every home or hotel we stayed in.

We were going to meet up with Victor the following day, so we settled into our place then headed out for food. Wandering around the streets of Paris, we got gelato and pedicures, and we visited some local markets to grab snacks.

When we met Victor and his mom, they welcomed us with open arms. She'd scheduled a boat tour for us along the River Seine that included dinner and sightseeing. It was such a fun experience, floating by Notre Dame and the Eiffel Tower, snapping photos as quickly as my fingers would go. We then jumped on a bus tour for an evening view of the Eiffel Tower, lit up and sparkling, plus other must-see spots around Paris. It was such a beautiful evening, from a dream.

IG POST: July, 2018

This evening, I took a tour around the city and sat next to an old woman, probably in her 80s. She was solo, headphones in, and quiet. I bumped into her by accident a few times, and after apologizing for the 100th time, we started talking.

She was from Australia and on a solo trip. She'd been to Paris before, but I was still intrigued to see her just sitting there, not taking photos.

She said, "This time, I just want to soak it all in..."

I smiled and said that was probably a good idea. I finished the bus ride, trying not to take many pics but watching her as she sat there, looking around and closing her eyes between sites, with the wind just blowing on her.

She looked so at peace. But I sat there, wondering what she was thinking about: her kids? A spouse who'd passed? An old lover she never took a chance on, a trip she never took, a promise she broke?

It brought tears to my eyes, just watching her and hoping, when I'm her age, I'll have the same experiences and the drive to get out and explore, not wasting a second.

We woke up the next morning and were off to Le Mans, France, where Victor's family lived. We spent the day walking around the city with Victor and his mother, as they gave us a tour. We stopped at the local grocery store to grab a few little things to go with dinner, and then Victor took me and Bobbi to every cute landmark for photos, stopping for drinks here and there at local pubs.

When dinner rolled around, I was feeling quite tipsy. I lay down in the bedroom they'd assigned me, feeling excited about the next several days, including a family wedding we were invited to join. Bobbi knocked on my door to let me know Victor's brother had arrived, and it was time for dinner.

I was sitting with Bobbi outside in their garden when the infamous brother walked out carrying a bottle of champagne.

"Holy hotness," I whispered to Bobbi, elbowing her. She laughed loudly.

"Bonjour!" Augustin said. We both smiled like teenage girls. She had an excuse, but I had none.

"Bonjour!" I replied, thinking how lucky I was to be able to spend the next several days with such a hottie whose English was only so-so.

I woke up nervous the next morning, as I got ready for the wedding. Bobbi had said we needed to really dress up, so my insecurities were flowing as I put on my little, gray, cotton dress fearful I'd be underdressed.

When we pulled up to the wedding venue, though, I felt right at home and perfectly dressed for the occasion. After the ceremony, we dove into dinner and the reception where the drinks were flowing, I could feel the chemistry between Gus and me. But I kept thinking, *Is it one-sided?* I reminded myself to just have a good time. *Yolo. Yolo.*

The reception dinner felt more formal than I was comfortable with. Bobbi and I sat there, downing glass after glass of wine, as members of the family and friends gave their speeches and well wishes for the newlyweds. When the music started and I stood up, I realized I'd maybe had an extra glass or two than I should have.

Bobbi and I made our way to the dance floor with everyone, not really knowing many of the songs being played. *I can't dance* is always the story I tell myself, because I often can't get out of my own head long enough to feel the music and move freely. But alcohol always provided me with the liquid courage I needed to fit in on the dance floor.

Gus was around, dancing with everyone and making them laugh, the life of the party. He was very fun to watch. *So free,* I thought.

After Bobbi and Victor's mom headed back to the hotel, I had opted to stay with Gus, his sister, and the other cousins my age, continuing the party. We were invited to stay overnight at a home on the property.

"Everyone will be back in the morning anyway, for breakfast," Gus told me.

So, I continued to live life. I sat with a group by the backyard, sipping drinks while they all spoke French. Every once in a while, Gus leaned over to translate for me.

Around 2:00 or 3:00 in the morning, lying on stones beside the pool, Gus and I were going back and forth about who was more adventurous, between the two of us.

"I bet you wouldn't jump in the pool right now," he said playfully.

"I have a dress on!" I laughed back at him. *And an ostomy bag,* I thought. My ileostomy wasn't something I could ever forget about, and it affected me every day. I'd made frequent trips to the bathroom during the wedding reception, so my tight dress didn't bulge out as my bag filled up. I limited what I'd eaten, too, so I didn't have to have a full bag through the night.

"So?" he asked, jokingly.

I stared at him, with his dark hair, beard, and half smile on his face. Then, I looked at the pool, kicked off my heels, and jumped in, fully clothed.

"*Woooo!*" I heard him scream. A few other splashes followed. Several of us playfully waded around in the water, laughing.

When Gus swam over to me, we held onto the side of the pool, paddling our feet as we moved closer and closer to each other. Time slowed as I wrapped my legs around Gus's waist. He grabbed onto my thighs, and we started kissing, holding tight as the weekend's tension released. We stayed there, soaking in the water, bodies pressed together like no one else was noticing, making out for what felt like hours.

"Ready for bed?" he eventually asked as we wandered out of the pool and tried to wring out our soaked clothes.

We were laughing as we made our way up to the house. When he reached for the door, it was locked. Gus laughed and said, "Let's try another door…"

We walked around the entire house, trying to find a way in with no luck. At this point, it was 4:00 or 5:00 a.m., and we had no way to get inside.

He said that the hotel was *possibly* walking distance, so I laughed and took my heels off, following him down the gravel road leading to somewhere. Still a bit intoxicated and very wet, we walked, talked, and laughed for what felt like miles before we spotted a barn.

"Do you want to just sleep in there?" he asked with his sweet accent.

"I guess so…" Laughing, I followed him into the random barn, where we climbed up into the loft and spooned together between some hay bales. We used his dry suit jacket as a blanket and soon dozed off together.

I woke when the sun was up, unsure how much sleep I'd actually gotten. My phone had died hours before, so I didn't know the time or whether Bobbi had tried to get ahold of me. Surely, she'd be worried I never made it back to the hotel.

Gus woke up right after I did, and we just laughed, moaning about how quickly morning had come and rubbing our heads, wishing the headache would go away.

"I have to go to the bathroom," I told him, holding onto my ostomy bag that felt full. We hopped out of the loft and wandered over to the house just down the road. Gus knocked on their door and, in French, spoke to the woman, asking if I could use her restroom. I laughed in my head, wondering how he was possibly explaining to this stranger why we looked ragged in nice clothes and needed to use the toilet.

We headed back up the gravel road to the house, where we could see the big tents. Just then, Victor, his sister, Bobbi, and their mom all pulled alongside us in the car. Gus's mom yelled at him in French while the others laughed from the back of the car. All I could do was grin and keep walking. Luckily, my suitcase was still in the car, so I changed and refreshed in the back seat after they parked. I still likely looked like a mess but luckily didn't have a mirror or camera to check.

We sobered up by having breakfast with the family and tried to act like normal humans again. Bobbi kept elbowing me with wide eyes, and all I could do was shake my head and smile. It had been quite the night.

The family had booked a little home in Brittany, a seaside peninsula in western France. The region seemed dramatically different from other parts of the country.

The home they'd rented looked like a beautiful little castle above sandy beaches and rugged cliffs, the perfect place to recharge for the remainder of our trip—which is exactly what we did. Gus and I didn't talk again about the night we'd shared. It remained our little secret.

Our goodbyes with the family were emotional. I was sad our whirlwind had come to an end. We'd arrived in Spain, gone to London, and then ended in France, and again I boarded the flight home feeling like a new woman.

These adventures were changing me, helping me release old stories and write new ones.

Life #28

Adventure

When I arrived back in Missouri to pick up the girls, Gus messaged me on WhatsApp, saying he'd had a fun time. I agreed.

I'm going to be doing a hike in September, if you'd like to join? It's called GR20. It's a 180-km hike across Corsica, France.

The word *YES!* flew through my fingertips. *I would love to do that!*

I immediately began to book flights back to France for those dates. This was one of the most difficult hikes in the world, but I had a lot of hiking experience in Colorado before getting sick, so *how hard could it be?*

Gus and I kept in touch over the next couple of months as I started to hike again at home, filling backpacks with anything I could to prepare for this trek. I was a little nervous, mostly because of my ostomy. There would be long stretches without showers, sleeping in tents, peeing and pooping in the woods—I mean, this was a serious adventure I'd signed up for. I purchased a large hiking backpack and sleeping bag, plus all the supplies in preparation for my trip.

The more Gus and I talked, the more he started to feel like a really good *friend*. I got a little nervous, wondering how he'd take the friend zone after our make-out session over the summer. Before the trip, I sent him a voice message explaining I didn't want to go out there with any pressure. I wanted to hike and go on this adventure as friends, nothing more—no expectations. He agreed.

When I met Gus at the airport in France, my excitement for the trip took off. Our next little flight took us into Ajaccio, the capital of Corsica. We checked into our tiny hotel room and explored the gorgeous city that night. In the morning, we'd take the train to the trailhead and begin our trek.

After organizing our backpacks and getting for bed, I was hoping for a full night of solid sleep before starting the journey. As I lay down in bed, though, my stomach sank. Gus had reached over to touch my leg then my stomach. I shook my head with a gentle smile.

How am I feeling guilty for saying no? I thought. My butterflies returned as I realized I might have to be more direct in saying no. Gus made another attempt, so I pulled away and said, "Gus, I don't want to. I told you, I just want to be friends."

He jerked back to his side of the bed. "Are you serious? Why did you come here then?"

"What do you mean, why did I come here? I'm excited to do this hike with you. I'm excited for the adventure. I told you before I left that I wanted to just be friends." I felt nauseous, nervous, and guilty all at the same time.

Mumbling something in French, he stood up quickly, put on a jacket and pants over his boxers, and then left the room. I lay there, thinking, *What in the fuck just happened?*

I had just turned him down. Yet, I'd flown here to see him, to hang out with him. And I'd spent my last trip making out with him so much, no wonder he'd expected more. I know now that his pain didn't mean he was right, but as I lay there, allowing my many thoughts to run through my head, I felt guilty, trying to process what had just happened. After an hour, Gus still hadn't returned to the room.

I grabbed my phone and called Ali, my new friend in Vancouver. We'd talked nearly every day since we met, and I'd grown to really love and cherish our friendship. I called her in tears and explained my situation, asking her advice.

I was in a country I'd never been to, about to do a hike I wasn't familiar with, and Gus was the only person I knew. "I'm fucked," I cried to her.

"Raina, breathe. You're not fucked. He's being a child. He's going to come back, and you're going to let him throw his fit. Then, you're going to wake up and go on this hike like a badass— for you!" she ordered, knowing exactly what I needed to hear. "You are there because you are a strong and independent badass. You don't need him to do the hike. You're doing this for you."

When we ended our call, I wiped my tears turned over to try to asleep, alarms set for 6 a.m.

Gus came back at some point, not sure what time. When we woke the next morning, I turned to him and gave him a nervous half-smile.

"I'm sorry," he said. "I shouldn't have acted like that."

"I'm sorry, too," I replied, "if I gave you the wrong idea. I should have been more clear before the trip."

After closing our backpacks, we set out for the train station. On our hour-long train ride, Gus shared the game plan with me: where we would start our hike, where we would set up camp each night, and where we'd end our hike, staying in an Airbnb for a few days. I started to feel excited again about the journey ahead of us. Ali was right: I wasn't going to let last night set the tone for the trip. I could change my energy, change how I reacted and responded to Gus, and allow this trip to be one I'd remember forever.

We got off the train at our first GR20 Le Refuge and started our journey. There was a mark painted on rocks and trees along the way, which we were supposed to follow. A white line above a red line signified the GR20 hike, so anytime we saw one, that's the direction we needed to go.

The first day, we hiked about seven hours, and it was amazing, full of waterfalls, green forests, and the tallest trees. I took so many photos, my phone died, and it'd be a while before I could charge it again.

At our Refuge for the night, we set up our tent overlooking the foggy mountains, a breathtaking view, made dinner, and enjoyed our first night in camp.

We hiked about eight or nine hours each day. One day was uphill and rocky, then the next day, we'd be scaling the side of a mountain. Another day, we jumped from boulder to boulder, followed by a day walking through flatlands.

On one of my favorite days, we scaled down the mountain and came upon a big, flat, grassy area with wild horses grazing in front of us. It felt so magical to see them. I walked slowly up to a white mare and was able to pet her neck, while Gus snapped photos. A beautiful experience.

Gus always walked a hundred or so feet ahead of me, often just out of sight, so for many moments, I felt like I was on the trip solo. I didn't mind it, though. I knew he needed the time and space to think, just like I did. I also had to slip off the trail occasionally to empty my bag, so I appreciated the privacy and solitude. Now and then, we'd pass another hiker or two and nod our heads, greeting, "Bonjour!"

Our solar charger worked here and there, so my phone had a constant charge of about twenty-percent battery. No service for days, though, so I was unable to talk to the kids or check in. Halfway through the trip, over five days in, we found a Refuge with actual bedrooms and a cold-water shower, like a mini-hotel. I really missed talking to the kids and felt the emotions boiling over.

When I got into my private room, I dialed home and thought my heart might explode when I saw the girls' smiling faces over FaceTime. I cried and wished they were with me, although they would have hated it.

We returned to the trail the next morning. One day, this hike felt like the most empowering decision I had made, and the next day, I was trailing behind Gus, crying because my body hurt so badly and I couldn't stop because we wouldn't make it to camp before dark.

One night, the hike was so hard, I cried uphill for hours, talking to all of the black crows who'd kept me company. We needed to hike for another hour or two. The sun was setting, and we had to set up camp at the top of a mountain. It was the worst night's sleep we had, too, because the wind was very strong, like our tent would blow off the side of the mountain at any moment.

I learned so much about myself on the hike. Not only did I impress myself physically—hell, I was just over six months post-op from my ileostomy surgery! I hadn't known what my body was capable of, but she really pulled through. I also felt so proud of my mind through it all. I did really hard fucking things. I climbed ropes up mountains. I scaled them with my fingertips, losing most of my fingernails, and I tiptoed across gullies with a backpack on my back. I lived off of bread, cheese, and weed for two weeks and stayed present. Completely and totally present. Not missing a moment of my journey.

When we made it to the end of the GR20, we started our journey backpacking up the coast. We found a commune called Calenzana, where we ate pizza, donuts, and beer. It was marvelous to be back in civilization again. From there, Gus and I hitchhiked to the train station and hopped on our train back to Corse.

In this beautiful coastal town, we set up our tents in a campsite and explored the area for the week. We spent time on the beach, washed our laundry, and showered with hot water for the first time in weeks. When I looked in the mirror, my skin was sunburnt and dry from days on the trail. Oddly enough, though, I liked the look. I felt incredible: strong and capable, empowered by what we'd accomplished.

Gus helped me find a tattoo shop when we made it to Calvi, another commune on the coast. I decided to get the white-and-red GR20 marker tattooed on me, along with a plant I'd kept seeing along the trail. Both are on my shoulder. We rented two bikes to travel around; I filled my bike basket with baguettes, cheese, and wine after stopping by little markets.

We hitchhiked to another train station and went farther up the coast to a beautiful Airbnb in Corse. It was a two-bedroom home that overlooked the ocean, very secluded with breathtaking views and only donkeys and goats for company.

When we finally arrived back to the Ajaccio Airport, I felt so homesick, I couldn't wait to see my girls. I had never been on a trip where I was so disconnected and removed from the people I loved and the business I'd created. It did take me a few days to really accept the fact that there was no choice *but* to disconnect.

IG POST: Monday, October 1, 2018

Well, it's afternoon here in Paris, and I spent a few hours this morning filling out an interview about my #GR20 adventure, while I sipped Starbucks and had some real food.

Back to reality - but reality is what we make it, right?

I didn't think I'd get so emotional as I filled out simple answers about the trek I did, but I had tears in my eyes most of the time as I typed.

What an adventure.

What a challenge.

What a crazy mind-fuck.

But here I am, leaving yet ANOTHER trip with a transformed mindset and so ready for the next phase of my life.

It wasn't just about a hike. It was about the challenge, mentally and physically.

TWO YEARS of not being able to do what I KNEW my body was capable of took a toll on me.

This trip was for ME. This trip was to prove to myself that I am capable of amazing things... and to show YOU that our only limits are the ones we set on ourselves.

It wasn't the trip I thought it was going to be, but it was the trip that I needed.

Life #29

Elements

I landed in Denver and didn't want to let my girls or my puppy
go. It felt so good to be home. I'd missed my bed, I'd missed my
balcony, I'd missed my food.

Yet my traveling year wasn't finished, nor did I want it to be.
Every trip of mine felt life-transforming, and I was hooked on the
growing process.

Ali, Amanda, Caitlin, and I planned a girls' trip in Tofino,
B.C., a little surf town on the island. Ali told us it was one of the
coolest places on Earth, so we got an Airbnb there for a few days.
Before, however, I wanted to spend a few days in Vancouver,
because I had fallen in love with the area and wanted my kids to
be able to see what all of my hype was about.

When the girls and I landed, we took an Uber to Deep Cove,
to stay with Caitlin for a few days. Her home was incredible, a
little three-bedroom home overlooking the cove. She also had two
big dogs, and my kids loved sharing beds and space with them.
Caitlin and her boyfriend were both working while we were
there, so we had lots of time to ourselves.

I didn't mind our quiet time together. The first day, we
walked around the strip in Deep Cove, with little shops and
restaurants that reminded us of Encinitas. The girls agreed.

We slept in the following morning, and I got a workout in as
they woke up slowly. We explored the city that day and rode the
gondola to the top of Grouse Mountain, which was a blast. Their

faces were full of excitement, joy, or awe, which put a smile on my face.

On their last day, the kids and I slept in then wandered down to Deep Cove for their infamous Honey Doughnuts. We walked down to the docks and beach, and they played in the water, my memory engraining the whole peaceful scene. I loved the experience of sharing this world with them. It became a part of my vision.

Someone mentioned World Schooling to me at some point, and when I learned more about it, I felt that little nudge in my belly saying *yes*. World Schooling involves families travelling together, using the journey and the travel experiences to enhance their kids' education. The philosophy is that kids can receive no better education than experiencing and interacting with the world around them.

I felt like, over this last year, I'd World-Schooled myself. I grew up in a very small bubble with quite limiting beliefs, not only of myself but of the world around me. In my hometown, racism and judgment toward people of color, those exploring another sexuality, or anyone not considered *normal* was the way of life. That's why I rarely chose to go home anymore.

And then there was religion. My family thought that anyone who didn't believe the way they did or who hadn't *really* given their soul to God was going straight to hell. And there was a specific strategy to being saved. If you belonged to a church where you read words to be saved, a repeat-after-me situation, that wasn't really being saved. You had to throw yourself down at the altar, crying and sobbing so God would really believe it, and beg for forgiveness for the laundry list of sins you've ever committed in your entire life. Without that, hell.

I felt like since I turned 30, I'd spent most of my days working to rewire what felt like brainwashing that I'd been surrounded by my entire life. Religion haunted me, even into my marriage as I was told that masturbating was a sin and sex was not something to be enjoyed, you do it because you're married, in order to reproduce.

So many stories that I needed a lifetime to rewire.

So many lives I've lived, that I needed to heal from.

I'd made a pretty significant change over the last two years because I'd let go of the people and places I needed to in order to grow. I wanted that opportunity for my kids, it was a part of the reason why I moved them to California in the first place. I wanted them to see the world, to meet all kinds of people from all different races and ways of life. I wanted them to then decide what they believed and what they wanted their life to look like. World schooling seemed like the perfect opportunity for that.

We took an Uber to the airport that afternoon and I waited for them to board the first flight they'd ever taken by themselves. I hugged them both, not wanting to let them go, knowing they'd be fine. They were going home where grandparents would be waiting for them, but I missed them already.

IG POST: Thursday, October 11, 2018

Spending the week with my girls in Vancouver has been an absolute dream.

There was a time in my life where I was living paycheck to paycheck and in serious debt - traveling, especially with two kids and a husband, was impossible. We barely had money for gas in our car, let alone plane tickets.

I started this business for my own accountability and it turned into an opportunity to provide my girls with a life that I only dreamt of.

When I filed for divorce, I had a sense of worry that my kids wouldn't be able to live out that life that I had worked so hard to build. I don't know why - maybe guilt for ripping their life apart and flipping it upside down.

And then I quickly snapped out of it because I BUILT THIS.

I CREATED THIS.

I MANIFESTED THE SHIT OUT OF THIS.
I am a better mom because of it.
A better woman.
A better leader.
A better follower.
A better friend.

And this opportunity that I have, changed my life in every way, shape, and form so I am going to take the freedom, the flexibility, the accountability, and I'm going to continue to give them a life that I didn't have.

As we approach 2019 and I think about #worldschooling, I just get giddy. I get excited to share my love for travel with them, to show them the world, to show them new places and experience new things... and groom them to be FREE - INDEPENDENT - EXPERIENCED - EMPOWERED women.

Here we go…

As I sat there, crying in the airport, watching their plane pull away from the terminal, my phone buzzed. *"We're here!"* Ali's text read.

I walked out to the passenger pickup with my suitcase in tow, drying my tears and ready for the final half of my trip. When I got into the car, the girls hugged me, understanding how hard it was to watch my kids fly off.

"Okay, energy shift now. We've got a girl's trip to focus on!" Amanda added as we all laughed and clapped. "Yes!" I loved their energy.

We drove our car onto the Ferry and got out to grab dinner fueling for the 3+ hour drive to the other side of the island to Tofino. By the time we got to the Airbnb, it was dark but we started the party anyway. Ali is the gift giver, she'd always packed something, so when she plopped out 3 little gift bags, no one was surprised but everyone was grateful. We slipped on matching pj's and started making drinks, while we all laughed, cried, talked about life and dreams.

We woke up the next morning and walked to Tofitian Coffee and sat outside planning the rest of our weekend. We headed over to a local surf shop to rent surfboards and wetsuits, strapping them to Amanda's little car. When we got to the beach, we unloaded the boards and made our way into the water.

I had never surfed before and was slightly terrified because of my ostomy, unsure how the whole process would affect my body. Our wetsuit was so tight, I knew my bag wouldn't come off but I did get nervous about the potential impact and leaking. Putting my worries in the back of my mind, we got on our boards and headed out past the waves. Ali, no joke, is nearly a pro surfer. Everyone has different lives within their lives, Ali used to surf and do all kinds of water sports, she was even sponsored by Roxy at one point, she knew what she was doing and we trusted her fully.

We all took turns getting coached by her, eventually standing up on our boards for at least 2 seconds. It was so funny cheering each other on, each of us standing for even a second, our screams and cheers filling up the beach. I felt hopeful, knowing that no matter what the past held, the age, the what-if's, new and beautiful core memories can be made.

We packed up all of our gear and took our wetsuits off outside of the house under the outdoor shower, one at a time, helping each other out of our suction-cupped fits. I pulled my suit down, pulling my arms out and as I carefully brought it down over my waist, I noticed that my bag had, in fact, leaked. "Ugh!" I moaned, "It leaked!" I whined as the girls continued to help me. I made my way into the house and into my bathroom to shower off, annoyed but accepting of the situation. *I just surfed in the Pacific Ocean off an island in Tofino. Cry me a river, Raina* - I thought to myself as I smiled in the shower. *I fucking did that.*

We spent the next couple of days waking up slowly, grabbing coffee at our now favorite shop, and playing in the water. We walked along the beach with a bottle of wine, handing it back and forth as we laughed and talked constantly. We'd go out to dinners and grab drinks, flirting with anyone Ali could get her eyes on. Happily married, she's also the best wingman and her sense of humor will pull anyone in. We played, for days, like carefree women and I soaked in every moment of it. On our drive out, we explored the vast forests and parks that the island had to offer, in awe of the massive trees and ferns that covered the forest floor. The ferns were just as big as I remembered when I did that first hike in Deep Cove with the girls - I knew what I wanted my tattoo to be.

We hugged, cried, said our "see you later" and I went with Amanda to her apartment where I'd stay for a couple of days before catching my next flight to Edmonton in Alberta where I was asked to speak for another event. Amanda went with me the next day to get my tattoo, Ali met us there just to say hi and grab food after. We went to the same tattoo shop we'd gone to originally, the same artist in Gastown I'd kept in contact with, and I laid on the bed as he shaved my head around my ear where he placed my new fern tattoo.

Everyone asks me how bad it hurt, the large fern tattoo that starts at the base of my neck and runs up the side of my head above my ear. Honestly, I nearly fell asleep. I think the loud buzzing put me in a meditative state where I - no joke - feel like I dozed off. It was one of the easiest tattoos I've gotten to this day.

Amanda and I played in Vancouver for another 24 hours before taking me to the airport. When I landed in Edmonton, it was a giant area of nothing much. I joked with the women at the event and they agreed, "You've gotta go down to Calgary, the views are incredible."

I had in fact made the plan to travel down to Calgary after my event. I wanted to explore Banff and all of the glorious scenic attractions the area had to offer. Social media came to my rescue again for this trip, introducing me to two of the coolest women I'd ever met. Bethany and Tarina picked me up from the airport and had offered their extra bedroom for me to stay for the 4 days I'd spend in Calgary. Not only did they offer up their home, they gave me a car to use. When I got to their house and settled in, we went out for dinner to get to know each other a bit more. I'd shared so much of my life on social media, it was really me learning more about the life they were building together.

We walked into the house after dinner and when I got out of the bathroom, I saw a Smirnoff Ice on the floor. *That's... extremely weird.* I thought as I turned the corner and saw them burst out into a laugh. "Have you ever been iced before?!" they asked, I had no idea what they were talking about when they explained the college game to me. I knelt down on one knee and chugged the Smirnoff Ice, the taste brought up memories of high school parties that ran through my head as I finished it off. It would now be *our* game. We spent the rest of the evening turning Mario Kart into a drinking game, taking a drink if we ran off the road. I loved them instantly.

I spent the next few days waking up slowly, grabbing a latte at Tim Horton's and making my way up into the mountains of Banff and Jasper. I felt so incredibly free out there, on my own, following my Google map and trusting the universe was going to take care of me. I walked along Lake Louise and Lake Minnewanka, sitting to stare into the water until my butt was numb. I went to Grassi Lakes and Moraine Lake in awe of the clear blue water I've never seen anywhere else in my life. I explored Bow Falls and drove Icefields Parkway in awe of the glaciers on my way up to Jasper National Park. I checked every box on my list and to this day feel like it's one of the most stunning places on Earth.

Bethany and Tarina helped me find a tattoo shop where I got a tattoo of mountains with bright blue *water* surrounding them, planting the vision in my mind and on my body.

IG POST: Thursday, October 25, 2018

New tattoo: Banff - The place for reflection (physically and mentally).

So, I got a tattoo to represent that (under my armpit).

I think I found the place that brings out the human, the soul, and the love in me.

#untilnexttime @bethany and @tarina - thank you guys for opening up your home (and car) to me, feeding me, all of the car karaoke, and showing me why you love #Alberta so much.

I finished out the fall with a trip to New Jersey with some of my friends and teammates for a Tony Robbins event, a trip home for Thanksgiving, and a visit to Dallas to see one of my good friends, Melissa.

Life #30

Dating

I had done it. I had lived my own version of *Eat, Pray, Love* and quite literally transformed from the inside-out. I explored the world, collected tattoos from every place my feet touched, I fell in love and released love, I met incredible people and built lifelong friendships, and I found a strength within myself that I never realized I had in me. Not only can I survive hard things, I can do hard things, I can grow from them, too.

I had always said I missed out on my 20s, but I think I did it right. I think waiting until I was divorced and in my 30s to explore and find myself was the way to do life. It was the way *I* needed to do life, at least.

Home and ready to settle for a little while, I pulled both kids out of public school and enrolled them in a homeschooling program in preparation for some traveling we wanted to do in 2019.

Looking back and knowing my vision, the timing wasn't quite right for me when I joined Tinder, curious to who and what opportunities were around me. My friends encouraged me to meet someone and I felt like I was ready, healed from my divorce and inspired by the relationships I'd built while traveling.

I nervously went on a few dates, messaging Ali, Amanda, and Caitlin with all of the person's info in case I didn't message them with updates when I was supposed to be home at night. Most of them were fun, good conversations, but I never felt the spark I wanted to feel. I talked for a week or so to someone I matched with, Chad. He seemed like a nice guy and one of the things on my list was someone in the medical field. Not necessarily because they'd have a stable job and make good money, but because I knew that they'd feel less affected and more accepting of the fact that I had an ileostomy.

I pictured sitting there on dates, wondering when it would be the right time to bring up the fact that *I don't have a butthole, oh and I poop in a bag that hangs on my stomach.* It didn't feel like the best dinner conversation so before I agreed to meet Chad for a date, I asked him to look at my social media. I was extremely open about my ostomy, taking photos each week that exposed my bag and telling the story of my health journey. "I already did, it's fine, I'm not worried about anything I saw…" he replied.

Greenlight. I text the girls on my drive down to Denver for our first date. "Here's his Instagram, this is the address where I'm meeting him, and the plan is to meet for tacos and have a drink or two. If I don't text you, call the cops." I texted as they responded with laughs, wishing that I'd have a good time.

I met Chad outside of his apartment around 4 p.m. and when I saw him, light brown hair combed over to the side and brown eyes, walking toward me standing about 6'2", I thought *that'll do.* He was wearing khakis and a button up shirt which I debated, thinking *Okay, Mr. President…* as I wore my cute overalls and a tank top for our casual date. I was hoping he wasn't as uptight as his outfit presented.

We walked down the block for a drink at a cool little hole in the wall bar in Denver.

"Let's meet early," he suggested, "that way if the date sucks, we can call it early and not waste the entire night." *Genius.* I thought. He ordered a cocktail and I ordered a shot of tequila. I wondered if that was the moment he fell in love with me.

We sat at the bar getting to know one another. It felt a bit awkward at first, I'd answer a question and he'd ask me the same one ten minutes later, maybe his mind was elsewhere. We walked a couple doors down to Machete's, a taco spot, to have dinner and another drink or two. I went to the bathroom at one point and later he told me the bartender asked if we were on a date. He'd told her yes and she had recognized him, apparently, he had a few other dates here. She told him that she thought I was really cool and very pretty, thumbs up - when I heard that, I mean - I knew that, but it made me wonder what the others were like.

After we finished our food, I went to the bathroom one more time to empty my ostomy bag. I didn't want to go in for a hug or quick make out sesh with a full bag on my stomach, how distracting. I walked out and he asked, "Do you wanna come over to my place for a little bit?" He lived just a few blocks away. "Sure." I replied, nervously.

I hadn't yet had sex with an ostomy bag on and I wasn't quite sure how it would work. I also don't know why my mind went directly to sex when he asked me over, it wasn't like me to sleep with someone on the first night, a one-night stand, none of it. It's not that I never thought of it, it's simply that I was trying to break this "sex = love" story I had wired in my brain.

We walked into his one-bedroom apartment, clearly a bachelor pad, untouched by any woman. Vastly different from my 5,000 sq. ft. home in the foothills. I didn't judge, just shifted my thoughts. *I fucking hate dating. This is so weird.* I sat on the couch soaking in the environment he created.

Chad sat down on the couch next to me and we awkwardly watched YouTube videos for 20 minutes before he finally leaned over to kiss me. We sat on the couch, making out like college kids for a while before things shifted a bit. Listen, I hate even writing about this but I think it's important, knowing the words that made me think, *I already love this man* before I left his apartment that night.

He knelt down in front of me, kissing me as he started to take my clothes off. I kept moving my right hand down to cover my ostomy bag, one hand on it at all times as he started hanging out down south. My right hand had one job: protecting my vulnerable attachment. After 5 minutes or so, I'm sure he noticed how I kept readjusting and moving my hand, keeping my little stoma safe and under cover. He grabbed my hand and looked up at me, holding me still and said, "Hey, it's okay." I smiled at him with uncertainty. "I mean it, let go, it's okay."

And I did. I hung out for a couple hours and then drove home with a ridiculous smile on my face. I got home safely and texted him as he asked me to do, "Thank you for tonight. I had a lot of fun. And thank you for accepting all the parts of me, it means more than you know." I said, hinting at how he'd handled my *ostomy* insecurity.

"I had a lot of fun too. You're beautiful and it doesn't define you. It's not a big deal to me, I promise. It's just an accessory."

I knew *then* that Chad would be a beautiful part of my story.

I went into dating, hesitant because of the amount of baggage I carried. Physically and metaphorically. Divorced, two kids, an ileostomy, a bankruptcy not yet off her record, I had a lot of things that, on paper, qualified me as a *no*. Chad, on the other hand, was the perfect candidate. On paper, he came from a good family from Richmond, VA with a college degree, a job in the medical field and a huge heart. I saw no reason to not pursue this *thing* we had.

IG POST: Wednesday, January 23, 2019

"My heart breaks after reading an article about a 10-yr old boy who killed himself over being bullied because of his colostomy bag.

What in the actual fuck is wrong with people? With kids? With these trolls.

I'm breathing because of this bag.

I'm walking because of this bag.

I'm smiling because of this bag.

I'm still a mom because of this bag.

I'm still fighting… because of this bag.

I would give anything to be able to meet that boy and hug him, showing him he's not alone.

He's unique, special, and worthy and like someone told me, it doesn't define him, it's purely an accessory.

We texted the next day, chatting about nothing and everything. I think it was just a couple of weeks later that he met the girls for the first time. We went to a giant arcade, and they played together for a couple of hours. Kenzie and Ella approved of my new friend, not really asking many questions.

I deleted old photos of Mike, hid photos of Tom, and archived albums with Gus, allowing myself to completely commit to the man in front of me.

And then, I dyed my hair red.

You know, we do that sometimes when life pivots. I felt like I needed a new visual to match the energy I was bringing into the relationship.

We continued to chat through the holidays and into the new year. I'd traveled to Kansas City, Maine, and Philadelphia for a few speaking events and continued to show up on social media for work, sharing my life vulnerably. There was always something in me that felt nervous, bringing Chad into my social media world. I felt awkward taking pictures of the two of us, not wanting to blur the line between work and love. We never took many photos together, I hated that.

When I was home, Chad would sleep over a couple nights each week if he didn't have to be at work early the next morning. It was an adjustment sleeping in bed with someone, overnight, with my ostomy. I would always wake up at least once in the middle of the night to empty my bag and by morning, it'd be full again.

I'd daydream for a bit, Chad lying in bed with me as we slowly started to wake up in the morning. He'd grab me playfully as a little spoon and we lay there cuddled up for a little bit.

Like a record scratching, that daydream was instantly interrupted by the thought, *That could never happen. He could never carelessly reach over and wrap his arms around my waist without worry.*

He could never playfully pull me toward him while I wrestled to escape his grip, playing hard to get. I will never be able to be that carefree.

We woke up one morning and it's like I'd manifested my worst nightmare. Chad moaned in acknowledgement of the sunrise and I laughed. He grabbed a fist full of the blankets, playfully pulling them off of me and onto him, I screamed. "Oh my god!" I grabbed the blankets back as quickly as I could and sat there, breathing in to see if you could smell the poop that was now covering the sheets we were sleeping in.

I took a deep breath as I peeked under the covers.

"What happened? Did I hurt you?!" Chad said nervously.

"No. No you didn't hurt me but I do need you to get out." I started calmly.

"What?" he questioned.

"I need you to get out." I repeated, nervously trying to decide how I was going to clean up the situation. I laid there for what felt like 30 minutes, letting my mind think about how I was going to get out of this mess. *Washer? I'd have to rinse all the shit off and that's too embarrassing. I could probably - no, trash it.* I stood up doing my best to contain what was left in my bag that was barely hanging on by the adhesive. I stepped into the shower and cleaned myself off, replacing my bag and getting dressed before I looked at the bed again. I grabbed the corners of my sheets and pulled them up, allowing each corner to swallow my big down comforter and rolled it all into a contained ball. I fabreezed the fuck out of my room and walked into the kitchen to make eye contact with my boyfriend.

"I was so nervous I did something to hurt you?" He met me quickly, touching my arms in an attempt to comfort me.

"No, you didn't hurt me at all, swear. You just pulled off my bag along with the comforter. I know you didn't mean to, it didn't hurt, it just made a bit of a mess." I assured him.

"I'm so sorry..." he said quietly. I could see the understanding in his eyes.

"Will you go with me to get new bedding today?" I asked.

Life #31

Shifts

You cannot heal in the same environment that made you sick.

—Unknown

The first time it happened, the pain woke me out of my sleep. Danelle and Jerry were sleeping over for the weekend, so they were in Kenzie's room while the girls shared Ella's bed. I sat up in my bed feeling like I couldn't catch my breath.

My stomach was cramping, and I couldn't force myself to breathe as a fire lit up my chest. I stumbled into the girls' room to wake up Danelle, crying, "I can't breathe. My chest hurts. I can't breathe!" I continued to sob between gasps.

The girls were awoken by the commotion, so Jerry helped me to my bathroom while Danelle put the kids back in bed.

"Call 9-1-1, Danelle!" Jerry yelled back as he got me into the bathroom. I knelt down in front of the toilet as vomit came out uncontrollably.

When the medics arrived, they took me out on a stretcher and into the back of the ambulance. I kept grabbing at my chest, saying, "I feel like I'm having a heart attack. It feels like my heart is on fire! I can't breathe!" They hooked me up to machines with wires all over my chest, while one medic started my IV.

After some scans in the hospital, they told me I had gallstones and a panic attack. The next day, I had surgery to remove gallstones from my intestinal tract and liver ducts, but they also nicked my pancreas, giving me a mild case of pancreatitis, too. I stayed in the hospital for a few days to recover.

I'd spent the last couple of years eating anything and everything I could to gain weight back after my ostomy surgeries. In the process, my gallbladder paid the price. I blame it on the fried wings and fries at the restaurant near our house, which I ate at least twice a week—they were the best.

When I got home, I knew it was time to clean up my diet and work on healing my insides, now that my outside felt good. The girls and I decided we needed to eat at home more, and after some research, I started a daily regimen of celery juice. I had my juice every day and shared a photo of it for accountability, like I did almost everything else I ate or drank.

Oh gross, how can you drink that? I tried it and almost threw up!

I read DM after DM like this from people, and I just replied, *I drink it because I'm a fucking adult.* I said this so often, I decided to collaborate with a woman on Etsy to make little cups decorated with *I'm A Fucking Adult.* Activating my Jane energy! I sold them on Instagram and was tagged constantly by people purchasing and sharing their cups.

I started to feel I needed a lifestyle change, a new season, a shift. My home had started to feel uncomfortable, like every room carried secrets about the life I'd almost had there. It reminded me of my ex, it reminded me of my illness, and I needed to find an environment that enabled healing for me.

I had lived in the country, the suburbs, the beach, and the mountains, but I had not yet had a downtown-city experience. I started looking at lofts in downtown Denver and fell in love with a building catty-corner from Coors Field. The inside had an industrial feel, with wood and white, and it had been remodeled beautifully.

We'd be in the middle of it all, and I craved that energy, I craved that life. I could envision every part of it. I could see us walking Dexter around the city, pausing so he could pee on the tree grates. I could see lunch breaks with Chad at the restaurants on the ground floor and drinks on the rooftop. When we toured the potential space, I could see my girls there, too, running up and down the stairs as we played music, dancing in front of the giant, two-story, floor-to-ceiling windows.

Not only did I want to move into a new home, I also didn't want to take anything with me from our current home. I wanted new couches, new beds, new pillows, and new rugs. I didn't want any of the energy transferred or memories associated with the furniture in my new place. It would be the first place that was *all* mine.

I gave a thirty-day notice and signed a lease at the new loft to start the beginning of summer. The girls and I spent the next month packing and taking pictures of all the furniture, listing it on Facebook and Craigslist for sale. I sold as much as I could and donated the rest, with the exception of one wooden table I'd picked out myself in Encinitas with the old, worn look. It was mine and the only thing I felt compelled to keep. Its memories were deeper. It would make a good TV stand or something—I'd make it work.

I moved in June 2019, and our summer started exactly as I'd envisioned. Chad decided to move in within the month, forgoing his lease, and the four of us settled into our two-bedroom, seventh-floor loft, with Dexter in tow. I'd picked out new furniture that was exactly what I wanted—my style, my vision. The loft was so light, so bright, and our orange couch really popped. I also hired a man to furnish my apartment with plants, adding a beautiful pop of green.

I'd never been able to keep a plant alive before this, but now, I had over twenty live plants accenting different areas of my loft. I was obsessed with how well it all came together and how energized I felt in that new space. I set up a little office for myself and settled in nicely.

IG POST: Friday, May 31, 2019
Thankful for the old… It gave me the confidence, healing, strength, experience, and growth that I needed. But fuck, I'm so ready for the new.

With our new little life falling into place, I felt the vision of world schooling starting to slip. I knew I was allowed to change my mind. I just didn't want to disappoint the kids. We talked about pausing the goal for a year or two, just to enjoy our new spot. We'd left everything behind, including gymnastics, dance, and any extracurriculars, and had been homeschooling for months by this point. I wanted them to plug back into activities and community. They agreed and were excited for the possibility of going back to school, so we enrolled them in a local middle school just a few minutes down the street.

I fell in love with the flow of the new space. I'd wake up and take Dexter down the elevators for our mini morning walk. We'd say hi to the regulars on our block, who shared the same pee path as we did, and greet Lloyd and Vinny, two homeless men who had also claimed our block. They slept in tents or on the benches on the street and were seriously two of the best men I'd ever met in my life. Vinny passed away months after we moved there, on the bench under our master bedroom window. It was the first time I'd ever seen a dead body.

Then, I'd take the girls to school. When I came home, I made my pre-workout shake and did my morning lip-syncing.

Yes, I said *lip-syncing*. Before TikTok exploded, I created a little morning performance that I put on each day. I'd make my pre-workout, flip on the sunglasses filter, and lip-sync to any song *requested* by my followers. Once a month or so, I'd post a question box labeled: *song requests,* and I'd get a hundred suggestions, ranging from eighties bands to nineties hip-hop (my favorite) to Taylor Swift. It was so silly but also so fun. It kind of became my thing. I have one-on-one clients now who say, "I've followed you since your lip-syncing days!" It always brought up my mood.

Every day right after lip-syncing, I started my thirty- to forty-five-minute workout up in the loft that I'd turned into my home gym. Then, I made my post-workout superfood shake and sat down at my desk under the stairs to start my calls or emails, whatever was on the to-do list. I'd pause to make my food, cook for Chad if he was home, and take Dexter out for another walk. Then, I could work for a few more hours until I picked up the kids up from school.

After school and on weekends, we roamed around the city. We'd either walk or ride scooters to the grocery store, or walk Dexter down to the art district for a spontaneous photo shoot. We'd wander up one floor to the rooftop and grill steaks or chicken, while we watched the city lights and listened to the noises of people making their way home from work. It felt nearly perfect. After I sent the girls to bed, I would wash my face, do my skincare, and slip into my pj's after. I'd eat a sleepy-time gummy while Chad turned on *The Great British Baking Show,* and we'd watch until our eyes felt heavy.

"Look at that glaze!"

"Oh, he baked that too long," we'd say, like we were judges on the show. We laughed so hard, watching our evening shows. Some nights, we'd fit in an adult snuggle sesh before bed, and sometimes not. But I always took it personally when we didn't.

Chad joined me that summer at our annual work event in Indianapolis. He really got to see me in my natural habitat: with my team, my best friends, being recognized for the work I did. It was always such a cool feeling, going to these events. I'd be stopped on the street, in bathrooms, and in hallways by people who shared how they followed me on social media and felt so inspired by my journey... Then they would ask, "Can we take a picture with you?"

When we headed home, it felt like I had all of Chad's support, if I ever wanted to push for a big goal again. I felt kind of burnt out at that point. I'd hit so many goals in the business, it felt like there wasn't much left to do. I felt boredom and dissatisfaction, and when I pushed for such big goals, success never ended up feeling as good as I wanted it to.

Chatting for a while with Ali, she'd told me she thought there was something bigger we could be doing. I didn't quite know what she meant, though. I didn't want to leave the company I worked with: I made too much money and enjoyed it too much to move onto something else.

"You don't have to leave," she explained. "I just think there's more."

We decided to start a podcast together, after we spent an hour on FaceTime, laughing at our own jokes and conversation.

"People really need to hear how funny we are," I said after another joke. We decided to reach out to a coach and friend, Linzy, to whom we had gotten really close while traveling over the last year or two.

Linzy, Ali, and I were quite the trio. Ali was the class clown and high school drama teacher. Linzy was the sober rebel with a fuck-you attitude. This resurrected my Shadow Jane energy, and I became the chameleon. We decided we only wanted to record in person, because, with the three of us, we wanted to include not just audio, but also the visuals. We recorded ten sessions at a time, traveling between Denver, work trips, and girls' trips. We'd schedule one trip each quarter and release episodes weekly.

We talked about everything. There was nothing off limits.

Sex.

Blowjobs.

Drugs.

Ex-husbands.

Prostitution.

Friendship.

We explored it all, and the dynamic between the three of us felt unstoppable. I loved our friendship; those two knew everything there was to know about me. They cracked me open.

I reflected on when I'd had such overwhelming energy for work, usually when I was pushing for a big goal. I experienced it again around our podcast and felt I'd really like it again in my work. But I would need to become harder, and I felt nervous to turn that *hustle* back on. The hustle changed me. I knew that. And now, with Chad in the picture, I didn't know if he'd understand or accept who I needed to become, in order to hit those goals.

If I decided to push for Top 10 again, it would require selling my soul to the Time Gods for a little bit. I'd have to put in more hours to recruit new team members, and I'd have to put a lot more energy into my team calls and mentorship chats. It would require early mornings and late nights. Sacrifice. At least, that's the story I told myself.

It wasn't about the goal of hitting Top 10 again as much as it was proving to myself that I could do it. I craved the mission.

Chad told me he was on board, so, as we rang in the New Year, welcoming 2020, I felt a fire inside me and a strong belief: *I can do it all.*

———— ◆●◆ ————

JOURNAL ENTRY: Monday, January 6, 2020

If I want to change, something must change. This process is so foreign to me, but I truly believe it's a missing piece in who I am and who I need to become.

Life has hardened me to an extreme.

"I don't care…" is a staple phrase, and I know it's not okay.

I've had my heart broken, ripped from my body, squeezed into mush, and thrown to the wolves… by many people.

Trust isn't something that comes naturally to me. I'm cold and do not show a lot of emotion, because I was taught to conceal feelings.

Instead, I hold everything in, causing stress, anxiety, false fears, and sadness. I'm a worrier. I'm in constant fear of losing everything I have because I've lost it all once, and I know it can happen again.

But…

I'm in love with an amazing man who really does have my best interest at heart. He has taken my kids in and wants to see them develop into strong and good humans.

He accepts me and all of my baggage and sees no flaws. He deserves a better me.

My kids are at the age where they know who their father is and what his issues are. They are also sponges who soak in every "attitude" I display, which isn't always the best.

They don't have passions because I have dropped the ball, trying to be mom and dad while trying to build a business. They deserve a more present mom.

I love what I do for work, and I know a lot of people don't get to say that.

I'm a tough-love coach, which is natural for me because of the life I've lived.

It's easy for me to say - suck it up and do your shit - because it's what I had to do.

But I realize it hurts a lot of relationships that could have really been great.

I need to slow down and become more mindful of who I NEED to become in order to grow the amazing things in my life and to influence the way I need to.

We spent the holidays in Virginia. It was the first year the girls and I hadn't been with Danelle, Jerry, and/or my family. It was a fun trip, but it wasn't home. I know the girls felt the same, slightly out of place at each dinner or outing. Chad's family was amazing and so welcoming. I found it interesting to see that side of Chad.

There wasn't much he did to help us feel included, and it always felt like we were in the way.

This could have been my own shit I was projecting onto him and the situation. I recognized that, so I did my best to stay present each day, falling into the flow.

We exchanged gifts. I received a little prompted mindfulness journal. I hadn't ever been consistent at journaling, but it was something I was ready to explore.

Ali and I shared a birthday month in February. We decided to get an Airbnb in Los Angeles, so we could record some episodes and celebrate our birthdays together. Ali and Linzy surprised me with a long weekend full of activities. Our plan was to record episodes during the morning and go into girls'-trip mode when afternoon hit.

Linzy was originally from the LA area, so she had several connections. On our first evening, she had a friend come give us a private meditation and sound healing. The next day, she had a friend give us tattoos in the living room. She was new at tattooing, and to this day, the little topless mermaid on my back was probably my most painful, mostly because she was heavy-handed.

The third day, we scheduled an interview with the CEO of our company. It is still mind-blowing that we got to do this. I'm sure I had a slight *in* with him, as I'd been in the Top 10 twice and had finished January 2020 as #10 in the company, but it was still surreal. We set up our microphones and computers in one of the empty office spaces at headquarters and had an incredible, energetic interview starting the moment he sat down. And truly, that interview and the things our CEO shared helped me fall deeper and deeper in love with the company I represented.

When we saw one of the trainers in passing, we hugged him and invited him out to our Airbnb that night. I didn't think he'd actually show up, but when he did, the four of us smoked a bowl and spent the next several hours talking about everything under the moon, laughing together, and creating silly TikToks until it hurt to laugh.

The next morning, I felt sicker than shit. In fact, we all had started to feel like death. Months later, I swore we were some of the first people to contract Covid. We guzzled tea with honey and any other natural remedies we could think of to ease the congestion and stuffy noses we were all struggling with.

I woke up to "Happy Birthday" singing while I stood there awkwardly in my pj's, smiling ear to ear with Kleenex stuffed in my nose. *Best birthday ever*, I thought as I hugged my best friends. We then changed and headed to the beach, where they surprised me with a sound bath meditation. We lay on blankets with four or five other people in a circle as the waves rolled in, listening to her play the most beautiful sounds. I started crying, releasing whatever needed to be let go.

I felt overwhelming gratitude for life at that moment. My kids, my health, my boyfriend, my home, my friendships. It felt like the hard shit I'd gone through was starting to pay off, and the appreciation I felt toward the universe oozed out of my eyes, soaking into the blanket beneath me, then evaporated into the sand as it met the Earth.

IG POST: Wednesday, February 12, 2020
I needed a good night's sleep to process everything that happened over the last 4 days.

Saturday, two of my best friends planned 4 days of birthday activities for me in LA.

If you don't know, I'm a slight control freak, and they know it - so they didn't fill me in on anything that was happening.

Each day, I woke up having no idea what I was in for.

In between podcast recordings, we hopped around LA, and it gave me life.

We had someone come to our Airbnb to do tattoos for us, an amazing woman I enjoyed really getting to know.

We had private meditation sessions including a sound bath meditation on the beach in Santa Monica.

That alone changed everything for me.

We got to do an amazing interview with our CEO, who really just solidified every reason for me being in the business I am. We got to hang out with amazing friends and grow stronger relationships with people in our lives through great conversations.

We laughed, we cried, and we really just got to be with one another, growing and sharing life.

Every time I leave those two women, I just think to myself: holy shit, that was life-changing.

Every trip I go on, I'm ready, knowing it's probably not going to top the last one… but it always does.

Thank you, girls, for being there, listening, and knowing how much I need to get out of my head, heal, and just be in a safe, quiet place.

The day after we got back from Los Angeles, I fell back into my flow feeling motivated and inspired, like I always did after a trip. I sent the kids to school that morning and sat down with my hot tea to journal:

JOURNAL ENTRY: Thursday, February 13, 2020

Prompt: "Like a child standing in a beautiful park with his eyes shut tight, there's no need to imagine trees, flowers, deer, birds, and sky; we merely need to open our eyes and realize what is already here, who we already are."

—Bo Lozoff

I love this quote so much. It reminds me of the Deep Bits *podcast episode we did with Amanda.*

She looked at me and said, "At what point, if any, were you able to just stop and realize that you don't need to keep fighting? That you can rest. You've proven what you need to prove to yourself and to others. When will you realize that you're exactly where you are meant to be?"

Even just writing that, I felt myself emotional and tearing up.

I've told my friends I feel like my entire life has been fight or flight.

It's like each day, I'm ready, in fight mode, armed and ready to battle, when I don't need to anymore.

For so long, I was waiting for things to fall apart.

I lived so long with this deep gut feeling of pain, loss, insecurity, fear, etc.

I spent years building walls to keep out people who would create more of that pain in my gut.

I cut people out as soon as they "wronged" me to protect myself, and unfortunately, it caused a lot of pain and instinct that I now carry around, when in reality, I don't need to.

Raina, you can breathe.

Let go. Let it all go.

Realize the multiple number of beautiful souls who have been brought into your life to help you grow, move forward, and to develop you into the person you are today.

That woman has always been inside you.

But, over the years, you've allowed people, experiences, and thoughts to change you. You put a mask on - to fit in, to hide, to cover up.

But you, you're a fire.

Stop. Breathe. Look up. Look at what you've created.
Look at what you've built.
Look at the women your daughters are turning into.
Look at the home you're providing.
The safety, the security, the man who loves all of you.
You're safe.

The truth was, the character I'd created on social media had started to feel less and less like myself. While I lip-synced and responded to DMs, behind the scenes, I felt unloved. *How could someone with so many friends and social media followers feel so lonely?* I wondered.

When I filed for divorce, my ex-mother-in-law repeated to me, "Whatever you don't take the time to heal will be carried into your next relationship." And that stuck. I feel like it's the reason why, even though I dabbled in *situationships,* I could never settle in. I stayed single and decided to travel. I needed to find out who Raina was without Bret, without a wedding ring, and I needed to mourn the life I'd lost in order to create a new one.

Chad and I got along well enough. We could do small talk better than any other couple I knew. Ali always said we could talk for hours about nothing. She was right. We'd wake up in the morning, take Dexter out to potty on sidewalks, and get ready for the day, saying a few words. We'd mostly listen to whatever podcast or YouTube video he chose that morning, commenting here and there on what they spoke about.

He'd maybe kiss me, maybe not, as he headed out for work and I started my day. After my workout, I'd navigate through my social media to make my post, connect with people, and respond to messages. I'd get my shots of dopamine, reading people's messages and comments, eager to soak in their words, so I could feel like I was making an impact and get the validation I needed.

When I picked up the girls from school, the energy would explode. They always loved to recap their days, talk about bullies, and share what they had for lunch. We had so much fun after school until Chad got home. When he walked through the door, it's like the three of us knew we had to drop the energy in the house in order to not throw him off.

He'd made little comments before about our energy. Our back-and-forth "fighting" or "bickering" just felt like *too much*. We never fought, though. We were just three dramatic girls.

It was a difficult transition for me to make: being the loud, energetic, tough-love coach by day and the dull girlfriend by night. We'd get into little arguments, and he'd make comments like, "I'm not your coach, Raina. You don't get to talk down to me..."

I'd find myself getting defensive about everything, an instinct from being on social media for a decade, having to justify every word and choice I made to strangers on the Internet. The dynamic just felt hard, and I wondered if it'd ever get easier.

He always "needed an hour or so" of quiet when he got home from work to wind down. The girls and I adjusted and eventually enjoyed that hour, knowing, without it, Chad would be more on edge and passive-aggressive in his comments. With it, and probably a quick hit of the bong, he'd walk out of the bedroom in a lighter mood.

His job was heavy. I understood that. He had people's lives in his hands more than he felt comfortable with. One wrong move and he could paralyze someone or shut off parts of their brain required to function. I could imagine the pressure he had, which oozed out of him every time he put on scrubs.

While Chad disconnected, playing with Dexter on the floor or watching TV, I'd start dinner, enjoying the process. While I was working hard to break the stereotypical gender roles, part of me loved cooking for my family, watching them eat, and then cleaning up after. I loved loading and unloading the dishwasher, mostly because I liked it all to be neat and organized. One of my pet peeves was opening the cabinet or the dishwasher and seeing something in the wrong spot or out of order.

I realize now that's a bit controlling, and also, I took pride in my home no matter where I'd lived. I thrived in an organized and clean space, regardless of how long I lived in the home. I wanted to create a clean, organized, and aesthetic space for my family, because it's something I never really had and had always provided for myself.

This would be a heavy topic for Chad and me.

"You would rather sit there, bleeding out, than ask anyone for help, ever," he said to me once, upset that I didn't make the kids help clean up after dinner.

"I'll ask for help if I need it, Chad." I tried to explain that I didn't mind doing it. I actually enjoyed it.

But that wasn't the way he'd grown up. His mom and dad had met in college and waited nearly a decade after they got married to have kids. They were both teachers and came from a good family, providing structure and safety for their two sons from day one.

"We were a team," he always said when explaining how his family had raised him.

"I've always been a team of one," I rebutted.

We'd watch a movie or episode of a TV show and then head into our bedroom around 8:30 p.m., showering and doing our skincare while we listened to a podcast or YouTube video before smoking a bowl. We'd plop into bed to watch one of our shows, and I'd lie there, wondering when he was going to touch me.

I hated sex between the ages of eighteen and thirty. Bret always had an overly healthy sex drive, hence the affairs. We had sex once a day for the majority of our marriage, and I hated it most days. It felt like a job, a duty, an obligation as a wife, so most of the time, I just lay there, counting dots on the ceiling and waiting for it to be over.

My first night with Chad gave me a taste of what a healthy, fun sex life could be. Our first several months together felt like that, like we could play and explore without judgment or pressure.

Once Chad moved in with us, though, those connections felt fewer and further between, and I built resentment around the lack of affection I was getting. Healing my *sex = love* mentality, I felt left with little. *If we don't have sex, how else will I know that you love me?* Just simply *being here* wasn't enough.

I needed more.

In our small arguments about the kids, my lack of delegation, or the affection missing in our relationship, I'd question whether we could make it work, long-term. We were raised in such dramatically different circumstances. Even our twenties and thirties looked night-and-day different, as we'd navigated life in completely different ways. This question lived in my head and in my body throughout every day. I smothered it with work, my kids, and my eagerness to try to make this successful. *Because, on paper...* it should be.

I slowly started to realize I was in a relationship that wasn't serving me, but I was determined to fight this truth. *I'm not going to be my mom,* was in the back of my head as we continued to argue over the smallest, simplest things. I was dating someone whom *I believed* saw me as Jane, as someone who needed to be fixed. It felt like he didn't agree with my parenting or my approach to life, and this started to create serious self-doubt in my mind. *Maybe I am doing things wrong...*

I started smoking weed hoping to quiet some of the thoughts.

JOURNAL ENTRY: Friday, March 13, 2020

Felt good to just breathe this morning.

Found out last night that, because of the coronavirus, the girls' school is letting them out on an "extended" spring break, March 13-April 7.

At first, I was frustrated, but Chad strategized with me.

I was worried about not being able to work like I have been the last few month, so instead of freaking out, we decided to get the girls on a schedule just like me.

It'll all work out. When Chad gets home today, we are going to order a bunch of groceries and just plan on a month of staying home, working, working out, and massive amounts of games and movies.

I also found out that I'm going to get refunded about $5,000, because our Punta Cana trip got canceled. I've talked a bit about my fears around money and lack thereof, just my spending habits, and I really feel like this is going to allow me to save this month and practice better spending habits.

We won't be going out and doing much at all, so, really, the only expenses I'll have is groceries. God knows I spend enough in that area anyway!

Thinking positive about all of this chaos.

It really did come out of nowhere.

People are freaking out. NBA, Disney, all shut down.

But this girl is going to use this time to grow.

Life #32

Pandemic

I've always been able to put anything bad happening in my life onto a side burner, to let life do its thing while I continue to push forward in other areas of my life. The global pandemic sat in the saucepan of my life, while, in the Instant Pot, I was working on my business.

We were a company whose foundation was built on selling home workouts, so, as you can imagine, business kind of boomed in 2020. While half of my team was worried about losing their jobs or being out of work, I encouraged them to continue to push through, making time for *this* business, because, in my mind, it was a no-brainer. I'd built wild success, so anyone could—I truly believed that—if they just stopped making excuses.

The big difference, I think, was my ability to maintain consistency through anything. I'd navigated divorce, single parenting, bankruptcy, traveling, dating, relocating—all of it! And I'd stayed consistent in my business, growing into the high-six-figure income bracket. It seemed like a no-brainer to me that people should just *go all in*.

On my mentorship calls, I listened to people share about how difficult their life felt, and I insisted it was simply their mindset. If they didn't believe they could change their life, they wouldn't. If they didn't at least put in action toward creating something different, they never would. It was a painful thing to listen to as a coach, so many women wallowing in their limiting beliefs and negative self-talk. My mind never went there at this time in my life.

This tough, business-focused mindset had been easy to adopt when I was married and hated my husband, when I was trying to escape my reality. It was even easier when I was single.

I think, because I'd hit so many of the goals I had set, anything felt possible. I did not understand the flipside, that if those goals hadn't happened, I'd probably not feel as motivated and inspired as I did.

With Covid in full effect, the world just exploded. Chad and I masked up, our latex-free gloves on, to drive to the grocery store, where we walked down empty aisles. I wondered what I could create for dinner with beets and noodles, feeling nervous about accessing the foods I'd been consistent about eating. The food I'd been eating was the reason why I felt so good. I was convinced of that. It was the reason I'd been medication-free for a couple of years by then and thriving with my health.

I stocked up on seven bundles of celery each visit, hoping I'd never run out. We were allowed to grab one package of toilet paper and baby wipes, so we created rules that our family could use no more than four squares each. Chad gave the family a tutorial on how to fold it, to maximize wiping capacity.

We were only allowed out of the house to grocery shop and take Dexter to the bathroom. We kept puppy sanitizing wipes near the front door, so we could wipe Dexter's feet off every time we came back inside, to ensure he didn't bring anything into the house on his feet.

I think being with someone in the medical field changed how we handled the virus. It consumed Chad's thoughts and our family along with it. On the other hand, my mom and dad just walked around Missouri, mocking people who were taking it so seriously. My friend, Carol, chose to keep her wedding date set for May and invited all of her family and friends to gather at their home in southwest Missouri for the occasion. She stopped talking to me when I told her I couldn't be her bridesmaid and wouldn't travel there to attend, because I wanted to keep my family safe.

I also have an autoimmune disease. This was a perfect example of how invisible my disease was, which I had to remind myself as I felt sad about how half of the world navigated this crisis. I had to protect myself. People were dying every day from Covid-19, and I didn't have time for that.

Ali, Linzy, and I continued our weekly podcast recordings. They became the thing I looked forward to the most. We'd brought in our friend Amanda as our fourth, so the four of us would connect for hours, recording for thirty to forty-five minutes then staying online to chat about our lives for the rest of the time. I'd share about how strict Chad was being and how we were navigating the virus, craving a release and the ability to travel again.

"Girl, it'll fly by. We'll be able to hang out by summer, I know it," Ali would say, kind of living in a bubble. She knew that, but I don't think she wanted to admit it.

Life #33

YouTube

I got a FaceTime call from Ali one morning as I was sitting down to work.

"Did you see it?" she asked nervously.

"See what?"

"Someone made a video about you and Linzy, from a team call…"

I wasn't a stranger to online hate and the troll world with its mission to bring down celebrities and influencers. I've always been quick to block on my social media, if someone starts to spew hate; this was a tool to protect my energy in the space that I called *work*. I knew there were Reddit hate groups created specifically for people I knew and was close to. My name had been mentioned here and there, also.

I never understood why so many of my friends even looked at those groups and read what was being said. I didn't want to see. I knew me; I knew my intentions. Their misconceptions and observations from the outside looking in didn't affect how I showed up each day. Ever since the situation with the women in my church, I'd had the ability to put blinders on and do my thing, whatever was required to move forward and prove them wrong.

"I'm going to send it to you. Just watch it. It's kind of fucked up. Someone apparently sent her one of our team calls, and she just tears you guys apart," Ali continued.

By this time, we'd joined Linzy in the call, and she was spitting fire.

"Fuck her. This is such fucking bullshit. I don't even give a fuck. What kind of person makes a video like this? She's doing it for money. Fuck her," Linzy continued as I sat there, pulling the video up on my computer.

Surely, it's not that bad. I mean, I'm firm and direct, but I haven't killed anyone, I thought. But my body was telling me I needed to start worrying.

Linzy hung up the phone, off to deal with this situation in her own way, while Chad sat next to me, holding Ali on FaceTime as I opened the video.

It was a private team call I had held a month or so before. It wasn't posted publicly on YouTube, none of my team calls were, so that meant someone on my team or with access to our private Facebook Team Page had sent this video to this woman, who had turned "anti-everything" into her brand. Currently, she was on a mission to expose those in network marketing organizations as the devil walking in a human body.

My stomach dropped as I watched her open the video while warning people about what they were about to see, as if we were about to witness a graphic murder. The team call started and immediately the *no-excuses* mentality was evident, as Linzy and I gave tough-love to our team, who were pushing for another year in the Top 10. As she continued to pause our call and insert her commentary, I knew we were fucked.

I started crying as I continued to watch. This YouTube host had cut, chopped, and paused at the perfect times, commenting over our video and making it look like we were the worst people on the planet. There were people getting away with rape, murder, tax evasion, and child pornography, while I was being excoriated in this small corner of the Internet for the way I mentored and motivated my team.

"The fact that she has cancer is why she needs this," the video began. I was in the frame, *supposedly* telling my team to target people with cancer.

"Wussup, fuckers!" Linzy chimed in on the video, as she always did.

"I feel like I've been playing it safe with you guys," I started again, *"allowing you to take this business slow and avoid inviting people. Well, guess what? Inviting is the only way you're going to grow this business."* I sounded confident. She kept pausing, to add her two cents.

I continued, *"Guys, I remember sitting on my couch next to my husband, miserable in my marriage, with my laptop on my lap knowing that I had a way to get out of this. I sat there, listening to training videos next to a husband that didn't support me, and I invited."*

She paused there to mock my work ethic, when I started my business.

My notifications started going off, with DMs coming in, when I opened my phone to take a breather. My inbox was flooded with friends asking if I'd seen the video, along with concerned teammates sharing the link with me, shocked at how it had been twisted this way, and followers and message requests from strangers who were flabbergasted at how I would *say what I said, behave how I behave, and speak to people with such disgust.* None of them gave me the benefit of the doubt.

I started to cry more, so hard I couldn't catch my breath. I put my head between my legs as Chad rubbed my back. Ali was there for it all on FaceTime.

"I can't believe this is happening," I cried, trying to catch my breath. Chad closed out of the video and wrapped his arms around me to calm me. I was having a full-blown panic attack, my mind blown at how misunderstood I felt.

Chad spent hours going through my DMs to delete and block people, so I wouldn't have to read their painful comments and hateful messages.

Kill yourself.

Shame on you…"

What kind of coach talks to people like that…?

It got so overwhelming for me that, eventually, Kenzie asked to clear the messages, filtering and blocking to protect me. She was the tough one in this situation. I think she felt like she needed to be.

The messages came in so consistently that I stopped opening my Instagram app. Once I'd calmed down a bit, nervousness set up camp in my gut. I'd felt the same feeling so many times before, that *fear of losing everything,* along with the realization that I'd been very misunderstood and misrepresented.

Danelle's words flooded back in: "Raina, if what you're doing and sharing, inside your heart of hearts, feels good—if it doesn't feel wrong or malicious or for the wrong reasons—then keep doing what you're doing. Allow it to fuel your fire."

But my fire had been snuffed out that day. Sara emerged to keep Jane safe.

I called corporate, just to give them a heads-up that the video was out there, hoping they'd have a tool in their high-level toolbox to help make this all go away. They asked if I had the original video, thinking it'd be helpful for the higher-ups to know the full context. I went on a hunt for it.

After an hour or two, I found it and pushed play, curious to see what the Villain didn't want to include in her video. Her version of our team call, of course, didn't include our story, which I'd opened the call with and that set a more inviting tone than the one presented.

She'd gone on to mock our breathing exercise, something we always walked our team through before starting our calls each week. We'd learned it at our Tony Robbins workshop the year before.

Her video didn't show the members of our team who asked questions like, *"Someone I know was just diagnosed with cancer, and I know she could benefit from the movement and nutrition. How do I invite her to join me?"* This was what had led to my cancer comments. It didn't share the encouragement from one teammate to another or the comradery we had as others chimed in, adding their two cents.

Watching our team call made me sad and angry all in the same breath, knowing the intentions of every person who sat there with us, listening.

After a couple of calls back and forth with my corporate representatives, it was decided they couldn't do *nothing;* it would look better to the FCC or *whomever* potentially came at them, if there was a "punishment" given. Corporate and compliance apologized to me and, in the same breath, shared that I would be given a six-week suspension without pay. Not because I'd said anything wrong, but because Linzy, a member of my team, had made health claims without a disclaimer, and that was against compliance. This meant that, while I was currently Top 10 in the company, I would disappear from all aspects of the business and leaderboards. It would appear to my team that I didn't even exist in the back office.

I wasn't allowed to communicate with my team, host calls, or teach them in any way, shape, or form until the end of my suspension. It felt like I was required to fall off the face of the Earth, until all of this lost momentum. My team had been my anchor, my lifeline for the last several years. That was severed, and I felt like I was in utter freefall.

Since 2016, the fear of *losing everything* had always lived in the back of my mind. This suspension only amplified it. Not only had I lost my business for six weeks, I felt like I'd lost my footing on social media. I also felt a sense of abandonment, when the people I'd grown close to in Corporate did nothing to help me. I didn't hear from anyone for my six weeks of suspension.

In my corner of the world, it felt like I'd lost a big piece of who I was, which caused me to question everything, from who I am to what I believed or what I valued.

That version of me, Jane, slowly died. Someone else, Sara, peeked her head up. It felt impossible to wake up every day and continue to show up as if nothing was happening behind the scenes.

The next week, George Floyd was brutally murdered, and the entire world watched it happen. My stomach, already in knots, couldn't handle the hatred oozing from every corner. I changed my profile photo into a black square and felt myself withdrawing from everyone and everything I knew.

I opened my windows and watch the streets below me fill with protesters supporting the BLM movement. I grabbed the girls and headed downstairs, so we could stand in support. My heart felt so heavy, so disgusted, so angry. It was hard for me to channel the anger I had into anything healthy. It even felt hard to eat.

I received texts from my family, like, *Hope you're staying safe while all that chaos is happening around you. This is why I didn't want you living in the city.* My dad imagined my life was on the line when these protests broke out. Little did he know I felt safer there, in the middle of that protest parade, with people giving voice to their stories of oppression, than I did in Missouri.

I fell into one of the deepest depressions I'd ever experienced. It felt like I was really losing it all: my income, my business, which I had so strongly identified with for the last decade, my voice, my platform, and the people who had been with me through so much of my life. At home, I was with someone I fought with constantly, trying to justify my choices as a parent and a confident woman, which was forcing me into dulling everything about myself.

Dulling. That is where Sara thrived.

With the Covid-19 numbers rising, we decided to try to get out of the middle of the city and into the suburbs for some air. I wanted a back yard and some space to myself, so we spent time looking for rentals on Zillow. We signed a lease not long after for a cute, little 1920s home in a nice suburb of Denver.

We finished out our current lease and moved into our new space in June 2020. The girls had separate bedrooms, which they were happy about, and Chad and I set our room up in the basement, so we could have some privacy from the rest of the house. We also set up our home gym down there, and once we settled, it felt quite cozy.

Because the house was a hundred years old, it had a lot of character and felt more closed off and dark than I prefer. There was no way to let in much natural light, so I strategically placed all of my plants around the house, doing my best to make the house a home for the next year, while things got crazier outside.

It felt good to have my space again, which allowed me to breathe a bit more. However, I had dulled myself so much to the point of breaking, I didn't even know how to show back up when my six-week suspension was lifted. I ghosted so many of my team members, feeling scared to speak publicly, and I stopped talking on my social media platforms. I switched to relying on mindless, humorous reels to try to grow my following, hoping to replace the people who had left over the last month.

Life #34

Darkness

While I worked to heal from the YouTube event, I thought Linzy was doing the same. We hadn't been talking as much since we'd both been suspended. We still connected on our podcast, but because things had felt so heavy, most of our recording days turned into crying sob sessions, as we all navigated what had happened.

I got a FaceTime from Ali and Linzy one afternoon as I was pulling into my garage. I parked the car and stayed there, feeling a heaviness from Linzy, along with the urgency to *share something*.

I'd known since the first time I met her that Linzy was on her own human journey, exploring gender roles, sex, and beliefs. She danced to the beat of her own drum, and I loved that about her. I think it's what drew me to her the most. She'd tell Ali and me stories of her past, the sexuality she'd explored, and the pieces of herself that she'd healed. I felt like I knew her more than I had ever known another human.

I always joked with her, knowing she was more attracted to those identifying as female "Why aren't you attracted to *me*?" I'd ask as she laughed. "You don't think I'm hot?"

She knew I was teasing. I loved her deeply and supported her in every way I knew how.

When she began to tell us that she felt the need to pull away, my stomach dropped, and my eyes started to water.

"I'm going to transition, and I just don't think you and Raina have ever supported me in that way," she began. "I also can't be part of a podcast called LadyBits, so I'm going to quit the podcast." The rest of her words started to muffle as I felt my watering eyes drip.

"*What?*" I started to say, as Ali said the same.

After Linzy ended the call, Ali and I stayed on. I asked, "What in the fuck just happened?"

"I have no idea," Ali replied.

I felt completely helpless, watching my best friend spiral and cut the cords that had tied us together. I mourned the loss of her friendship for a long, long time.

> *"I lost my identity when the character I was playing stopped."*
>
> —Unknown

I spent each day falling into the routine that had once lit me up, but feeling nothing. I wanted to work out and not share it. I wanted to eat a meal and not tell anyone. I wanted to hide and not worry about a knock on my door. I numbed with weed, craving quiet.

It was the first time in so long that I'd begun to feel hopeless. It was the first time in my life I'd ever had a hard time creating a vision for my life, a hard time picturing what life could look like a year or two from then. I could barely see past tomorrow. It was the first time in my life when I'd ever had thoughts of, *If I did decide to kill myself, how would I do it?*

I was still paying $5,000 bankruptcy payments and a $4,000 rent. I'd lived this lifestyle for the last several years, one that I loved and my kids were used to. I felt so fearful, realizing that what I'd worked so hard to build could be taken from me at any moment. Even though it was *my business,* it wasn't my business. I remember Mike telling me years before that I should really start thinking of another stream of income, another business, in case something ever happened to the company. *I should have listened to him.*

Intrusive thoughts took over. *What if I lose my job? What if I can't pay rent? Will Chad be able to? I can't ask him to do that, they're my kids. What if I had to get another job? What job would I get? I'd lose all the freedom I've built… What else would I do? I'm a college dropout.*

As quickly as the thoughts came in, I tried to release them. I began to drown myself in self-help books, trying to snap out of the negative thinking and spiraling funk I felt trapped in. I fell in love with Rebecca Campbell and her outlook on life, and I read every Dr. Joe Dispenza book I could get my hands on, obsessed with his belief in the power of our thoughts. It became my focus, to shift those.

Chad's birthday was approaching, and we'd been talking about getting a dog together for the last couple of months. We discussed different breeds and what to name it, just daydreaming. I think, subconsciously, I thought that a puppy would act as the glue to many things in my life at that time. Maybe it would create a stronger bond between Chad and me. Maybe it would be good to have something else to focus on. Maybe it would bring more joy and laughter into the family, something I felt was really lacking.

The girls and I got Chad a card for his birthday, explaining that we'd bought a golden retriever puppy, and he was soon to be a dad to Archibald, one name we'd joked about choosing. We'd call him Archie for short.

We picked up Archie the day before Halloween. At age eight weeks, he fit in the palm of Chad's hand. Dexter wasn't quite sure what to think of the tiny new addition to our family, but we were patient, knowing their love for each other would grow. We spent every day on our hands and knees, playing with Archie and Dexter, watching them use tug-of-war toys, and exploring the home.

We decided to enroll in virtual obedience training, since we were still in a lockdown with Covid and unable to take any classes in person. We met with our trainer, Christina, each weekend, and this became the highlight of our week. Watching Archie learn to sit, stay, walk next to us on the leash, etc. made me feel like a proud mom. I know Chad felt the same. I would always joke with Ali, saying I was getting a sneak peek into what Chad would be like as a dad. It was crazy obsessive. Not a bad thing, I supposed.

One weekend, as we sat in training with Christina, watching Archie walk around, she asked, "Is he walking a little funny?" She tilted her head to one for a closer look. Chad had mentioned this a couple of times, but with his *obsessive parenting*, I'd pushed it off, figuring he was overreacting.

When you looked closely, though, Archie *was* in fact walking with a little bit of a limp, kind of like a pirate on a peg leg. Christina suggested we take him into the vet, just in case, to have him looked at. So, we did.

We were referred to a veterinary hospital in Ft. Collins for x-rays and tests, to see what was going on with his back left leg. When the vet showed us the images, I felt nauseated. It looked like his left leg was completely detached from his body. The ball and socket in his leg hadn't developed, so it was attached only with cartilage and muscle. My heart sank. *Of course, I picked a broken puppy for Chad.*

We spent the entire hour-long drive home quietly crying between guilt trips put on me for not taking Chad seriously, when he'd originally expressed concern about Archie's legs. I felt guilty enough! The added pressure made me feel like the worst dog mom in the world. When we got home, Chad left and I took Archie downstairs and lay with him on the floor, sobbing and apologizing to him.

"I'm sorry, Arch," I cried. "But you know what, Momma is broken, too. We'll get through this together, and you'll be just fine." He just looked at me, unsure why everyone was so upset.

We spent the next couple of months in and out of the vets, at appointments for scans, injections, physical therapy, and anything else we could do to both ease his pain and help him live the longest, healthiest life possible. While it all felt terrible, I also felt lucky that I'd been chosen to be his mom. I knew no one would take care of him like I could.

Ali, Amanda, and I decided to keep our podcast going, changing the name of it and doing a bit of a rebrand with just the three of us. I looked forward to it every week, though we often gave up recording and instead, vented about life and cried to one another about things we were working through. It became a therapy session most weeks.

When we did record, we always tried to interview people as a way to take the pressure off ourselves and to expand our reach. We interviewed mediums, psychics, spiritual women, coaches, and any other inspiring woman we knew. Each time we had someone on, I'd hear the words "slow down" from them.

Ha! What a luxury, *slowing down*. Must be nice to be in that space, could never be me. I'd been living in hustle mode for most of my life, so I didn't know how else to live. Even in the midst of this identity crisis, I set my work hours and worked mindlessly on anything and everything I could to keep my mind busy.

One of the last coaches we interviewed was a life coach who said to me, after I'd explained some things going on in my head, "Girl, it sounds like you need to slow down."

I lay down on the floor with Archie after crying. While he pounced on his toys playfully, I heard the words in my head: *You weren't going to slow down, so the Universe did it for you.* I just whispered, "Thank you."

When I get a *memories* pop-up on social media, flashing me back to 2020, I can see the darkness under my eyes and the heaviness on my face, the numbness I was craving. I also wish I could give her a hug. It felt like everything I'd ever known had crumbled, and I needed to dramatically rebuild. I had to find my way into a new season, I just didn't know where to start.

Life #35

Pause

"It's impossible to develop your identity and be online at the same time."

—Emma Chamberlain

JOURNAL ENTRY: Tuesday, December 1, 2020

Today felt off, slightly. It felt fake. Today, I felt like I needed to act like everything is okay, like nothing hurts too much.

Yesterday was hard. "Heavy," as I explained it. It felt like I couldn't take a deep breath without tears beginning to well up.

It even happens now, as I bring attention to it.

Today was my first official day off of social media. How sad, as a grown-ass woman… "My first official day off social media" sounds like I'm some whiney-ass influencer who got her feelings hurt.

It's deeper. Way deeper. Yet I feel like only a handful of people know the feelings coming up for me and how hard this severing really is.

Chad or even my therapist can't comprehend how deep the pain, feelings, worry, anxiety, and doubt goes.

So, I write.

I wonder why "what everyone else thinks" matters to me.

Feeling like this may be the only way to get it out and process it.

Today, it feels like mourning.

It feels like a relationship. One I invested in every single day, throughout the day, for 2,790 days.

One that allowed me to "be me."

One that listened when I had something to say.

This relationship told me I was beautiful on days when I felt less than.

It made me laugh when I needed to smile.

It went with me through heartache and love, equally as deep.

It also caused me so much pain every day that it became my outlet.

It told me how ugly and unworthy I was.

It told me to "eat a cheeseburger" when I was suffering with my illness and to cover up my "disgusting bag of poop" as I shared vulnerably, all in one breath.

It forced me into comparison games that caused me to change everything I knew for one single like or comment.

It clouded every thought, every emotion, and it eventually broke me.

I just really have no idea who I am.

I've been cheated on.

I've been lied to.

I've been called names.

But this relationship with social media has got to be the one that broke me the most.

My heart breaks. It aches. Yet a part of me, way deep-down, is already breathing just a little bit lighter today.

Tomorrow may be different, but today is just okay.

Since April 12, 2013, I had been plugged into social media, sharing my life, every single day. I began sharing when I was twenty-five years old, inviting people along as I grew and evolved into the human I was supposed to become. It felt like such an important part of my day. So, when I decided to take the month of December off, it required an adjustment.

Days into the hiatus, I started to have physical withdrawal symptoms: shaking, sweating, overwhelming anxiety, and tightness in my chest. It took a couple of weeks before I started to feel the quiet relief of being unplugged and my heart rate steadied.

My days slowly began to shift. Without the pressure of showing up on social media in any certain way, I felt free to experiment with my day.

Archie was still so little. We had to be up with him at least once in the middle of the night, followed by a 4 a.m. wake-up. Chad and I would take turns getting up with him in the morning, letting him outside, and then finishing what sleep we could get on the couch in the living room.

JOURNAL ENTRY: Sunday, December 6, 2020
We measured the dogs today. Their height on the doorway.
We all smiled then.

I was up solo with Archie around 4:45 a.m. He fell asleep on my neck when we lay on the couch. That made me smile.

I haven't even had my pre-workout yet!

I inhaled "peace" today.

Exhaled "worry."

I tried to visualize a bit this morning during my meditation.

Visualized us, the four of us, super-peaceful and joyful, smiling and laughing without worry.

Then, in my visualization, I thought about feeling no worry in regards to my job... When I started thinking about my job, the worry hit again.

I kind of came to and realized that I'm living that visualization right now, but that worry does seep in.

It's so heavy, like someone sitting on my chest with their hand on my throat.

I've been hearing myself think, "You need to start healing the old shit. Write about it. Journal about it."

While social media is a huge reason for these "episodes," I can't ignore all of the trauma I went through and woke up with for the last 33 years.

I don't even know where to start. Do you go to your easiest memory? I don't have many, and I know that so many of my answers are tucked away in those memories.

I remember telling my mom how I don't remember a lot from my childhood. She says, "Was it that bad?" And we laugh.

Funny, Kenzie and Ella tell me sometimes that they don't remember much from certain situations, and all I think is, "Thank God."

Maybe what upsets me, too, is knowing that, one day, they're going to be in my spot, hurt, sad, misled, and in need.

But they chose me for a reason, and I think it's to teach them strength and how to overcome the hard shit.

Every page I journaled felt different than the page before it. I'd write about an argument that Chad and I had one day, putting down all of the things I wish I had said. The next day, I'd explain how we'd had sex, so things felt a little better than they had yesterday. I'd write out my day on the next page, working to fill every bit of time I had with something that made me feel like I was moving forward. I battled the guilt that popped up around feeling the need to keep myself busy, while sitting there watching Netflix while my mind called me a *lazy piece of shit.*

I worked daily to rewire and release those engrained *hustle* behaviors. I had such twisted thoughts around rest, recharge, and reflection. My therapist said to me, "Rest could be playing with puppies, recovery could be your workouts, and reflection could be journaling. It could be the therapy you are in weekly."

I worked toward releasing the negative self-talk and replacing it with positive acknowledgement. I was moving forward; it just didn't look like it used to.

I read in one of my books, *Think Like a Monk,* "Our lack of gratitude is what makes us feel unloved." When I read that, something shifted. I had been focusing so much on the things going wrong. If I wanted to start to regain control of my life, I needed to acknowledge the things that were good, right in front of my face. Most days, that was easier said than done.

I journaled every single day, vomiting my thoughts onto paper and reading it back with curiosity. I wanted to know why I was thinking the way I was. *Where is this thought coming from? Where is this feeling coming from?* I continued to question what I wrote, looking for the lessons or sparks that would allow me to shift.

I swear to God, my mind started to change and shift quicker than I thought it would. But one constant remained: *is this the right relationship?*

------◆◉◆------

JOURNAL ENTRY: Thursday, December 17, 2020

Sometimes the silence is unbearable. We were just sitting in the gym. Cleaners are here, and we said two words.

It just sucks, and it doesn't feel good. This can't be normal. Maybe it's normal, but I don't want normal.

I want to feel loved, appreciated, respected, and safe. I don't feel any of those things.

Maybe that's why I turned to social media so much.

In an instant, I could share a struggle and feel loved.

I can share something that helps me and feel appreciated.

I can share what I've overcome and accomplished and feel respected.

Because of that, it felt safe in so many ways.

The negativity came in right alongside it, which caused the pain. It was like a parent saying, "I love you, and you're doing such a good job," then telling you how shitty of a person you are in the same breath.

Confusing and unsteady.

So, remove the distraction.

Remove that negativity.

I felt excited to make the emotional switch, depending on myself and my family to provide the love, appreciation, respect, and safety.

Actually, it's quite difficult and unrealistic.

So, I'm supposed to find this in myself? And be fulfilled?

It seems far-fetched, especially when it doesn't feel like it's coming from anything external.

And it's exhausting.

And it's overwhelming.

And it's incredibly lonely.

I'm reading a book now called Disconnected. *It's all about the real underlying issues and solutions to depression.*

I don't know if I'm depressed. The first chapter nearly had me in tears, because I related so much.

Lonely.

That's all.

I started to think about the difference between where I was and the old version of me who felt like she could do anything. Life had stripped me of that belief, and I was realizing that it was my responsibility to get it back.

"If you aren't obsessed with your life, change it," the quote goes.

I wasn't in a healed-enough space to create a vision for my life, but I could start by creating a vision for my day. I was supposed to go back onto social media in January 2021. This was the goal I'd set for myself. I scheduled two photo shoots for myself that month, so I'd be able to share in a different, more confident way when I returned. I wrote:

JOURNAL ENTRY: Friday, January 1, 2021

Before I go back, I need to cast a vision.

I need to get crystal-clear on what I want in my life and in my business.

I haven't cast a vision since 2015.

Coincidence that, after that year, the decline started?

I was crystal-clear on California and that vision. It woke me up every morning. But it was deeper. It was getting my family out of Missouri.

Why?

Because I knew we were "capped" in growth there.

I wanted my daughters to experience more, and I wanted to be there for it all. Showing them what hard work looks like.

And now, they talk about college in Korea and Japan.

The independence and vision they have inspires me. But they got that from me.

Now I need to figure out what that new vision is, to reverse-engineer and grow.

I sat down on Monday morning and wrote some more. This was really becoming my superpower. I decided to write out two scenarios, as detailed as I could do them.

The first prompt was: *If nothing changed, what would life look like in one year?*

I wake up to my brutal alarm, anxiety creeping in immediately. I look over at Chad, nervous to start the conversation, so I get up and take Archie outside without saying a word, consumed by nerves. I make my morning drink as I try to slow my heart rate, because I can already feel my heart beating out of my chest.

I send the kids to school, missing them already but glad to have a day full of quiet time, so I can focus on work. I've already shared on social media a few times that morning, feeling dread and "shoulds" around what I've posted, clicking back to it every couple of minutes to see if anyone commented, which distracts my thoughts for the next couple of hours.

I make my pre-workout and do my workout, because I should, not because I actually enjoy it anymore. I half-ass my workout and do enough to post a video after, to social media, feeling like I'd just rather sit down and start working, so I can make sure my bills are paid.

I work all day, feeling pulled between social media and my email inbox, when in reality I should be working on finding new clients. Instead, I procrastinate on Instagram, labeling it as work. I end the work day when the kids get home, feeling like I didn't do enough, so my phone is in my hand while they talk to me. I'm not really even there.

When Chad gets home, we barely talk and definitely don't touch. We've gotten used to the way our relationship is, accepting it. We sit down for dinner, and all I'm thinking about is work and how I'd rather be anywhere else. I clean up dinner, feeling resentment because no one helped, but I also didn't ask for help. I turn on music and head downstairs to fold some laundry, because it's quiet and no one will bother me.

After I wash my face, I lie in bed, exhausted and wishing for a hug that never happens. Closing my eyes, I drift off to sleep, hoping I don't wake up in the morning.

The second prompt is: *If I started to make small shifts, what would life look like in one year?*

In one year, I wake up without an alarm, excited for the day ahead. The heaviness in my chest is gone, and the nausea has dissipated. I turn over, smiling at Chad as his eyes open. I snuggle Archie as I greet everyone, 'Good morning!"

We playfully jump out of bed and head outside to let the boys go potty, while I start my morning drink, looking forward to what's on my calendar that day. I wake the girls up, fully present, and help them get organized and ready for the school day. I send them off to school as Chad leaves for work, I give him a kiss on the cheek, wishing them all a good day, before I head back downstairs to get my workout clothes on.

I make my pre-workout shake and do a quick little check-in on social media before I start my workout, not because I have to, but because I get to. After my entire workout is complete, I make my post-workout shake and get dressed, eager to start work. I spend the day working with my clients one-on-one. I'm no longer doing group work, and instead,

I've created courses that people can work through at their own pace, in order to reach more people. When I finish my one-on-one calls, I'd spend some time on my emails before heading out to take Archie on a walk.

We welcome the girl's home and spend some time together, connecting and catching up on their day before Chad gets home. When he does, I hug him, excited for him to be home. I give him his time to turn work off and disconnect. The girls help me make dinner, and we sit down as a family to eat, sharing our highs and lows of the day before we all pitch in to clean up.

Chad and I sit down with the dogs to watch an episode of the show we're watching, relaxing together without judgment. I head downstairs to shower, cleaning off the day, and lie down in bed feeling accomplished, like I've checked every box I needed to.

Chad jumps into bed, allowing me to be the little spoon, while we watch TV and fall asleep, Archie above my head on my pillow.

Exhale.

The difference in energy between these two visions felt like night and day. I wiped the tears off my first entry, acknowledging that the future I'd described was the life I was currently living, just amplified.

Tiny shifts. All I needed to do was make tiny shifts in order for the second vision to become my reality. When I looked at it, I noticed how similar both visions were. The main difference was my mentality and how my work day was structured, so that's where I started.

When I thought about my job, even before the entire YouTube fiasco, I felt the frustration return. It didn't matter how many meal plans or food pictures I shared. It didn't matter how many workout videos or transformation pictures I shared. People struggled with something bigger: consistency.

It was also one of the main questions I got in my DMs:

How were you able to stay so consistent through your divorce?

How were you so consistent while you were sick?

How were you so consistent, even when you traveled?

The question was asked weekly. Now that I'd been doing a deeper dive into my mindset and thoughts, realizing how powerful a tool journaling had been for me, this became something I wanted to share more about.

I knew I could easily transition and start talking about that kind of thing on my social media, but something in me felt I wanted the title or certification to back it up. I did some research online, browsing different options. I hated school, and I didn't want to enroll in anything that would take me years to complete, so I settled on getting my Life Coach Certification.

JOURNAL ENTRY: Monday, January 25, 2021

In books and random places, I've been reading a lot about our "current reality" and how it is so incredibly dependent on what we think.

I've had so much negative self-talk and doubt, it causes me to "feel" it physically.

I'll stay sad, carry my body slouched, and think constantly about how I'm being perceived.

I'm doubting everything I do, down to the way I meditate in private.

It's all part of my routine.

Whoa.

That word is used negatively as an example of our reality. While routine *allows us to think, negativity in routine can paralyze us.*

We are in a cycle we can't get out of, because it's our habit, our routine, a ritual we "need" for peace.

Peace how?

Comfort is what it is. Even if we are in a constant state of hating ourselves, it's comfortable there.

Well, no way I'll be able to go back now. I know too much.

Another book suggested: "Live as if you are the future self you envision."

The one who let go of the fears, doubts, insecurities, and past. What does she look like?

How does she carry herself? She's confident.

She cares what people think in a sense, without feeling the need to change who she is because someone may do something differently.

She smiles. And even if it's forced, it turns into a real one because, deep-down, she knows she has everything she needs, no matter how the current moment feels.

Do you hear that?

It's quiet inspiration, not black noise.

Darkness, negativity... She's out of it, because she knows how strong her thoughts are now.

I felt so confident after completing my Life Coach Certification, not because of the paper, but because of the process. Connecting with other Life Coaches and figuring out what I wanted my *thing* to be brought up so much excitement and energy in me. I was motivated by something new.

Life #36

Reinvention

I was doing it. Creating something that was mine, something that could never be taken away from me. It was step one in becoming the next version of myself. With my new photos, my new title, and an improved mindset, I decided to start showing up as *her*.

I opened my Instagram app and logged into my settings, erased "rainavsfood" and typed in "its.just.raina." For the first time, it was no longer *me* against anything. I wanted to just be me, and I'd share the process of figuring out who she was without the fight. I later changed it to "raina.odell," ready to reclaim myself.

I found someone to help me create a website for myself that aligned with where I wanted to go. I posted options for people to book one-on-one calls with me, and I began creating my first course around journaling. I wanted to share my journey over the first thirty days of my journaling process and how quickly it had started to transform my mind. With all of that, I slowly started to phase myself out of my fitness business.

I was still earning a weekly paycheck, a perk from the ten years of work I'd put in up to then. I remembered something I'd told Danelle years before, when she asked what my goals were with the business. I'd told her, "I just want to go all-in to grow it and get to a place, years from now, where I can take a step back to focus on and build something else that I love." I had done just that. I got chills, remembering that conversation.

I restructured my team page a bit, removing team calls and the group work we'd been doing. Instead, I went live, telling people they had the tools they needed. Now, it was simply about putting in the work. With that, I released the old *need* I had to handhold my team, and I delegated, letting go in a new way.

I did all of that within the month, tiny shifts toward my vision—check! I knew I just needed to continue what I was doing, especially the mental work. Then, that vision I'd created would no doubt be my reality.

JOURNAL ENTRY: Tuesday, April 6, 2021

I cannot let my day be affected, mentally and emotionally, by someone else.

Why give anyone that power over you?

Why choose to stay in a mood of heaviness, anger, frustration, annoyance, ego?

That's all it is.

Ego.

So now, we let it go.

Let it go.

Breathe and decide how you want to feel right now...

I had gotten really good at dodging the negative thoughts and feelings I was beginning to absorb from the people around me. I had felt the wear on my body and emotions because of how much Chad and I continued to argue about life, parenting, and our future. Part of me metaphorically threw my hands in the air, surrendering and releasing the thoughts that came in. The other half felt more and more concerned as each day went by, wondering if we'd ever fall into alignment.

I knew I didn't have the best track record with relationships, and I also knew in my gut that something was wrong. Something inside me was shifting. It felt like, if Chad and I didn't get on the same page, I'd outgrow him, just like I had Bret.

JOURNAL ENTRY: Friday, April 23, 2021

100 pages today.

I started on December 1, 2020. The year that broke me.

It's April 2021. It's flown by.

The book this morning was right: Every rock-bottom I've ever hit felt possible because of all the lessons I've gained from other rock-bottoms.

Bret taught me strength and independence.

My illness taught me patience.

My single parenting taught me true love and loyalty.

Archie showed me how to slow down.

2020 was the hardest rock-bottom.

Social media got the worst of me.

It tore me down, along with the climate of 2020.

Had the video not been made, I'd still be in survival mode.

I'd still be telling myself that tough-love is how I thrive.

I'd still be telling anyone who disagreed with me to fuck off.

I'd be surface-level.

I wouldn't be with Chad. We wouldn't have Archie.

I wouldn't have the home I do.

I wouldn't have the routine I do.

Mornings would look different, not in a good way.

They'd still be rushed and rigid.

I'm thankful for this journey. I can breathe now.

I can see now.

I can feel now.

All new senses I removed to fit inside my bubble were fake.

Chad said it once: I lived this "IG" life, and it was an act at first. Soon, it became who I was.

This year, I learned more about who I am without all of that to cloud me.

And I love me.

I'd convinced myself that, if I could continue to work on myself, most likely I'd grow into someone who would be less affected by interactions and differences with Chad. Surely, if I kept working on myself, the parts of me that still felt the need to be defensive or dull would heal, also, right? I knew I loved him, and I wasn't ready to throw in the towel, but some things really needed to shift. I'd control what I could and surrender the rest.

The harder part of it all was watching my kids build resentment toward Chad, too. Being quarantined together for over a year created a lot of tension at times. Kenzie was getting older, and if you don't have teenagers, well, they start to speak their mind more at a certain point in their life. That new instinct, along with Chad's personality, caused explosions that left me in tears, feeling like I had to choose sides.

The fact of the matter was, I'd always choose her. I could never say that out loud, but it was the reality. There would never be anyone or anything that could come in between me and my kids. The relationship tried, it tested, and the tension it caused felt hard to handle most days.

As Archie started to grow, Chad and I did our best to turn our house into the most pet-friendly home on the block. We added ramps in the back yard to reduce the number of stairs Archie had to use, and we kept an eye on how much he ran around in the back yard, afraid the impact from the stones there would cause more damage to his legs. Living in the 1920s house had started to lose its appeal. We kept having to change and upgrade things in order to make it fit our family.

I also felt lighter. My personal life and inner journey felt lighter than ever, while the house we were in felt like a dark shadow I couldn't escape. I needed natural light again. I needed the sun again.

Chad and I decided not to renew our lease there and instead start looking for a new place. We'd talked about buying a home together, but there was always resistance and tension in those conversations. I wasn't great at keeping my cool during talks around finances. We eventually settled on renting for another couple of years, until the bankruptcy I was still paying on had been paid off. The rental house hunt began.

I spent a month setting up appointments with realtors to see different homes all over the Denver area. We weren't set on a specific area as much as we were looking for a good back yard and light. In my free time, I went on Zillow to browse all the rentals in our price range, looking for a space that inspired curiosity in me. I left house after house feeling just *meh*. I knew, when I found the one that I was supposed to be in, I'd feel it. My gut feeling had never been wrong, ever.

One day, I got on the interstate and headed north to an area I had not been to before. The farther north I got, the bigger the mountains were. I liked that. As I drove down the street just minutes from the next house, I was in awe at the 180-degree view of the Rocky Mountains and how big the sky was. I got the same feelings, remembering how I'd felt when we found our home in Encinitas. There were new developments going up all around me and a giant high school nearby. This felt like a promising area.

I looked at the listing again, just to refresh my memory on what to expect before pulling down the driveway. It said, "no dogs." *How in the fuck did I miss that?* I sent a quick text to the realtor I was scheduled to meet in just ten minutes.

Hi, I'm on my way, but I just saw in the listing that dogs aren't allowed. I'm so bummed. I have a little maltipoo, and we just got another dog. I just wanted to make sure it was an option.

Why don't we view the house, and if you're interested, I can talk to the owners to see if it's a possibility! she responded.

Hell yes.

When I pulled up to the house, I was in awe. It was bigger on the outside than any house I'd lived in to that point. When I walked in, it smelled like a brand-new home and looked perfect, with crystal light fixtures and chandeliers. The yard was massive, with a giant patio. There were sunrooms, extra space, and when I paused to inspect each room, I could already see how the rooms would be set up, with all of our furniture fitting in perfectly. I could picture us there in that home clear as day.

I'd also been working on releasing expectations around almost everything, so before I left, I told her I was extremely interested, and I'd love to have her talk to the owners about my two good boys. I went home, smiling from ear to ear, knowing it would be the next space I called home.

JOURNAL ENTRY: Friday, July 2, 2021

Well, we skipped several journaling entries that probably would have started with, "I'm so fucking tired."

We're moved in! Yes, smiling, because the house is perfect. The move itself was pretty stressful, movers and the move- out drama with the old landlord.

I'm glad it's done.

The first couple days in the house, Chad and I got along well. Surprising, with the chaos of the move.

The normal Chad-and-Raina bickering started around day 3, lol.

Yesterday, he told me to "call one of my fans, I mean, friends…"

We started talking about rugs.

I asked him if he thought seven feet would be long enough for the kitchen.

He quickly responded with, "I have no idea and don't order without finding out."

I told him I obviously wouldn't order without measuring and asked him if he'd lie on the floor so I could measure.

He didn't laugh when I did. Instead, he got mean, ending with that statement about calling one of my "fans" for help.

Random and unnecessary, it actually really hurt.

Then, my Internet didn't work. I sent a text to the family thread, asking for help, and he responded privately with, "Don't ask me to check on shit today."

I responded with "K."

Is this what a normal relationship is? Misunderstandings to miscommunication that leaves someone feeling useless, alone, heavy, and damaged?

I've compromised so much for what?

The more I compromise, the more it weighs me down.

Everything feels heavy - my permanent frown is causing crater-sized wrinkles on my face.

Ty came over last night to see the house, and he said, "I could tell you were tired and drained."

I wanted to correct him when he said it must be the move.

No. That part feels good.

The shit look on my face is because of months of compromising who I am in hopes it will make someone love me more.

Breathing extra today.

And doing what feels good to me.

Life #37

Joy

"There's hope, even when your brain tells you there isn't."

—John Green

In summer 2021, I felt like I was finally able to breathe.

We had successfully moved into a new home, mostly for Archie. In our new town, it felt like the sky was so big. I stepped out onto our patio each morning as the sun peeked her head over the horizon, pinks and oranges filling the massive sky, while I planted my bare feet on the ground.

The house was so open, so light. I felt like I was finally going to be able to drop my shoulders and settle. I arranged all of the furniture exactly the way I'd seen it in my head a couple of months before. I set up my office, my home gym, and helped the girls organize their spaces however they requested. I loved helping them get excited and organized in their rooms. I knew how good that felt: a safe space of their own, like my bright-pink hand-painted bedroom in my mom's house.

I worked patiently each day to figure out a routine that would work for me. With the girls home for the summer, this was a temporary flow, but I knew I thrived on ritual. I set my work hours and started to fill my calendar with one-on-one clients, releasing my imposter-syndrome thoughts and just pushing forward.

Each morning, before journaling, I got nervous. When I dug into where this was coming from, I discovered a lot of pressure to help people I'd connected with for my one-on-one work. I didn't want to let them down. I didn't want to let *myself* down.

Just show up, Raina. Just listen to what they need help with. You've got the tools. I gave myself this pep talk on paper each morning.

I knew this was the new direction I wanted to take my business. I saw this clear as day in my vision. But still, I had to deal with the uncertainty of it all, while still feeling slightly fearful to show up on social media like I once had.

Journaling continued to be the biggest tool in my toolbox, I talked myself through work changes, parenting roadblocks, and routine restructuring. Yet, I found myself still mostly journaling on a common theme: *Is this the relationship I'm supposed to be in?*

I pulled out old journals and flipped back to 2021, to the page where I wrote out my year vision. I had written how I wanted to feel and how I wanted my day to flow. In that moment, it hit me: everything I had written had become my reality within the span of one year. The work flow I wrote about, the way I wanted to spend my mornings and evenings—all of it looked now as it did on that paper, written in the depths of my depression. I had successfully created a vision, identified the action steps needed for it to become a reality, and it had worked.

Everything except for my relationship. This was the one thing that didn't fit. As I journaled, I would write about the heaviness and anxiety I still carried, trying to put my thumb on the cause. Work already felt good. The answer, it turned out, was right under my nose.

Ali and I talked almost every single day. For the last year, I'd been unable to see her because of the pandemic and travel restrictions, especially in Canada. It had been hard. When she got the greenlight, Ali booked a flight to Denver. We needed some face-to-face friend time. I'd missed her so much it hurt. No wonder I felt like the last year hadn't been fun. I hadn't laughed, because I wasn't around Ali.

When she landed, we hugged for so long, we both started crying. Then, we spent the drive from the airport, venting and catching up in real time. She knew every piece of my life, but being able to explain to her how unhappy I felt in my relationship and what had been unfolding was the best therapy.

We played the whole weekend she was here. We sipped cocktails while talking about life. We always joke, when we're together, "We solve all of the world's problems," and it really did feel that way. We spent time with the family and hung out with Chad. But my favorite time was just the two of us, driving down the road to wherever, talking.

"Raina, I think a big issue here is that you guys have been cooped up together for over a year, and you're not doing anything you love!" she said as we got into the car.

Suddenly, it hit me: I didn't really know what I loved, anymore. I felt part of me had died and the other half was dulling herself into Chad's life, attempting to be accepted. I thought back to other seasons of my life when I had become this chameleon.

I used to hike. I used to go into the mountains every weekend. *I used to do all kinds of fun things*, I thought.

"I don't even know what I'd do for fun anymore," I admitted to Ali. "Chad travels so much for work again now, when he's home, he doesn't want to do anything, so we end up just staying home. But you're right, I'm really fucking bored."

My mind started to wander as I drove.

When was the last time I remember doing something just for me, for fun? When's the last time I had a smile on my face because of something I was doing for the joy of it? Horses popped into my mind.

I used to love riding horses. We often went to my aunt and uncle's house. I'd run out to the barn and stand on the wooden slats, leaning as far over as I could to pet them and say hi. My uncle saddled them up and took us out into the woods in Missouri, where we created our own trails. I remembered so much joy and laughter, playing follow the leader on horseback.

"What do you think you'd do, if you could do anything," Ali asked.

"You know what I just thought about? Riding horses…"

"Raina! Yes!" She was excited at the image.

Part of me was looking for permission to do something for *me*, something that felt unrelated to my current life. Ali's encouragement gave me that permission.

I hated dropping her off at the airport after that visit. It felt like a little piece of me was leaving.

JOURNAL ENTRY: Friday, September 3, 2021

I keep feeling this, like a rush of nerves before the anxiousness kicks in.

It never goes into full-blown anxiety or worry, because I'm in a constant state of reminding myself that I'm safe, fine. No work calls even.

Nothing to be worked up about.

Today, I get to chill and check off boxes.

Everything on my list I enjoy, I love. So, it's just this weird feeling I have that pops up as I start the day.

So, deeper breathing.

I've been tethering Archie to me for training.

Brain wandering.

I want to train him to be a therapy dog.

Mostly, well, two things: deeper training and the ability to fly with him.

And the daydreaming - imagine him as a hospital therapy dog, like the golden that came to me when I had my surgeries.

I think he'd love that so much.

Ali texted me last night: Your assignment for tomorrow is to book horse riding lessons. *And to send her the confirmation.*

So, I'll do that.

That, to me, is something for me.

It actually makes me tear up, if I picture it for too long.

When's the last time I did something for me that wasn't work-related or more stress?

Like, hop on and just ride?

The connection with the big being—it'll be like a giant Archie.

I just think a lot of quiet, peace, and clarity is going to come.

Ahh, yeah, it makes me excited.

———— ◆●●◆ ————

Life #38

Decisions

I'd been thinking more and more about the conversation Ali and I had had about doing something for *me* again, something I would find joy in. I'd fallen so deeply in love with Archie that the thought of him doing therapy work lit me up. I knew that would be something we could do together at some point, so I let that float in the back of my mind.

The more immediate joy, I knew, would come from horses.

The area we'd moved to was full of new developments bordering old acreage that had always home to cows or horses. There were ranches on nearly every road I turned on. It was hard to focus as I drove by!

"Da babies!" I'd say out loud as I drove past.

I searched for nearby ranches that offered riding lessons and set up a first lesson at one just five minutes down the road. I already felt giddy.

Chad was supportive and the kids were not interested in what I was doing. But none of that even mattered. It felt *so good* to have something to look forward to again. Something that had nothing to do with my job or how I made money.

On an entrepreneurial podcast that week, the host said, *"Not everything you do has to bring you an income. Some things can be for fun, just for the joy, just for the disconnection it brings you."* I needed to hear that.

Because I'd been an entrepreneur for so long, I believe my brain was wired to look for ways to monetize anything I was doing. I'd been an *influencer* for too long, and really looked forward to outgrowing that, but my instinct was tied to creating safety.

I put on my skinny jeans, an older T-shirt, and my Timberland boots. Walking into the barn, I felt confident and excited. I had no idea what to expect, but I wondered if I could still trot on a horse. When a tall man in a cowboy hat walked toward me, I smiled. "Hi, I'm Raina! I'm here for lessons!"

"I'm Sean. Nice to meet you." he said with a roughness to his voice. He had kind eyes, a gentle smile, and a sense of humor that immediately comforted me. He felt like home after knowing him for just three minutes.

Sean walked with me through the barn, showing me the tack room and the arena and introducing me to all the horses. We grabbed the mustang for my lesson, Taz.

Taz was a chestnut mustang with a little white blob on his forehead shaped like the Tasmanian devil, hence his name.

"That one's Rocket," Sean said, pointing to the horse beside Taz. "Guess where he gets his name!" He laughed. "You won't wanna ride him just yet."

We put a halter on Taz and led him up to the barn, attaching ropes to his halter so he'd stand in place while we grabbed his grooming box.

"Go ahead and brush him out," Sean instructed, pointing out one of the brushes.

I eagerly started brushing the horse, while we chatted. I told him about my horse experience and how I'd owned a Shetland Pony at one point and ridden in the woods as a kid, but hadn't been on a horse in a couple of decades.

He handed me a hairbrush to detangle Taz's mane and tail.

"Have you ever brushed a horse before?" he asked me.

I blushed. *What did I do wrong?* I wondered.

"I probably have." I laughed nervously. "Not in a long time."

"You have daughters, right? How do you brush their hair?"

I was not really sure what he was getting at.

"You brush from the bottom up, right? To help with tangles?" And, yes, I did brush human hair like that.

I started to brush Taz's hair with the gentleness and attention I used on my kids. Next, we led Taz into the arena, where I stood next to Sean as he talked me through basic groundwork. I'd never watched someone do groundwork before, outside of movies, and it was kind of fascinating.

"We won't be riding until you can earn the trust from the horse and master this groundwork. Everything we do with horses starts on the ground," he explained.

Great. I'm not even fucking riding, I thought, fighting the need for immediate gratification and trying to stay positive. The image I had in my head of what this was going to be wasn't accurate. It became more than I could have imagined.

I stood next to Sean, tense, my excited energy oozing out of me. I felt wired, almost like I was putting on an act, trying to *be* a certain way to fit in. As good as I thought I was at trying new things, I wasn't.

He turned away from Taz and looked at me. "Whatever you've got going on outside the barn needs to stay outside the barn." I'm sure I looked shocked at that.

"Taz can feel your energy. Horses have a beautiful way of mirroring back to you whatever you're projecting. Horsemanship is more about energy and your breath than anything else."

I felt tears sting behind my eyes. *It is exactly what I need.*

JOURNAL ENTRY: Monday, October 18, 2021

I just need to shift - my head keeps going to my riding lessons at 11 a.m. It's nerves. My head immediately goes to technique and worry, but then I shut it down quickly - making myself think about something else.

What if I stopped doing that?

But instead let myself think.

I think about my job and dogs all day, why not horses?
I'm new.

There's embarrassment and fear of not being good.

But those thoughts aren't real or true, because I'm just starting, I am new.

They're causing me worry and nerves for no reason.

I will catch and shift that into energy and excitement for the opportunity to remove myself from my thoughts.

It's not about me, it's about the experience.

The freedom, the disconnection, the deep breaths, the energy exchange, the confidence boost, and the fun.

Breathe.

JOURNAL ENTRY: Tuesday, October 19, 2021

Horse lessons went well yesterday - I reminded myself of what I journaled on, and it helped me get out of my head.

Sean even said it was my best lesson yet. I told him it's crazy to have others read and share what my energy is looking like. He mentioned self-awareness, saying I'll get really in tune with mine.

That justified to me the importance of making sure I show up to these.

When the next girl came in for her lesson, I sat and watched for a bit.

She saddled her own horse, brought him into the round pen, and Sean helped her, spoke to her, coaching her just like he does to me.

It helped to see that this is an adjustment, a learning experience for everyone.

JOURNAL ENTRY: Tuesday, October 26, 2021

Focus today. Monday is now my light day.

I realized yesterday how little time I have for work on Mondays with riding lessons.

I sat on Taz! Haha.

We rode in the round pen, and it was slightly terrifying.

I didn't hold on at all, and I couldn't squeeze with my legs or else he'd run - gah!

I could only get into the motion. I was so tense, and I felt it.

He told me to exhale and release my tight gut, haha.

Breathe and flow with him.

I tried, but I caught myself squeezing between breaths - my fear kicked in - what if I get kicked off?

Or worse - bounced off, because I can't chill the fuck out?

I'll get more comfortable, but breathing, knowing I'm new.

He even said again - everyone bounces - the tightness in my body made me bounce really hard.

My butt-bones hurt, haha.

As hard as it was to become a student again, I looked forward to Monday and my lessons all weekend. Because 11 a.m. was kind of in the middle of my work day, I struggled to figure out a flow for that day and always got home feeling like half my day was gone, which it was.

Instead of fighting it, I decided to flow with it. *Maybe I'll categorize my days,* I thought. Instead of every day looking the same, maybe I'll slap a theme on each day. That'll prevent me from getting so bored.

Mondays would be my self-love day. I'd spend Monday mornings especially slow. After my workout, I'd head to the ranch for lessons. After lessons, I'd have two hours before I had to get the kids from school, so I'd use that time to work on my social-media content, allowing myself to get into a creative flow state.

I'd make Tuesdays and Wednesdays the days when I did my client calls. I opened my calendar from 10 a.m. to 2:30 p.m., and if a client couldn't meet within that time frame, I wasn't the coach for them. I'd be firm and steady about the boundaries I'd set.

Thursday would be my writing day. I'd use this time to work on content, write my newsletters, maybe even start blogging or write a book. I had fallen in love with writing the more and more I journaled, so I really wanted to incorporate that into my business more.

Friday, my catch-up day. On Fridays, I'd catch up on emails, call notes, to-dos that had piled up through the week. I'd allow myself to stay focused Monday thru Thursday, leaving the odds and ends of my business to-dos for Friday. It worked so well. By the end of the week, I felt as if I'd checked all the boxes I needed to. I got off on the thrill of productivity, feeling like I was moving forward.

Saturdays would be my "adventure day," and I didn't care if I had to adventure *solo* or not. I was going to get the fuck out of my house. I found Saturday morning Farmers Markets and made brunch dates with some of the people I'd lost connection with over the last couple of years. I loaded up Archie and went for a drive into the foothills to take walks, or I invited the girls out to Costco and Target, and we spent hours there. Chad joined in occasionally, but it definitely became *my thing*.

Sundays became my favorite days of all: Silent Sunday. In order to put better boundaries around social media, I decided to take one day off each week. There were not many jobs that required you to be on, plugged in, seven days a week from 7 a.m. to 10 p.m., yet I'd followed those hours for a decade. Taking Sundays off would give me that disconnect I craved without having to take a month off again. I didn't post, I didn't scroll, and I didn't even open the app. The disconnect was addicting and life-giving.

When the world had *mostly* opened back up since the pandemic, we made plans to travel to Richmond, Virginia for the holidays, to see Chad's family. We had gone out there in 2019, a really good visit, meeting most of his family for the first time. We spent the holidays of 2020 in lockdown, which was extremely hard for Chad, who'd gone home every year. This year, I knew it wouldn't even be a question as to where we'd be traveling.

The holidays had begun to feel triggering for me. I never really shared that with Chad or the girls, trying to keep the holiday cheer to a maximum. Especially since divorcing Bret, the holidays had changed so much. The holidays we'd spent with Jerry and Danelle and all of our extended family had felt like one of the best times of the year. The girls always had so much fun, their faces full of joy during the week we spent with Grandma and Grandpa. It was painful to take that away from them.

We tried to continue the traditions in 2017 and 2018, after the divorce, but it just wasn't the same. Especially with the hate I began to develop for Bret, when he journeyed through new girlfriends and families. There was no way I'd be able to sit on the couch, opening presents next to his flavor of the month.

In 2019, I had the talk with the girls, explaining how we'd be going to Richmond to join Chad for the holidays, and promising we'd stop in Kansas City on the way back to Denver, so they could at least see their grandparents for a couple of days. They agreed, nervous, just like I was. I made it work. I brought some of our traditions with us to Virginia, like our matching pj's and monkey bread on Christmas morning. It wasn't the same, but his family made it beautiful.

2020 was the hardest holiday to date. We'd had to celebrate on Zoom. Chad was an emotional mess, which caused a lot of tension in the house. It was also the first time we'd ever celebrated at home without family, just with Chad. I did my best to bring the holiday spirit into our home, but it lacked any spirit at all.

I had high hopes for 2021. We wanted to take Archie and Dexter with us, so, instead of flying, we decided to do a road trip out and back, figuring it would be nice to have our car, too.

It was a two-and-a-half day drive out. We stopped in Charlotte, where his brother lived, before continuing to Richmond. On the way back, we stopped in Kansas City, so the girls could spend a day with Danelle and Jerry before the day's drive back to Colorado.

JOURNAL ENTRY: Thursday, December 30, 2021

Twelve days on the road.

I space out when I think about what to say, because it wasn't the road trip I was anticipating.

I'm so disappointed, sad. It's like things that may have been rocky before were all of a sudden heightened.

Chad was an absolute asshole - the whole trip, because, well, I don't know the real reason.

But it started because his expectations were off, too.

There was also an extreme lack of communication as to what his expectations were.

Instead of communicating how he wanted the road trip to flow, he got frustrated, mad, disappointed, and, in an immature way, took it out on us the entire trip.

3 days on the road were absolute hell - silence, rude comments, character attacks, parenting attacks, and then we arrived in Charlotte.

I pasted on a smile to be the girlfriend I needed to be, and we had a great time. Nights at the hotel were filled with the same silence and passive-aggressive assertiveness, but as soon as we got around others, we could act happy.

Isn't that what psychopaths can do?

We had a 4.5-hour drive to Richmond, and all felt well when we were with his parents.

They've raised kids, they've had teens - funny that everyone I talk to seems to get that, and they laugh about how hard and chaotic it is, everyone except Chad.

He seems to think that Kenzie is the "most disrespectful person in his life."

No, she's 15.

We spent 5 days with his family, and honestly, I had so much fun with them. They're funny, light, understanding, and patient.

Anything the teens did or said could be chalked up to them just being teens.

They get good grades, they aren't out doing drugs or having sex - I'm actually very proud of who they are.

Being made to feel the opposite or to question that is hurtful.

I'm going to be reminding myself of that.

The way home was the hardest, mentally.

I sat up, awake, to spark more convo and to chat, to help engage him to try and make the trip easier, but most of the time, I was met with an energy that stung.

The way home, we were to stop in KC. Bret would be there. My nerves were already shot. But I couldn't expect Chad to understand, even though I tried to explain it.

He doesn't get it and lacks any empathy or compassion for the situation, because, in his eyes, "I allowed it."

Tuesday (28th) was Ella's birthday. We were driving and on the road.

It was hard not giving her what she maybe wanted - I mean, even on Christmas Eve, I cried, because I had to set up a mini-Christmas tree in the hotel room.

It's so different for them - of course they'll be a bit off.

I took the girls. We stopped in Columbia and surprised my little brother, Ivan.

I am tearing up, remembering his face and genuine excitement and surprise to see us.

That made my heart really happy.

A piece of joy in the middle of sadness.

Back on the road to our hotel in Excelsior, where we'd meet Bret and his family.

I was nauseated the whole time but I can't show it, for the girls.

Today of all days, I needed a support system in Chad.

I needed a friend, a partner, and a hell of a lot of empathy and compassion.

Kenzie was nervous to see her dad and spent the two days prior trying to talk it out with me, I felt so sorry for her.

It's so painful to know how much change and trauma they're working through and not be able to help control any of it.

Chad and I met up with them for cake and ice cream. It went okay.

Bret "looked" fine. But there's so much anger there - I deflected with jokes.

We stayed for an hour, then Ella stayed the night.

Kenzie came back with Chad and me.

I tried to open up to Chad, telling him how hard this situation was, the pain, the emotion - and it was just passed over.

We left KC, heading home - and I'm so done, so tired.

One last spat between Kenzie and Chad just 30 minutes from home, and he was a dick again.

Kenzie was, too - so I said something, but of course it's never enough.

This morning, breathing deep.

We had a spat. The first thing he said to me was, "I'll be waiting for an apology."

I'm so done. I feel it to my core.

We are waiting for a therapist. I'll try that.

But if there's no shift, I have to wipe my hands clean.

I fell out of love with Chad on that trip. I could feel it slipping through my fingers like slime. We got back home, and I felt so defeated, realizing I needed to stop *thinking* about making changes in my life and actually do it.

It was hard to wake up, knowing I was in the wrong relationship. I'd spent nearly four years with him, trying to shift everything about myself, in order to be the person with whom he needed to be.

That's exactly what I'd done wrong. That's what *Sara* did to *Jane*.

At what point did I stop listening to myself, to my gut, to my inner knowing? At what point did Sara tape Jane's mouth shut, forcing her into the basement of my body, to not be seen or heard?

I'd lost my spark, my fire. It wasn't just work that had caused my light to go out. It was also my relationship.

My therapist stopped me at one point, correcting me. "No, Raina. Chad, a relationship, another person—no one can 'make you' feel any certain way. You're allowing it. You're choosing those feelings based on their words or actions."

Fuck.

JOURNAL ENTRY: Monday, January 10, 2022

Gaping emptiness. That's dramatic.

But patiently waiting for couples therapy has been so hard.

My head is just creating scenarios and situations, and if not that, I'm planning my escape.

The book… Someone said the secret to a long marriage is that the people in it see it as a "life sentence," so leaving isn't an option.

Does that mean, no matter what, we fight to hold on?

Through it all?

Well, that's the mindset I had in marriage #1, and it nearly killed me. I can't. Won't. Repeat it.

So, how do I know?

How do I know when to hold on because it's the right person or when to let go because it's not?

Is there even a "right person"? Or is that something we live our entire lives searching for?

Some of us settle and some find it.

But I bet a lot of people die, craving it.

Horrifying, lol.

I'm just sad; I guess that's all I can say now.

I feel sad knowing that I may be settling.

Sad that two lives I crave, being their mom and having a loving relationship with Chad, seem impossible to coexist.

I feel sad that one has to go, if meshing isn't possible.

I feel sad that visions I'd created of us working won't work.

Like I told him, a future "here" seems impossible.

Has too much been said?

Too much damage done?

Probably happened last year, when I told him I hated him. That probably broke his heart.

Maybe that needed to be said, because I felt it.

Hate for lack of compassion, sympathy, love, romance—everything I wanted.

Why does it seem so impossible to get?

Breathe.

I think a part of me felt so nervous to leave because I had no idea what life would look like without him. Again, I needed a vision.

I didn't need a big vision, just a daily one. Similar to the exercise I did back in early 2021. What did I want my life to look like a year from now? I sat down in my big journaling chair, the dogs snuggled in around me, and I wrote. There were two options: one vision with Chad in my life, and one vision without him in it.

I filled up two notebook pages with daydreams. When I put my pencil down, the answer was incredibly obvious. I needed to follow through with some hard decisions. I now knew that life with him would be harder than life without him.

Ali and I booked a trip back to California for our birthdays, because we both felt the need to clear our heads and spend February on a beach. We booked a little bed-and-breakfast and spent the days surfing, walking along the beach, eating, and drinking at all of my favorite spots. Also, crying a lot.

I'd shared my decision with Ali, along with my fears and hesitations around staying in a relationship that no longer fit me. She loved Chad. Of course, she felt sad, but she supported the decision I was making for me and the girls.

I got home from the trip with the solo vision in my head. I journaled on it quite a bit, trying to figure out who I needed to become now. The "solo me" had a different energy. She carried herself differently. There was a confidence about her that was contagious. I needed to prioritize *Jane*.

JOURNAL ENTRY: Wednesday, March 2, 2022

One month ago, I flew to San Diego. Ahh - inhaling the peace I got from that trip.

I'm feeling myself this week.

Literally and metaphorically. Getting in touch with me.

Who is she really - behind it all?

Is there a "behind it all," or is what you see what you get with me?

Confidence popped in my head this morning.

I can kind of turn it on like a switch. I can inhale deeply and turn on a "do not fuck with me, watch me do this" attitude of I AM FEMALE - HEAR ME ROAR.

Do you think I need you? No.

As I write, I realize a lot of those can be negative things, and while putting the words on the page, I can feel the shame in the words explode up through my chest.

Silly, "who do I think I am" thoughts popped in, dulling my excitement for the meaning and intention in those words.

Where does the need to "dull yourself down" come from? I think of Ella, because of how often I tell her not to "be so dramatic." I tear up thinking that I've let her dull her shine.

When did I first dull it?

It used to be what made me smile the most. Why am I dulling?

Why am I projecting that on my daughter? Why don't we dance in the kitchen anymore?

I'm finding it hard to finish the page now, like I'm avoiding something, but my mind just wanders to and from events when I remember feeling the need to dull.

We felt like "too much" at times for Chad.

With Bret, just making me feel like an idiot so often or picking fun at vulnerable moments or feeling "too much."

From the YouTuber - whom I let steal my voice.

So POWER is what I'm reclaiming.

No more dulling.

It would take me another year to completely remove the dull "hangover" I felt after deciding to separate from my boyfriend. The woman I used to be felt like a figment of my imagination. Part of me felt fearful to allow her back in, while the other part knew I needed her to survive.

We survived so much before the dullness wave clouded my vision. We accomplished more than I could have ever imagined, and it had felt easy. I knew, before I could ever think about letting him back in, there was a lot of healing work I needed to do around what had developed over the last three years.

Who I was three years ago isn't the same person I am today, thank God. I was thankful for the evolution, for the growth, for all of it. It was needed.

JOURNAL ENTRY: Wednesday, April 27, 2022

Ex-fucking-hale. I think that the more I think, the more I realize Chad and I needed to pause. It hurts to think of the potential of what "could" be and let that go, but I don't think he's capable of being who I need.

And vice versa.

I think I've written that 200 times in the last 3 years. When am I going to learn to listen to my gut?

A couple years ago, he told me what a "red flag" it was that I'm so driven to "go with my gut" and whoa! How did I ignore that flag?

I talked to Ali yesterday, and she reminded me that I'm not tied to anything.

We didn't get married, we do not have kids together, no mortgage (thank God), or anything else that means I'm stuck.

I'm like butter, baby!

I can move when I wanna move and flow when I wanna flow. The images I envision, the ranch with a horse and chickens, can be mine whether Chad's in the picture or not.

The little 2-bedroom condo in Encinitas can be mine, as well. With or without him.

All I have to do is decide.

Of course, it would have been nice to share that experience with him, but who he is, is not the person I'm envisioning with me there.

He has too many reservations, too many hesitations, too many questions that I would rather jump on (with planning) than hear him say, "Oh, that's not realistic.'

I'm a dreamer and a doer.

With balance and a level head.

The level head without a dream is an over-analytic realist, but that's also not enough to break up.

I want someone madly in love with me. A man who can't help but stare at me when I'm cooking and who comes up behind me to move to the music we're listening to, while holding me at the stove.

He'll be cautious around the kids, sure, but he will be unapologetically in love with me.

He will calm me, ground me, nurture me, and touch me.

And because of that, all my walls start to break, because I feel loved and safe, cared for and appreciated. Beautiful and strong.

He makes me shut off work and go for a bike ride.

He wants to be in nature on the weekends and off his phone.

He wants to capture memories and snaps imperfect photos of us constantly.

He winds down with me and kisses me every night before bed.

But also, being real, we aren't perfect, but we hear each other, we challenge each other by asking questions with love, empathy, and compassion, knowing neither of us are perfect.

When my trauma shuts me down, he opens me back up.

Not from a place of judgment or impatience, but from a place of curiosity.

Ex-fucking-hale.

Today will be, it just will be.

I can do this, even with the girls and two dogs. I can do it, and I have the resources.

Thank God for my business. Without it, phew - no idea. I wouldn't have made it this far.

So, I'm inhaling, soaking up the sunshine, and exhaling extra-long today.

Inhale belief.

Exhale doubt.

Chad started to look around at apartments and moved out a few weeks later. I had to go through a mourning period, and I allowed myself that, while intentionally diving into anything I needed in order to fall back in love with myself.

I've learned not to have any regrets in my life. No doubt, things were really hard, and if I'd made other decisions in the midst of the chaos, things would have been different. Different how? Who knows?

I never regretted not leaving Bret before I did. If I had, I wouldn't have the kids I have. I also wouldn't have started my business, moved my family to California, and probably wouldn't be in Colorado right now. I'm happy I stayed, I needed to, in order to become who I am today.

I didn't regret the choices I made for my health. I still believe the stress in my life caused the severity of my Ulcerative Colitis, so it just had to be a part of my journey. Without it, who knows if I would be taking my health as seriously as I do now? I sure as hell wouldn't have the energy or respect for my bodily functions, like I do.

I don't regret falling in love during my dating experimentation. If anyone else had been by my side as I navigated the pandemic and the loss of my identity, I don't know what my life would look like today. There's just so much.

Instead of regret, I feel thankful for the journey.

When I talk to my clients and help them create a vision for their life, I call this the Beautiful In-Between. Life right now is the beautiful in-between of where we are and where we want to be. The in-between is going to be full of so many ups and downs, so many pivots, so many obstacles, all meant to be there. All on purpose, in order to help you transform into the person you need to be, so that your vision can become a reality.

When Chad moved out, I needed to reset—mentally, physically, emotionally, and environmentally. I was done numbing, done dulling. I threw all the weed, pipes, and bongs I had, ready to feel again.

JOURNAL ENTRY: Saturday, May 7, 2022

I have an energy healing session with Cindy at 9 a.m., and I have no idea what to expect, but I'm going 100% in.

I chatted with Ali yesterday, after she watched my entire 60-minute session (ha-ha, I'm so lucky to have her) with Alea. So many takeaways, yet the most powerful was – okay, what are we manifesting?

What new, good, aligned, beautiful, empowering, magnificent, and exciting things are we doing to do/start?

Today's chapter was so good. Community and the importance of it, my own bubble. Noted.

Relationships, love - getting crystal-clear on what you're needing, wanting, and unwilling to settle on, while not shutting doors on what's trying to come in.

Everything I'm ingesting feels to be so aligned.

So, I finished the parenting audiobook and now, with everything else, feel excited to implement, with the understanding that the learning and growth is never over.

I downloaded my next book, Manifesting with Alignment - *and just the intro, I'm like, fuck - okay!*

Shifting and controlling and manifesting the external only works if you shift the internal - noted.

It's time to get quiet, Raina. And soon, you'll have nothing but quiet.

Soon, you'll have a space filled with full alignment, safety, security, and peace.

Yes, you hoped you'd have that with Chad, but I believe he came in to slow you down, just like Archie, way more than you would have otherwise. And now, he's got to exit, so you can expand - internally - into the next version of you.

Be accepting of that. Welcome it, knowing that he - and you - both needed to go through this.

So, what's next?

Step one: create your "safer" space.

You have a completely blank canvas to make it everything you and your daughters need - to heal, to grow, to move forward.

Do some rearranging - I'm moving my bike back, opening up the gym.

New TV in the living room. I'll have a ton of space in my bedroom, so move the meditation cushions up and create a corner.

I feel a new nighttime routine coming on. Whew - that feels good, because now, it's fear- and boredom-based.

I get to journal and think, what does my perfect evening look like?

I'll dig into that. I'll move my desk to the office, new mirror in the hallway? Yes.

I'm cleaning out the storage unit next weekend and will be able to fill my office with all of my awards, so I can remind myself of what I'm capable of.

All new - all mine - cleared space.

I'll be rampant with sage.

JOURNAL ENTRY: Wednesday, May 11, 2022

Journal prompt from my Homecoming *book:* Imagine yourself emotionally and spiritually at home with yourself - exhale. What will that look like? How will you breathe, speak, move through life, make decisions, love, manifest your purpose, and rest?

What will your laugh sound like?

What will shift within you and around you?

"Welcome home" - exhale.

When I imagine it, it feels peaceful. I can take naturally deep breaths without having to force it.

A gentle inhale with a deep exhale. It's a weight off my shoulders. I feel light.

Smiling comes naturally, not forced.

My face is relaxed, and my teeth aren't clenched.

All the muscles in my cheeks and forehead just are.

I speak in alignment, not forced or for show and not dulled to please whoever is in the room, I'll carry confidence and knowing.

I will enter a room without worrying about saying or doing the right thing, because whatever comes "is" the right thing.

I will walk through my day without deep-seated worry. If it comes in, it's immediately calmed because of the confidence I have in where I'm headed - the bigger picture will gently flow into my mind, easing away any pain that may try to seep in.

I will love hard and without fear.

I will be clear about what I want and need in a partnership and love those in my bubble without fear of abandonment or fear of losing it.

Raina loves hard - but also requires hard love in return and clearly communicates that.

That alone feels in full alignment with what my needs are to get to the big picture.

Daily positive manifestation will be a focus - realizing there's no room for that negativity in her space.

She has big dreams for her bubble. There's no more space for those who want to criticize it.

Rest will be a daily non-negotiable, along with intentional recharge in nature. Daily walks, gardening, weekly adventures, and monthly hikes will all be prioritized, so I can connect with Mother Earth.

Grounding and manifesting in meditation daily.

My laugh, I haven't heard her in a while.

She's deep-belly delivered, and she is unapologetically contagious. I miss her.

That will shift - surrounding myself intentionally with a community that brings out the best qualities in her. Those who hold space for her, ask deep questions, and allow her to take a big breath.

She moves like fluid, she flows, yet - she's knowing and determined, hard-working and harder playing. My energy will shift in ways that are contagious, and my bubble will expand.

Full of love, joy, kindness, care, compassion, and energy.
Oh man, I can see it clear as day.

The next few months felt really confusing to navigate. On paper, I could reclaim my life, but when my ex wanted to hang out, I felt weak and unable to turn him down. He'd moved into an apartment about thirty minutes away. I brought Archie over once a week or so, and we spent a few hours with him, usually only talking about things revolving around the dog.

I would call his new place the "sexpartment," because it was all we really did there. Each time I left, I felt more confused than when I arrived. I hated how it started to make me feel, like backtracking. That wasn't the direction I wanted to go.

Life #39

Horses

I continued to do all the things for me, enjoying my newly rearranged home and dabbling in the things I knew, at the time, brought me joy: my dogs, my work, and riding horses.

I looked forward to my weekly riding lessons so much, I decided to add on another one. Mondays and Fridays became my self-love days, when I committed to twice-a-week lessons with Sean.

I had gotten good at riding Taz, so Sean suggested I start riding Cesar more, a little red roan Mustang with a mustache. He was adorable, with a big barrel belly, but he was a bit more stubborn than Taz. I was a good challenge for me, as I continued to learn more and settle into my riding technique.

While I was riding Cesar one morning, Sean and I were talking about the little filly who had just been born on the farm to an unhandled mustang named Fiona. The mustang and baby, Carina, were being adopted by a woman who frequented the ranch. This sparked so much curiosity in me.

"What does it actually take to adopt a horse?" I asked. "Like the baby, just anyone can adopt them?"

"Well, yeah. They'd go through an adoption process, and then boarding and training, basically, depending on what their goal would be."

"I want to adopt a baby horse!" I said like a little girl wishing for a pony on Christmas.

Sean told me there were a few other recently rescue mares, some of them were also pregnant. My eyes lit up. He explained boarding typically looked like and what was involved after adoption. Owning a horse felt like a bigger deal than owning a dog.

On September 1, a little colt was born. Sean let me know he would be going up for adoption and asked if I was interested in checking him out. It was a hell yes.

On Sept. 19, I drove down to Morrison, Colorado to meet with the woman who owned the mustang rescue. We met at the little barn where the colt was staying with his momma, Honey. Honey and Fiona had been rescued together; they thought the same stallion had fathered both babies.

I pulled up to the barn and couldn't wipe the ridiculous smile off my face, watching the wobbly little guy make his way over to the fence to check out the weird humans who were baby-talking to him. At the paddock, he came right over to me and let me pet him and scratch between his ears.

Horses are mirrors. They will reflect back whatever you show them. When I looked at him, I saw someone who needed to be saved, so I saved him.

"I want him. Can I put my name on the list? Has anyone else claimed him?" I asked eagerly. "I want him."

She smiled and told me I was first in line. I could have sobbed right there, but I controlled it, knowing how much horses absorb our energy. I didn't want to freak him out the first day I met him.

I went down to see him every weekend, using the forty-five-minute drive as an opportunity to catch up on some inspirational podcasts before spending time with my soon-to-be horse. I fed him, ran around in the paddock with him, and took my journal in and wrote, just be there, letting him get used to me and comfortable with my presence.

My dad had told me to gently blow in his nose, "It'll help him imprint on you," he swore. I'd sit there, staring into his eyes while allowing him to sniff my coffee breath. I fell in love, hard.

JOURNAL ENTRY: Sunday, October 2, 2022

And joy. Speaking of joy - when I think of joy, I think of my boys: Dexter, Archie, and now the horse. I still haven't gotten the adoption stuff finalized, but she said he's mine. No rush. I'm going to go see him after I take Kenzie back home after work. It's a 45-minute drive there and back. Even if I just get 10 minutes to pet him, it's worth it. I've been putting on a podcast and just enjoying the drive.

Joy.

So, I decided his name. It's been in my head for weeks. I've pushed it back, but it keeps coming up. When I think of him, I think of joy. And if I put myself in that space, the vision, he's trained (by me) and cuddly and such a ball of goofy love - the baby voice comes in - Joooyyyyy. Joooeeey. JOEY.

Yes! Joy = Joey.

Joey. My horse.

I'm naming him Joey.

Dexter, Archie, and Joey. It makes me smile, so it is. I'll tell Sean when I see him, I'm excited to get back there tomorrow, excited for lessons. Friday's ride was so fun. We trotted a lot, and I learned how to lean in and flow with the trot. Made me smile so hard.

Anyway, my intention this week is health, my course, my kids, my joy.

Dexter, Archie, and Joey.

Exhale.

I started to sense a bit of anxiety as we got closer to the holidays, unsure how we'd spend them or who we'd be with. I knew I didn't want to spend them with Chad in Virginia. That was a big

306 & RAINA O'DELL

no. I didn't want to go back to Missouri, either. That just felt like a space I no longer fit. *If we didn't spend it with family, where would we go?*

I had the conversation with Kenzie and Ella, asking their feedback on how they'd like to spend Christmas and New Year's. It was unanimous: let's go to our favorite place in the world.

I booked an Airbnb right on the beach in Encinitas, and it was decided. We'd spend our holiday in California. Even though we had road-trip-trauma, I talked the girls into driving out. It would be easier to bring the dogs and have a car there, so we could do whatever we wanted.

While the girls finished up their last week of school, I hopped on a weekend flight up to Vancouver to see my best friends. Ali and Amanda and I spent the weekend together, walking around Stanley Park and Granville Island, having dinners with other friends, and happy hours, where we continued to solve all of our problems. When I got home, I packed another bag, and we hit the road to California the next morning.

Our road trip included stops in New Mexico and Phoenix. Everyone did amazing. I figured out I could only drive for about seven hours before my eyes started to get too heavy. The last hour, I'd have to stop at a gas station and get Chewy Sprees to eat, while I listened to the *Call Her Daddy* podcast to keep me awake.

When we checked into our Airbnb, we were in awe of the 180-degree view of the Pacific and excited to call the place home for the next couple of weeks. The girls and I went to Target to get any Christmas decor available and give the house a stronger holiday vibe. I had so much anxiety built up around this holiday, which felt so different from any other, so I wanted to do everything I could to help the girls feel that Christmas *spirit*.

I've always been really good at traveling and settling into any space like I lived there. I think that mindset helped me adjust and settle into my wellness routine with no glitches. The teenagers slept in until noon, so I was able to wake up and start my day in a way that just lit me up.

It felt so good to be in my routine and in Encinitas again, so much that I hopped on my therapy appointment from the balcony, telling her that within four years, I wanted to move back.

I didn't have a relationship holding me in any one place, and I could work from anywhere. The reality I was living that week could be mine all the time. *What was stopping me from moving back?*

I knew how powerful a vision was in my life. I'd proven, over and over to myself, that if my vision is strong enough, I will make it a reality. It just takes time, and that's something I've got plenty of.

JOURNAL ENTRY: Tuesday, December 27, 2022

I live in Encinitas, California. I just bought my first home, and it's got a 180-degree view of the Pacific Ocean from most windows. I wake up with the sun. Nature's alarm clock is the sound of waves crashing into the shore outside of my home.

Archie and I slowly roll out of bed to make matcha and open the doors, so the breeze and smells can roll through the hallways. We sit out on my balcony and listen to the waves as I read my one chapter and write my one page. I take a moment to close my eyes and let my brain clear out, expressing gratitude for the environment I've created.

I get my workout clothes on, and we take an hour-long walk around the beach and through the town, grabbing a green juice before we head back to the house to do some work.

Once we're back, I sit and work for a couple hours, do one-on-one calls, check in with clients, writing and creating. It feels like a beautiful flow I've spent the last few years creating. I pause for lunch, and we enjoy it out on the patio, watching the surfers catch waves, ride them in, and fight their way back out. I do another couple of hours of work before we close the computer and head out the door to the dog beach.

I watch Archie living his best life, running his heart out and going as fast as his little legs will let him. Pure happiness.

We load up and get home to rinse him off, then I head out to a yoga class.

I've prioritized getting out and into our new community and have fallen in love with yoga. I do an hour class every other afternoon to turn my brain off and give my body some love. On the opposite days, I head out to the stables to work with Joey.

I get home and feed Archie his dinner before heading out with him to one of our favorite restaurants. I sneak little bites of chicken to him under the table as people greet him when they walk by. I smile, in love with this city and the people who fill it.

We walk back home and start our evening wind-down routine, massaging Archie's legs before I hop into the shower, then we read in bed before falling asleep at 10 p.m. while the sound of waves continues to crash, creating a meditative state.

Before I know it, the sun has peeked her head back up to the east, and we get to do it all over again.

It's beautiful, reading back over that vision, knowing how much my life changed within just a year of writing that. I wrote that vision and read it back, completely and totally convinced it was possible to make that happen, because I had once before.

Once the vision was clear, I knew I had more transforming to do.

JOURNAL ENTRY: Saturday, December 31, 2022

What do I need to leave behind in 2022? Fear.

I'd like to take fear to the beach with us today and hold her underwater until she can't breathe anymore. Not the good fear my book talked about, which you get on the way to good growth, but the trauma-induced fear that keeps me playing safe in relationships, business, and life. I want her gone.

I want to leave behind self-doubt. Those thoughts that peek in, telling me what I'm doing isn't working or won't work, the doubt that floods in when I need to be more vulnerable in a relationship, the doubt that creeps in as I work my business and parent my kids. I want to trade it for a knowing. A knowing that I am capable of making good choices for myself. I am capable of parenting and raising two strong humans (because I already am), I am capable of growing a business that exceeds every dream I have (because I already have one), and I'm capable of finding love and building a beautiful friendship inside of an exciting and passionate relationship (because I'm worthy of it).

And I want to leave behind worry. Worry has consumed me for most of 2022, and I'd like to not let her take a step with me into 2023. With that, I'd trade her for trust.

Trust is my word for 2023. I picked trust because, to release fear, doubt, and worry, trust needs to be at the forefront of my mind.

Trust in the universe - a trust that she is going to take care of me. She knows what she's doing and already knows the outcome and life ahead of me. I don't have any way of seeing how things will play out in my future. However, she does, and she's aligning everything for me perfectly, to get to the place in my life at the right time.

Right where I need to be.

I'm putting my trust in her entirely.

Trust in myself next. I've always listened to my gut, my voice, my intuition, and have put a lot of trust in it, while accompanying it with doubt.

If doubt is gone, I'm going all-in on what feels right for me - inside - and trusting whatever comes up.

And, trust the process. I've learned that everything I need, I have. The universe and my gut will continue to pave a path for me. It won't be without heartache or pain. I know that - and I will continue to trust that the path is exactly for me, leading me somewhere greater. I'm ready, 2023.

Life #40

Manifestation

"Nothing is more energizing than making progress toward your vision."

—Arnold Schwarzenegger

It was easier to move on from Chad after creating my 2023 vision. I could see how beautiful life was going to be on my own. This was like gas to the fire that I thought had gone out.

When I got home, all I could think about was my vision. I told myself I'd make the move in four years. That would be long enough to grow my business to the point where I needed it to be. By then, both of my kids would be graduating from high school.

That was a big reason why I'd decided to stay after the holiday: the girls didn't want to move yet. We'd lived in so many houses over the course of their lives, which meant they'd been enrolled in many different schools. They didn't mind the changes at first, but eventually, they got tired of having to start over. I understood that, though I think, after having been in the same school from kindergarten through senior year, I wanted them to have a different experience.

Four years: that was the goal. There was no need to rush anything. I had plenty of time.

JOURNAL ENTRY: Thursday, January 5, 2023

Missed yesterday. Giving myself grace as I start my four-year journey. Obviously, it won't end there. I'll be in a constant state of dreaming and manifesting and for the next 4 years. I'll be intentionally focused, resting, aligning, acting, and implementing.

I'm in a new phase, a new season - creating a new "beautiful in-between."

Being home feels good. I know I can't snap my fingers and be somewhere else, so I'm in a deep state of gratitude, being home, realizing how beautiful this life I've created is.

I won't take it for granted.

I won't spend my days wishing it away. Instead, I'm going to embrace it, knowing it's exactly where I need to be.

I pause to look up, and I feel so safe and cozy in my space. I've got two girls at home with me who, in 4 years, won't be, most likely.

So, I'm going to soak it in, even on hard days, knowing it's all temporary and part of each of our growth journeys.

I'm going to experiment this weekend with what feels good. In the 100 Essays *book - I wish I could recap it all easily, however, the energy is implanted.*

I want to focus on me, spend time with me, adventure with me, slow down with me, date me, hold me, laugh with me. I want to create all of those things for myself.

The book said, "Whatever you're craving or upset about not getting in your relationship is what you need to focus on giving yourself."

Exhale.

I felt that. As much as I love the safety of my routine, I <u>need</u> to play a bit more, get out a bit more. Encinitas helped me see the insane joy I experience when adventuring out, even for a juice or coffee, even for a long walk or a lunch date with Archie.

I need to romanticize myself first. Over the next couple of weeks, I'm going to play with that, let myself play, experiment, adventure. I want to go see baby Joey more, take longer walks with Archie, go on lunch dates to write, and be surrounded by people. It's all going on the calendar.

Just exhale, Raina.

So much possibility in 2023, so much potential to make a big shift in you, in business, in finances, in energy. My mind is just racing as it all floods in, yet I remember, 3 years ago how, it felt impossible - dreaming, creating a vision for the future, not seeing the options in front of me, feeling stuck.

Releasing it all because there are always options and a new direction - go.

Something inside of me was reignited. I could feel it pouring out of me.

"Whatever you're upset about not getting in your relationship is what you need to focus on giving yourself..."

Okay, I thought. The next day, I made a list of all the things I felt like I was missing in my relationship and/or life:

* Adventure
* Laughter
* Affection
* Excitement
* Spontaneity
* Joy

I settled down with the list I'd made, deciding I could always add on later, if I thought of something else, but those seemed like the big ones. I then wrote next to them some ideas or ways I could give myself those things:

Adventure: *Don't skip your Adventure Saturdays. Plan the month with things on the calendar no matter what.*

Laughter: *When do I remember laughing the most? With my friends. I need local friends. I'm going to get out into the community and connect with people my age. I'll sign up for yoga weekly and send a text to people I'd like to reconnect with, putting lunch dates on the calendar.*

Affection: *I just want physical touch. I think that's my love language. Maybe I'll get massages. I'll start with once a month, splurging on a full-body massage.*

Excitement: *This ties in with adventure, I think. All of the above, really. Just thinking about it all makes me excited.*

Spontaneity: *I want to say yes more. As my community grows, trips come up, etc., I will say yes to the things that light me up.*

Joy: *Joey. Easy. Joey, my other boys—I feel the most joy when I get to spend time with my animals. Get outside with them. Allow them to be a piece of your adventure and spontaneity.*

"Live each day as if it were on purpose."

—Hitch

I put massages on my calendar, signed up for the yoga classes, and started doing what I did best: putting in aligned action.

I kept looking over the vision I'd created and remembering: *Be her now.*

What could I start doing now that will allow me to have the same feelings of joy and happiness that I know I'll feel in that vision?

I went back through my vision and created my new daily flow, using it as my inspiration, and focusing on what I *could* do versus what I didn't yet have the ability to do.

I may not have a 180-degree view of the ocean when I wake up, but I can still wake up with the sun and ocean sounds. I downloaded the Insight Timer app, so I could play ocean sounds before going to bed. I set them to turn on when I woke up. Perfect.

Archie and I slowly rolled out of bed to make our matcha and opened the door to let fresh air in. It may not be ocean air, but it was mountain air and would do for now. I could sit in my cozy little space I'd created just for journaling, to read and write my morning pages, then pause for a moment of gratitude for the space I'd created.

I could get my workout clothes on and still take that long walk with Archie. I'd miss the ocean views, but the snow-capped mountains weren't bad to look at. I could keep my phone put up and enjoy our walks and the quality entertainment I get by watching him explore the world.

I could get my green juice delivered, grab it as I headed up to my office to start my work day, hop on my one-on-one calls, and begin to implement the things I want to start doing in my business.

I can take intentional pauses for lunch, to disconnect and give myself a break, watching the people in my neighborhood walk their kids and dogs around the big park I see from my porch.

After another couple of hours at work, I can take Archie to the dog park and watch him chase all of the other dogs, running his little heart out. He follows along behind me while we walk. I love that time we have.

I can sign up for yoga. My future self loves yoga, so I might as well start exploring it. One class a week to start, and I can do some at home. We'll see where that goes. After yoga, I will swing by to visit baby Joey, brushing him and doing some groundwork with him. He is literally a ray of sunshine—pure joy.

I'll come home to make dinner, eating out once a week, but enjoying the process of cooking. I'll put music on and allow myself to dance in the kitchen like no one but the dogs are watching. I'll massage Archie's legs and do my skincare before I plop into bed with my smut book, falling asleep with my ocean sounds on by 10 p.m.

One day at a time, I did it all. Every bit of what I *could* do, I did, keeping my vision in mind while enjoying this beautiful in-between I'd created.

Slowly, my self-love and confidence returned. Loneliness, which had felt so crippling before, started to fade, as did my attachment to the relationship I was in. All along, I was the only person who could give me what I needed. *Imagine how much time and energy I could have saved if I'd believed that from the beginning.*

JOURNAL ENTRY: Friday, January 27, 2023

Ocean sounds on. Breathing. Started my period. I'm nervous/anxious.

I'm trying to figure out if it's coming from dinner with Chad or my trip. Well, I suppose it's obvious. And - I'm an adult, and we are "friends," but I know he wants to be more.

I'm not able to give him more right now.

I'm sure we'll sit down, have a fine convo. My nerves are just telling me what I need to know, I think.

Otherwise, it would be exciting, right?

So - guides, What do I need to focus on today?

"Truth. That's what you must lead with - living it, sharing it, walking it, talking it. Truth"

Okay. Yes. I don't live in my truth when I'm with Chad, for some reason. I'd rather hide, go within, shape-shift into another form of Raina, into Sara, who is passive and unheard. Why?

What is it about him that causes me to do that?

Experiences we have had. His know-it-all or analytical side doesn't allow the silly dreamer in me to play or explore.

She's made to feel silly in a negative way, which made her guard her silly and dull herself.

Exhale. Raina, you know you don't have to do that anymore, right?

You know you get to do and be anyone you want and opinions of others are nothing more.

You naturally have a beautiful energy and light that you carry around. No more will you dull it to make others feel comfortable.

It's what makes you, you.

Notice the energy this evening. Notice how you shift and allow yourself to catch it before it happens. Be you, genuinely. Knowing that this man may not be your best partner, but he can be a great friend. He can be a sounding board and a resource. Act like it's dinner with a friend. You know what you are and nothing more. Go and be a friend.

If the conversation goes in a direction that makes you uncomfortable, you notice and speak your truth. What would it feel like to be totally honest?

You aren't responsible for his feelings, only yours.

Go move, ride horses, be.

After dinner that night, we left with car doors slamming and screeching tires pulling out of the restaurant parking lot. I had a pit in my stomach, and *I knew better than this.* Was my body trying to tell me something, or what?

I was unable to be authentic with Chad, something I didn't realize until we'd broken up. He never got me, the real me, and instead of throwing out regrets or ways I wish I'd acted differently, I trust, knowing that our journey is exactly what it needed to be. I needed it all, the good days and, even more so, the bad, in order to become the woman I am today.

---◆●◆---

JOURNAL ENTRY: Friday, February 17, 2023

Exhale. I got an email this morning. Right as I sat to write about why I have resistance toward stepping into ownership as a business owner.

It was about the YouTube video.

I'm "mean," and the video was "very telling" about who I am.

I couldn't help but release a little laugh, more like a deep sigh.

Fuck. Really?

No. No, it's actually not "very telling about who I am." This experience is why I'm having a hard time.

The fact that my "tough love," which people signed up for, was used to turn me into a monster.

But Raina, you can take a moment and accept what happened.

Do it.

It happened. You can't change that, and now it lives forever on the Internet.

So, what now?

You just give up?

You just coast along as you let the old business and the new barely grow, because you're not stepping into who you are?

Stop.

That is not who you are, and if you continue to believe that, you're going to stay stuck.

You teach this!

What would you tell a client?

I'd say: that's a story. Stories can change. What's the new one you're going to write?

What's the new impact you're going to leave?

If people think that's who you are, let them.

You can't change how they perceive you. You can only change how you show up.

That's all.

So, who will you be? No, not even that - <u>Who are you?</u>

I am an entrepreneur.

One who has gone through addiction with a spouse, divorced said spouse, dealt with bankruptcy, raised two kids by myself, illness with UC, surgery and hospitalizations, ostomy, dating, moving, all the while growing my businesses that quite literally made it possible for me to survive all of the above.

My business and vision have been my anchor as the world around me burned down, year after year. It was the thing I had control of, the thing that kept me grounded, hopeful, creative, and growth-focused.

Through those things, those events, sure - parts of me hardened.

Hell, I have a brick wall tattooed on my chest. No one will get through.

Wait, no one will get through?

Is that what I want? No - so, I had to learn how to soften, slow down, release, overcome, transform, and grow.

As a person, a mom, a friend, and an entrepreneur.

That is what I did, and that is who I am.

Ever since, my focus has been to continue to live in that space of focusing on who I am becoming. Who I used to be doesn't matter. Those are old stories that will keep me in old patterns, if I allow them to. I've always found healing in solitude. For a long time and in some seasons, I labeled it as haunting loneliness. In order to change that narrative, I had to reach back and hold the hand of *little me* to help her see her worth, the vision I had for us, and our value.

I decided I was ready to live life again. Wait—not just live it, but *love* it. I woke up each day asking myself what I needed and gave her that. As I woke up to my ocean sounds and navigated my slow morning, journaling and playing with my puppies, I fell deeper in love. As I sat down for work, feeling like I had direction and confidence, I fell deeper in love. As I ended my work day, took my dogs on a walk, and then headed to the ranch to play with Joey, I fell deeper and deeper in love.

I was falling in love with my life and hadn't even achieved the vision I had in my mind's eye. At some point, I had learned more about Human Design, realizing I was a Generator.

"We are the life force, the energy beings, which gives me the power to do, create, build, and persevere," I read. "We are here to master what we love, and if something doesn't bring us joy, it's not for us."

I felt that to my core, deep in my belly. It all made sense, and I decided I had nothing to lose by living in that space, following what I loved. Slowly, I cleared out what didn't fit that description. I paid attention to my energy during my day, noticing what lit me up and what drained me, mentally or energetically.

I hopped on a call with one of my one-on-one clients to whom I'd grown pretty close through our work together. She asked me about my Encinitas vision and how it was going. I paused, soaking in the question before responding.

"You know, something crazy is happening. As I've had this focus of incorporating habits from my vision into my *now*, I'm starting to fall in love with my life now. So much that I don't even know if that vision is *the* vision, ya know?"

Part of me felt like I was *cheating* on "California Raina," while the other parts of me knew that vision was allowed to change. There was, in fact, a giant piece of me so in love with Encinitas and the possibility of living there again. I'd later heard a medium say that our souls can be drawn to people and places we knew in past lives. I felt that—as if there was a piece of me who felt so incredibly connected to that little town on the coast, like I'd spent a beautiful lifetime there.

I just don't think it's this lifetime. In this lifetime, my vision was shifting.

I spent every single day at the ranch, beginning to really love the little community I was building there. In addition, the weekly yoga classes had transitioned into for or five days a week of Pilates, because I'd grown really close to one of the teachers there, Andrea. It felt like I had little families and little villages all around me, and there was safety in that, which I think was missing for a long time.

All of these little villages, most of them not connected at all, gave me the confirmation I needed to know I was on the right track.

I grabbed breakfast with Andrea after Pilates one morning, as we do a couple of times a week. I live for it. If you were to ever label someone as "woo-woo," Andrea is that person, so connected spiritually to this world and to others. I think, in another life, we had to have been sisters or best friends, because our friendship just felt so right and easy.

"So, I think I want to start doing women's retreats, and I'm curious if you'd want to run them with me," she asked while I dove into my bacon.

"Are you kidding me?" I replied, excited. "I would love to do that!"

Years before, I'd hosted several retreats for my team and loved it. I always felt so energized upon leaving those retreats, feeling like I'd developed insanely beautiful connections with my community. Part of me craved that again.

JOURNAL ENTRY: Friday, June 9, 2023

Exhale. There's no rush.

I've felt uneasy or anxious this morning, like there's not enough time.

Funny, because today I've got all the time.

This week, this month, this year - nothing but time.

I did have a beautiful day yesterday. We did an 8:15 a.m. Pilates class, then we went to breakfast after.

Andrea and I talked a lot about doing retreats together, like Tulum retreats, 10-15 people - spiritual, expansive, aligned. It was a yes!

This is a way to expand and make an impact.

Deeper than just online.

I've seen people hosting retreats, waitlists, giving people an experience.

AND adventure was one of the things I want more of.

It felt exciting. She sent me links to a ton of homes yesterday. It felt so beautiful.

I wanna talk about vision, clearing energy, and realignment for manifestation.

Organizing your <u>now,</u> so it's creating what you truly want your life to look like.

What's holding them back? Journal, write, clear the space.

I just paused for a second to send that to Andrea for her feedback, and while I was talking via voice memo, a yellow butterfly landed on my peonies.

I saw it, kept talking, and it flew in front of my eye line, then off.

I think that's a sign, right?

Yes. Like confirmation?

Yes. Thank you.

Whoa, thank you. This feels like another deep vibrational yes.

Thank you. I'm going to take a walk with Archie for today's movement, grab a coffee at Fox Dog, listen to the rest of my podcast, then go to the ranch to work with Joey.

Home for lunch, then work till 4-5 p.m. I've got the Yoga and Cider Sunset thing tonight, and it will be beautiful, too.

Yes, yes, yes, thank you. I could cry. This aligns – so, so much.

———————————— ❖◆❖ ————————————

Within a week, we'd booked the Airbnb for our first retreat in Mexico. It sold out within a few days. I carried that high with me every day as the vision for my life slowly started to drift.

I went to the ranch for my lesson and felt the energetic shift, even around the horses. I felt calmer as I stepped into the realignment, and while no one probably noticed, I feel like I walked with a little more confidence. I put the halter on Cesar and led him up to the barn, where I gave him kisses in between brushing him. When his saddle was on, we went into the round pen to do some groundwork, before I hopped on and rode him around the arena.

It felt easier now, like it was flowing just as it should be. Sean and I talked about anything and nothing while I rode, but it felt like I was somewhere else. Home. I put Cesar back into his paddock and walked down with Sean to peek in on Joey and his sister, Carina. We'd moved Joey up to my ranch in March, and he'd been weaned at the same time as the other baby, so we put them in together. Turns out, they're actually half-brother and half-sister. It's been a cute friendship to watch evolve.

Joey and Carina were eating and playing with each other in between bites, so Sean and I sat down on a couple of plastic chairs under a big tree, watching some of the other horses run and play in the pasture.

He took a deep breath and said, "I think I'm going to have to leave soon." I felt pieces of my heart break. "There's just so much going on here, I think I need to start over somewhere else, probably sell the ranch."

He'd shared a lot of what was transpiring around the ranch. This peaceful spot I'd called my second home wasn't as peaceful for him as it looked. That's his story to tell, but I held space for him to share and open up about as much as he wanted to, knowing that his pain, his worries, and his stress needed to be released.

"Maybe out East? I've been looking at places in Virginia. You can get so much property out there for a faction of the price in

Colorado." He pulled up a Zillow listing on his phone, so I could see a piece of his vision.

As he scrolled through the app, I asked, "What about the horses? Will you take all of your horses with you?"

"Most of them. Some of them won't be able to make the trip. I'll probably have to sell a few," he said with a little sadness in his voice. *I hate this for him,* I thought.

He leaned over to show me the listing, a cute home with a massive barn and acreage, the most expansive green pastures I've ever seen. There were little cabins in the corner of the property, just like the dude ranch in Heartland.

"Sean, that's gorgeous. You know, my friend Andrea and I just booked our first women's retreat in Mexico. Imagine, if you got that property, you and I could host retreats with the horses!" I had that idea as soon as I saw the little cabins.

"Now, Raina, that's an idea!" he said in this deep cowboy voice. We daydreamed a bit together about what that would look like. Him leading trail rides and teaching energy and breathwork with the horses, me bringing in my life-coaching tools and knowledge of vision manifestation, I fell in love with the idea before we even finished the conversation.

We sat quietly for a bit.

"Sean, if you do end up leaving, would you let me adopt Cesar?" I asked, as tears welled up in my eyes.

"Raina, nothing would make me happier than to know that Cesar was with you." he replied, staring out into the pasture.

We sat there for a few more minutes, smelling the smells and enjoying the moment. I probably would have sat for a while longer if I'd known that it would be our last conversation before everything in his life changed.

Weeks later, Sean was gone, and the farm was listed for sale. I had to mourn for a bit, realizing that such a healing space for me would be no longer. I signed papers with the brand inspector, and ownership of Cesar was transferred over to me. I cried the day I got to call him mine. It's hard to hold in the tears even now, thinking about that day. I had so much gratitude to Sean. I wouldn't have Joey or Cesar without his guidance and mentorship.

My old story, *you can't do this on your own,* tried to pop in, but I trusted myself, knowing that Sean had provided me with the knowledge and resources to take care of my two boys on my own.

I grieved my life at the ranch while I worked to find a new place to board my two guys. I wanted to keep the babies together, so I teamed up with Jackie, baby Carina and Fiona's owner, to tour some other ranches. I looked at quite a few before a spot fell into our laps. Jackie had sent out an email to friends asking if they'd keep their eyes and ears open for any opportunity that came up for horse boarding.

Her hairdresser got the email when the client sitting in her chair had just closed on a small private ranch with a nine-stall barn and would be looking for boarders, kind of a co-op situation. The two connected with Jackie. We also learned there was a third woman looking to join the co-op who currently hosted equine retreats.

I got chills all over my body and told Jackie, "This is it. This is the barn we're supposed to be at." We moved our horses over there later that month.

Jackie connected me with an animal communicator, a woman named Annette who'd studied at the Heart Math Institute. She's a beautiful soul, so connected and smart. I felt very excited to talk with her and see what came up as she tapped into Joey and Cesar, curious about the energy they were absorbing as they made the transition to the ranch.

"Oh, wow, Cesar is so sweet," she began. "Gentle giant. That's how he's showing up for me, a gentle giant."

It was exactly how I'd describe him.

"He's absorbed a lot from the old ranch," she said as she worked to clear some unwanted energy from him. "He's very happy and grateful to be with you, Raina."

I couldn't stop the tears at this point.

"Oh, wow," she continued. "You've actually had four lifetimes together, you and Cesar. He is your soul horse."

There they were, fully flowing tears.

"I see," she said. "Cesar feels very grateful to Sean. He was the vehicle to get Cesar to you."

Cesar was here to be my grounding horse, my old soul, the horse who would slow me down and help me stay connected to the present moment. There was never a rush with him.

Joey was here to bring me back to life. My joy, my silly, energetic, possibly ADHD boy, who put a smile on my face every day when I see him. I loved these boys and saw the reasons why we were together, right in my mind's eye.

The co-op deal we had with the ranch felt like the perfect transition time for me, if I was going to own my own property one day. I'd rotate shifts with the other women in our co-op, working two or three evenings a week, cleaning out the stalls for the six horses we had in total, feeding them, and sweeping the barn. It became so meditative for me.

I'd spend two or three hours there each evening. I put headphones in and listened to any book I could find about training and working with horses. Horsemanship, energy work, I became intrigued by all of it, feeling the urge to make this pivot in my career, my soul mission.

I went down a rabbit hole of books, downloading five by Mark Rashid, an author with a beautiful story. He wrote about his journey into horsemanship and how it started as a young boy. The "old man" he eventually started to work with and volunteer for took him under his wing, teaching him everything he knew about the equine world.

At one point in the book, Rashid shares that, after disconnecting from the old man for a few years, he saw him again at a gas station when he was a teenager. The old man had lost his farm and was heading west to see family. The old man caught the boy up on his life and shared how he'd once given a gift to someone long ago, something that he hoped would be passed on.

The boy, a little confused, didn't realize what the old man was referring to until he found out, months later, that the old man had died. The boy realized the gift the old man was referring to was the lessons and knowledge he'd passed down to the boy. The boy then became one of the most knowledgeable men in horsemanship, using the gift the old man had given to him.

I stood in my barn, headphones in, holding onto the broom, as tears rolled down my face. I had a long way to go in horsemanship, but the story reminded me of Sean. Sean the old man, me the boy who absorbed all of the lessons. I was so grateful for the time I had with Sean and all of the knowledge he'd instilled in me. I was going to pay that forward.

> ## "Horses have the ability to reconnect us with ourselves and slow down moments."
> —Mark Rashid

I smile when I think about the vision I wrote out in December, just months before. I had thought there would be a way I could live a life without having my horses in my back yard. I could see Archie running out my back door to greet his giant brothers, Joey and Cesar. The three of them running around in the pasture, playful, energetic, and living their best lives.

I could see the little cabins out on the far edge of the property I owned, the cabins where my guests would stay while I hosted my own equine retreats for people who wanted to reconnect with themselves. Joey and Cesar, professionals at the deep work we did, and Archie, the goodest therapy dog that ever did live.

I could see it all clear as day, and the vision created a deep knowing that ran through my veins like fire. There it was, *the fire*.

As I worked on this manuscript and made it closer and closer to the end, my weekly therapy sessions were extremely helpful in helping me to navigate what was coming back up for me. Time traveling was extremely hard some days and emotional the next, making me laugh and cry in the same breath.

"I just don't want this to be a relationship book," I told my therapist, as I shared how much of my manuscript included stories and journaling entries about Chad and all of my exes.

She smiled as she always does when I don't catch on to something that she has. "You don't want this to be a relationship book, but it is," she said. "It's about the one relationship you never had time to focus on. The relationship with yourself."

But truthfully, I think it's why Adam, Mike, Tom, Gus, and Chad never worked out. I needed to learn to love myself first.

I've spent decades living in self-doubt, not really knowing the woman in me.

I'm surely doing it wrong, I'd think. I'd live my life craving external validation or confirmation that I was making the right choices. I didn't trust my inner knowing, the gut feelings that tried to send messages to me through my body or other people.

Once I became unconvinced about all of those old stories I used to tell myself, everything around me changed.

Once I realized I could no longer give up my flame in order to light someone else up, everything in me changed.

"Seems like all I do is start over. It ain't nothin' to find no starting place in the world. You just start where you find yourself."

—August Wilson

Acknowledgments

I've wanted to write a book for years. It's been something in the back of my mind for as long as I can remember and something I kept pushing off, thinking, *When life settles down...* or *When I reach a certain goal or level, I'll take a break and write a book.* Life never settled down, in truth, and each goal or level I strove for just kept getting bigger and bigger, like one of those little black snake fireworks I used to watch expand, as a kid.

I'd first like to thank my publisher, Samantha Joy, for pushing me off the ledge and helping me to realize that my story needed to be shared *now*, not later.

To my two daughters, you make me feel like a superhero every single day. Your belief in me has fueled me in more ways than you'll probably ever realize and has been my greatest source of strength.

To my best friend and biggest cheerleader, Ali, whose boundless optimism, late-night deep dives, and genuine friendship have kept my head above water during the best and the worst seasons of my life.

A special thank you to my therapist, Mary, for being a beta reader on this manuscript and helping me make sense of the chaos in my head. I'm not sure I would have been able to reignite my flame without you.

To Sean, I hope this book finds you. I hope you read my words, realizing the impact you had on me at a time in my life where nothing felt certain. Thank you for helping me find my joy.

Lastly, though I know you'll never read this, I want to send an energetic thank you to my most loyal companions: Dexter, Archie, Rockie, Joey, and Cesar. You boys have no idea the amount of joy your invaluable lessons and affection have brought me. In your presence, I have found solace, peace, and a deeper understanding of myself.

About the Author

Raina O'Dell is not just a life coach; she's a beacon of resilience, empowerment, unwavering determination, and a devoted single mom to two girls, three dogs, and two horses.

With over twelve years of experience working with entrepreneurs and a background in wellness coaching, Raina has dedicated her life to guiding women to envision their ideal lives, amplify productivity, and infuse each day with abundant joy.

Her passion for animals runs deep, and she believes wholeheartedly in their ability to serve as mirrors, reflecting the paths to healing and growth. Through her work, she shares the profound lessons she's learned from her four-legged companions, painting the picture of how their presence can guide us toward self-discovery and inner peace.

Raina's journey hasn't been without its challenges. She's navigated divorce, illness, bankruptcy, and more. But through it all, she's emerged stronger and more resilient. Her mission is to empower women to realize that their current circumstances don't define their future and that, with self-love and determination, they can create their own safety and stability.

In her book, *Bare*, Raina offers a roadmap for transformation, drawing upon her own experiences and the wisdom she's gained along the way. Through her guidance and inspiring insights, she invites readers to embrace their power, rewrite their stories, and step into lives filled with purpose, passion, and boundless joy.

Connect with Raina on Instagram (@raina.odell) or visit her website to embark on a journey of self-discovery and empowerment today.

www.rainaodell.com

Made in the USA
Monee, IL
12 May 2024

58368477R10196